BEGINNING CSS

I0600806

Continues

BEGINNING

CSS

Third Edition

Pouncey, Ian.
Beginning CSS :
cascading style sheets f
c2011.
33305225412018
la   08/30/12

BEGINNING

CSS

CASCADING STYLE SHEETS FOR WEB DESIGN

Third Edition

Ian Pouncey

Richard York

WILEY

Wiley Publishing, Inc.

Beginning CSS: Cascading Style Sheets for Web Design, Third Edition

Published by
Wiley Publishing, Inc.
10475 Crosspoint Boulevard
Indianapolis, IN 46256
www.wiley.com

Copyright © 2011 by Wiley Publishing, Inc., Indianapolis, Indiana

ISBN: 978-0-470-89152-0
ISBN: 978-1-118-12177-1 (ebk)
ISBN: 978-1-118-12176-4 (ebk)
ISBN: 978-1-118-12178-8 (ebk)

Manufactured in the United States of America

10 9 8 7 6 5 4 3 2 1

No part of this publication may be reproduced, stored in a retrieval system or transmitted in any form or by any means, electronic, mechanical, photocopying, recording, scanning or otherwise, except as permitted under Sections 107 or 108 of the 1976 United States Copyright Act, without either the prior written permission of the Publisher, or authorization through payment of the appropriate per-copy fee to the Copyright Clearance Center, 222 Rosewood Drive, Danvers, MA 01923, (978) 750-8400, fax (978) 646-8600. Requests to the Publisher for permission should be addressed to the Permissions Department, John Wiley & Sons, Inc., 111 River Street, Hoboken, NJ 07030, (201) 748-6011, fax (201) 748-6008, or online at http://www.wiley.com/go/permissions.

Limit of Liability/Disclaimer of Warranty: The publisher and the author make no representations or warranties with respect to the accuracy or completeness of the contents of this work and specifically disclaim all warranties, including without limitation warranties of fitness for a particular purpose. No warranty may be created or extended by sales or promotional materials. The advice and strategies contained herein may not be suitable for every situation. This work is sold with the understanding that the publisher is not engaged in rendering legal, accounting, or other professional services. If professional assistance is required, the services of a competent professional person should be sought. Neither the publisher nor the author shall be liable for damages arising herefrom. The fact that an organization or Web site is referred to in this work as a citation and/or a potential source of further information does not mean that the author or the publisher endorses the information the organization or Web site may provide or recommendations it may make. Further, readers should be aware that Internet Web sites listed in this work may have changed or disappeared between when this work was written and when it is read.

For general information on our other products and services please contact our Customer Care Department within the United States at (877) 762-2974, outside the United States at (317) 572-3993 or fax (317) 572-4002.

Wiley also publishes its books in a variety of electronic formats and by print-on-demand. Not all content that is available in standard print versions of this book may appear or be packaged in all book formats. If you have purchased a version of this book that did not include media that is referenced by or accompanies a standard print version, you may request this media by visiting http://booksupport.wiley.com. For more information about Wiley products, visit us at www.wiley.com.

Library of Congress Control Number: 2011926318

Trademarks: Wiley, the Wiley logo, Wrox, the Wrox logo, Wrox Programmer to Programmer, and related trade dress are trademarks or registered trademarks of John Wiley & Sons, Inc. and/or its affiliates, in the United States and other countries, and may not be used without written permission. All other trademarks are the property of their respective owners. Wiley Publishing, Inc., is not associated with any product or vendor mentioned in this book.

To Mum and Dad.

Thank you.

ABOUT THE AUTHORS

 IAN POUNCEY, author of this revised edition of the book, is a web developer living in London, England, and working for the BBC. He has been working on the Web for over 11 years, building a wide range of websites, from small sites for local businesses to the latest version of the Yahoo! home page. He is a W3C Web Accessibility Initiative Education and Outreach Working Group member and a web accessibility advocate. Ian maintains a personal website at http://ianpouncey.com, where he writes about all aspects of the Web.

 RICHARD YORK, author of the previous editions on which this edition is based, is a web developer for Westlake Design, a company specializing in website design and development, product branding, marketing and identity. He wrote his first book, *Beginning CSS: Cascading Style Sheets for Web Design* (Wrox Press) in 2004. Richard lives in Camby, Indiana with his wife, Lisa, and three cats: Gandalf, Merlin and Caesar. He maintains a personal website at www.deadmarshes.com, where you can learn more about his professional and personal interests.

CREDITS

EXECUTIVE EDITOR
Robert Elliott

PROJECT EDITOR
Tom Dinse

TECHNICAL EDITOR
Steve Webster

PRODUCTION EDITOR
Daniel Scribner

COPY EDITOR
C.M. Jones

EDITORIAL DIRECTOR
Robyn B. Siesky

EDITORIAL MANAGER
Mary Beth Wakefield

FREELANCER EDITORIAL MANAGER
Rosemarie Graham

ASSOCIATE DIRECTOR OF MARKETING
David Mayhew

PRODUCTION MANAGER
Tim Tate

VICE PRESIDENT AND EXECUTIVE GROUP PUBLISHER
Richard Swadley

VICE PRESIDENT AND EXECUTIVE PUBLISHER
Barry Pruett

ASSOCIATE PUBLISHER
Jim Minatel

PROJECT COORDINATOR, COVER
Katherine Crocker

PROOFREADER
Nancy Carrasco

INDEXER
Ron Strauss

COVER DESIGNER
Michael Trent

COVER IMAGE
© iStock / Vitalina Rybakova

ACKNOWLEDGMENTS

I MUST FIRST THANK THE PEOPLE who gave me the opportunity to work on this, my first book: Nicholas Zakas for recommending me and Scott Meyers for taking his advice.

Thanks also to my editor for being so patient with me. Thanks Tom.

Many thanks also to my tech editor and friend, Steve Webster. Possibly the smartest web developer I have had the pleasure of working with.

Finally, love and thanks to all of my family, especially to my parents, who set me on my path by buying me my first computer and supporting me no matter what.

CONTENTS

INTRODUCTION

WELCOME TO *BEGINNING CSS: Cascading Style Sheets for Web Design, Third Edition.*

Cascading Style Sheets (CSS) are the tool that web designers and developers use alongside markup languages such as HTML and XHTML to build websites. CSS provides web browsers with the information they need to control the visual aspect of a web page, such as the position of HTML elements, text styles, backgrounds, colors and images, and much more.

Advanced CSS techniques give website authors the ability to tailor layouts and designs for mobile web browsers, as well as the skills they need to create websites for regular desktop browsers. I will introduce you to the basics of writing CSS for mobile devices.

WHAT'S NEW IN THE THIRD EDITION?

The second edition of this book, written entirely by Richard York, provides very thorough and complete coverage of CSS at the time of its writing. Possibly no other CSS book for beginners goes into so much detail and depth.

For the third edition, I have taken Richard's work and streamlined it to focus on the techniques that professional authors of CSS use every day to create the wide range of sites on the Web today. My intention is to provide an introduction to CSS that is easy to dive into and enables you, the reader, to get up, running, and productive with CSS as quickly as possible.

Many of the words you will read are Richard's, but I have attempted to mould them around my own experience as a long-time author of CSS used on websites big and small, complex and simple.

While some attention is paid to the older browsers still in use today, I have chosen to spend more time on the newer crop of browsers and those likely to be significant in the future, providing you with up-to-date knowledge and skills.

The code in all of the examples is syntax highlighted for easy readability, and the exercises that you will encounter are inspired by real-world uses of CSS and HTML, helping you to write CSS in the right way from the start.

I encourage you to have fun with each exercise, learning not only by following my instructions, but also by experimenting with the properties and values that I introduce you to.

WHO IS THIS BOOK FOR?

This book is for anyone looking to learn how to use Cascading Style Sheets to style websites. Designers, in particular, will benefit from a good grounding in CSS, as it is the key to producing websites from their designs.

To get the most from this book, experience with HTML is useful. While all of the HTML you need to follow the examples is provided, you will gain a greater understanding of the best methods for using CSS to create websites if you already know how to write markup.

WHAT DOES THIS BOOK COVER?

This book covers portions of the CSS Level 1, 2, 2.1, and 3 specifications. These specifications are created by an independent, not-for-profit Internet standards organization called the World Wide Web Consortium (W3C) that plans and defines how Internet documents work. The majority of the book is written using what is defined in the CSS Level 2.1 specification, with a sprinkling of CSS 3 to make things interesting.

This book leads you through how to write CSS so that it is compatible with all of the most popular web browsers. I have focused on all of the following popular browsers:

➤ Microsoft Internet Explorer 8 and 9 for Windows

➤ Mozilla Firefox 3.6 for Mac OS X, Windows, and Linux

➤ Google Chrome 10 for Mac OS X and Windows

➤ Safari 5 for Mac OS X and Windows

➤ Opera 11 for Mac OS X, Windows, and Linux

The preceding browsers make up over 99 percent of the web browser market share at the time of this writing. For your convenience, this book also includes an integrated CSS feature reference throughout the book, as well as notes on browser compatibility. A CSS reference is also included in Appendix C.

HOW THIS BOOK IS STRUCTURED

This book is divided into three parts. The following explains each of these three parts in detail, and what each chapter covers.

Part I: The Basics

Throughout Chapters 1 through 4, you learn the founding principles of CSS-based web design.

➤ **Chapter 1, "Introducing Cascading Style Sheets":** In this chapter I talk about what CSS is and the advantages it has over outdated ways of styling content, give a brief overview of the history of CSS, and then show you how to make a web page with HTML and CSS. The chapter finishes with an overview of the major web browsers available today.

➤ **Chapter 2, "The Bits That Make Up a Style Sheet":** In Chapter 2, I look at the component pieces of CSS and how they fit together. I introduce rules, selectors, declarations, properties, and values, and show you the range of value types that can be used in CSS. Next are the various methods of including CSS in HTML documents and finally a discussion of why good HTML is important.

➤ **Chapter 3, "Selectors":** In Chapter 2, I introduce you to the simplest form of selectors. In Chapter 3, I talk about the other basic selectors that you will use throughout this book.

➤ **Chapter 4, "The Cascade and Inheritance":** In Chapter 4, I look at the cascade, a fundamental principle of CSS, and how inheritance and precedence works. You will learn how to calculate which styles take effect when rules conflict, and how to use the cascade to your advantage.

Part II: Properties

Throughout Chapters 5 through 13, you learn about properties that are used to manipulate the presentation of a document.

➤ **Chapter 5, "Applying Font Faces":** Part II starts with one of the first things you are likely to want to do with CSS — style text. Chapter 5 shows you how to set a font and size for text to be displayed in, and how to make text italic, bold, or small caps.

➤ **Chapter 6, "Manipulating the Display of Text":** In Chapter 5, I showed you the basics of styling text. Now I move on to further properties for styling text, such as adjusting the height of lines of text; controlling the spacing between letters and words; text alignment; and other variations like underlined, overlined, or strikethrough text. I also show how to control the case of text by making text all lowercase, uppercase, or capitalized.

➤ **Chapter 7, "Background Colors and Images":** In Chapter 7, I move on to the CSS properties that control the setting of background colors and images, as well as properties that allow you to adjust the position of background images, the way they tile, and how to fix them in place so that they remain static even when you scroll the browser window.

➤ **Chapter 8, "The Box Model: Controlling Margins, Borders, Padding, Width, and Height":** In Chapter 8, I cover an important part of CSS, and the key to creating layouts: The Box Model. You will learn how to set margins and padding to elements, as well as borders, width, and heights.

➤ **Chapter 9, "Floating and Vertical Alignment":** In Chapter 8, I introduce you to some of the properties that will allow you to create layouts with CSS. In Chapter 9, I will show you how to take this a step further, by creating columns of content with `float` and `clear`. I also discuss the `vertical-align` property, which is used to create effects like subscript or superscript text, as well as to control vertical alignment in table cells.

➤ **Chapter 10, "Styling Lists":** Lists are a common element for marking up content, including creating site navigation. In this chapter, I look at the properties CSS provides to control presentation of ordered and unordered lists: how to use predefined list markers and custom list markers and how to control the position of list markers.

➤ **Chapter 11, "Positioning Content within a Document":** In chapter 11, I cover the final method for creating layouts, positioning content relative to other page elements or the viewport itself, as well as show you how to create layers of overlapping content.

➤ **Chapter 12, "Styling Tables":** In Chapter 12, I present the different properties that CSS provides for styling HTML tables. The properties presented in this chapter let you control the spacing between the cells of a table, the placement of the table caption, and whether empty cells are rendered.

➤ **Chapter 13, "Create a Complete Layout":** In the final chapter of this Part, I give you an opportunity to put the CSS that you have learned so far into practice as we create a complete layout, from HTML to CSS. I also introduce you to some more advanced CSS: using custom fonts and setting gradient backgrounds.

Part III: Advanced CSS and Alternative Media

In Part II, I cover the basics; in Part III, we move on to advanced techniques, which give you more fine control when styling content, and show you how to style for different media types such as print and mobile, as well as introduce a few more properties.

➤ **Chapter 14, "Advanced Selectors":** Chapter 3 introduces you to the basic selectors that you will use to write CSS. In Chapter 14, I show you more advanced selectors that don't have good support in older browsers, such as Internet Explorer 6, but can be a powerful addition to your toolkit. I cover selectors that allow you to style elements based on their position in a document and based on the value of HTML attributes.

➤ **Chapter 15, "Styling for Print":** In this chapter, I discuss what steps to take to use CSS to provide alternative style sheets to create a printer-friendly version of a web document.

➤ **Chapter 16, "Customizing the Mouse Cursor":** In this chapter, I show you how you can change the user's mouse cursor using CSS, how you can customize the mouse cursor, and what browsers support which cursor features.

➤ **Chapter 17, "Controlling Opacity And Visibility":** In Chapter 17, I show you how to make HTML elements transparent or even invisible, while still affecting the elements around them

➤ **Chapter 18, "Styling Content for Mobile Devices":** Chapter 18 shows you how to target web pages displayed in mobile phone browsers, giving mobile users a more tailored experience.

➤ **Chapter 19, "Closing Comments":** I finish Part III with an overview of what you will have learned by the end of this book, as well as some of my thoughts on the future of CSS.

Appendixes

The final part of the book is the Appendixes:

➤ **Appendix A, "Answers to Exercises":** Here I give you the answers to all of the questions asked at the end of each chapter.

➤ **Appendix B, "Additional CSS Resources":** Appendix B provides you will all of the links contained within each chapter, as well as links to other resources that I think are worth reading to expand your knowledge of CSS.

➤ **Appendix C, "CSS Reference":** The CSS reference is where you can look up which browsers support what properties.

➤ **Appendix D, "CSS Colors":** Appendix D provides a reference to all of the named colors you can use within CSS.

WHAT YOU NEED TO USE THIS BOOK

To make use of the examples in this book, you need the following:

➤ Several Internet browsers to test your web pages

➤ Text-editing software

Designing content for websites requires being able to reach more than one type of audience. Some of your audience may be using different operating systems or different browsers other than those you have installed on your computer. This book focuses on the most popular browsers available at the time of this writing.

I discuss how to obtain and install each of these browsers in Chapter 1. The examples in this book also require that web page source code be composed using text-editing software. Chapter 1 also discusses a few different options for the text-editing software available on Windows or Macintosh operating systems.

CONVENTIONS

To help you get the most from the text and keep track of what's happening, I've used a number of conventions throughout the book:

 WARNING *Boxes like this one hold important, not-to-be-forgotten information directly relevant to the surrounding text.*

 NOTE *The pencil icon indicates notes, tips, hints, tricks, and asides to the current discussion.*

Examples that you can download and try out for yourself generally appear in a box like this:

TRY IT OUT

The *Try It Out* is an exercise you should work through, following the text in the book.

1. They usually consist of a set of steps.

2. Each step has a number.

3. Follow the steps through with your copy of the source code.

How It Works

After each *Try It Out*, the code you've typed will be explained in detail.

As for styles in the text:

➤ I *italicize* important words when I introduce them.

➤ I show URLs and code within the text in a special monofont typeface, like this:
`persistence.properties`.

We present code in two different ways:

```
We use a monofont type with no highlighting for most code examples.
```

```
We use bold to emphasize code that is particularly important in the present
context or to show changes from a previous code snippet.
```

Also, code editors like Notepad++ provide a rich color scheme to indicate various parts of code syntax. That's a great tool to help you learn language features in the editor and to help prevent mistakes as you code. The code listings in this book are colorized using colors similar to what you would see on screen in Notepad++ working with the book's code. In order to optimize print clarity, some colors have a slightly different hue in print than what you see on screen. But all of the colors for the code in this book should be close enough to the default Notepad++ colors to give you an accurate representation of the colors.

SOURCE CODE

As you work through the examples in this book, you may choose either to type the code yourself or use the source code files that accompany the book. All the source code used in this book is available for download at `www.wrox.com`. When at the site, simply locate the book's title (use the Search box or one of the title lists) and click the Download Code link on the book's detail page to obtain all the source code for the book. All the Try It Out example code is included in the download files for the book at Wrox.com. In addition, any other code snippets that are included with the download files are highlighted by the following icon:

Available for download on Wrox.com

Code snippets include the filename as it appears in the download files in a code note such as this:

code snippet /path/filename

 NOTE *Because many books have similar titles, you may find it easiest to search by ISBN; this book's ISBN is 978-0-470-89152-0.*

After you download the code, just decompress it with your favorite compression tool. Alternatively, you can go to the main Wrox code download page at www.wrox.com/dynamic/books/download .aspx to see the code available for this book and all other Wrox books.

ERRATA

We make every effort to ensure that there are no errors in the text or in the code. However, no one is perfect, and mistakes do occur. If you find an error in one of our books, like a spelling mistake or faulty piece of code, we would be very grateful for your feedback. By sending in errata, you may save another reader hours of frustration, and at the same time, you will be helping us provide even higher quality information.

To find the errata page for this book, go to www.wrox.com and locate the title using the Search box or one of the title lists. Then, on the book details page, click the Book Errata link. On this page, you can view all errata that has been submitted for this book and posted by Wrox editors.

 NOTE *A complete book list, including links to each book's errata, is also available at* www.wrox.com/misc-pages/booklist.shtml.

If you don't spot "your" error on the Book Errata page, go to www.wrox.com/contact/ techsupport.shtml and complete the form there to send us the error you have found. We'll check the information and, if appropriate, post a message to the book's errata page and fix the problem in subsequent editions of the book.

P2P.WROX.COM

For author and peer discussion, join the P2P forums at p2p.wrox.com. The forums are a web-based system for you to post messages relating to Wrox books and related technologies and interact with other readers and technology users. The forums offer a subscription feature to e-mail you topics of interest of your choosing when new posts are made to the forums. Wrox authors, editors, other industry experts, and your fellow readers are present on these forums.

At http://p2p.wrox.com, you will find a number of different forums that will help you, not only as you read this book, but also as you develop your own applications. To join the forums, just follow these steps:

1.   Go to p2p.wrox.com and click the Register link.

2.   Read the terms of use and click Agree.

3.   Complete the required information to join, as well as any optional information you wish to provide, and click Submit.

4.   You will receive an e-mail with information describing how to verify your account and complete the joining process.

 NOTE *You can read messages in the forums without joining P2P, but in order to post your own messages, you must join.*

Once you join, you can post new messages and respond to messages other users post. You can read messages at any time on the Web. If you would like to have new messages from a particular forum e-mailed to you, click the Subscribe to this Forum icon by the forum name in the forum listing.

For more information about how to use the Wrox P2P, be sure to read the P2P FAQs for answers to questions about how the forum software works, as well as many common questions specific to P2P and Wrox books. To read the FAQs, click the FAQ link on any P2P page.

PART I
The Basics

1

Introducing Cascading Style Sheets

WHAT YOU WILL LEARN IN THIS CHAPTER:

- ➤ What CSS is
- ➤ The history of CSS
- ➤ How to create a CSS enhanced HTML document

Cascading Style Sheets (CSS) is a language designed for describing the appearance of documents written in a markup language such as HTML. With CSS you can control the color of text, the style of fonts, the spacing between paragraphs, how columns are sized and laid out, what background images or colors are used, and a variety of other visual effects. One of the major benefits is that the same CSS can be used by more than one page, meaning that the style of an entire website can be adjusted without having to change each page individually.

The most common use for CSS is to style web pages, and in combination with HTML or XHTML (which is used to describe content) and JavaScript (which is used to add interactivity to a site), CSS is a very powerful tool.

The history of how CSS came to be isn't actually all that relevant to CSS authors of today, so you can skip the next bit if you're in a hurry. If, like me, you're interested in the nitty-gritty, read on.

In the early days of the Web, nine different proposals were made to the World Wide Web Consortium, the main standards organization for the Web which is more commonly known as the W3C, for a style sheet language to help separate the visual appearance of a document from its content. In 1994, Cascading HTML Style Sheets was proposed by Håkon Wium Lie, now CTO of Opera Software (a company you'll meet again later in this chapter), but at the time he was working at CERN with Tim Berners-Lee and Robert Cailliau, the two men who invented the World Wide Web. CHSS became CSS because CSS can be applied to more than just HTML, and in December 1996 the CSS level 1 Recommendation was published.

Since then, three more CSS specifications have been published by the W3C. CSS 2 became a recommendation in 1998, with CSS 2.1 (which fixes a few mistakes in 2), and CSS 3 currently existing as candidate recommendations.

Although CSS 3 is still under development, CSS 2.1 is likely to become a fully fledged recommendation in the near future and is well supported by all modern browsers. In this book, you will cover CSS 2.1 as it stands today and take a look at some of the new features in CSS 3 that you can use in browsers today.

In the rest of this chapter, you will learn the advantages of using CSS and then get started with your first Cascading Style Sheet.

ADVANTAGES OF USING CSS

By using CSS for the presentation of a document, you can substantially reduce the amount of time you spend composing not only a single document but an entire website As you'll discover, CSS is much more versatile than the styling mechanisms provided by HTML alone. The versatility of CSS, when harnessed effectively, can reduce the amount of hard disk space that a website occupies, as well as the amount of bandwidth required to transmit that website from the server to the browser. CSS has the following advantages:

➤ The presentation of an entire website can be centralized to one or a handful of documents, enabling the look and feel of a website to be updated at a moment's notice. In legacy HTML documents, the presentation is contained entirely in the body of each document. CSS brings a much needed feature to HTML: the separation of a document's structure from its presentation. CSS can be written independently of HTML.

➤ Browsers are beginning to support multiple alternative style sheets, a feature that allows more than one design of a website to be presented at the same time. The user can simply select the look and feel that he or she likes most. This could only be done previously with the aid of more complex programming languages.

➤ Style sheets allow content to be optimized for more than one type of device. By using the same HTML document, different versions of a website can be presented for handheld devices such as PDAs and cell phones or for printing.

➤ Style sheets download much more quickly because web documents using CSS commonly consume less bandwidth. Browsers also use a feature called *caching*, a process by which your browser will download a CSS file or other web document only once, and not request that file from the web server again unless it's been updated, further providing your website with the potential for lightning-fast performance.

➤ Users of a website can compose style sheets of their own, a feature that makes websites more accessible. For example, a user can compose a high-contrast style sheet that makes content easier to read. Many browsers provide controls for this feature for novice users, but it is CSS nonetheless.

These features, along with the power of the cascade, which you will read about in Chapter 4, makes the planning, production, and maintenance of a website simpler with Cascading Style Sheets than with HTML alone. By using CSS to present your web documents, you can cut days of development and planning time.

HOW TO WRITE CSS

To write CSS, just as is the case when writing HTML source, you will need a text editor. Word processing programs such as Microsoft Word aren't ideally suited for CSS, because they automatically do lots of things that are helpful when writing a letter or book, such as correct spelling but get in the way when writing code.

Instead, you want something that doesn't make any changes that you don't want to what you type but lets you write and save plain text.

The Windows Notepad program is one example of a text editor that is ideal for composing source code. To launch Notepad, choose Start ➪ Run and then type **Notepad** in the Open textbox.

On Mac OS X, the Notepad equivalent is TextEdit, which can be found in the Mac OS X Applications folder.

There are more advanced text editors that will do useful things such as color your code so that it is clear which parts do what (this is known as syntax highlighting) or automatically complete code for you when you've started typing.

Editors available for Windows include:

➤ Notepad++: `http://sourceforge.net/projects/notepad-plus/` (free)

➤ Crimson Editor: `www.crimsoneditor.com` (free)

➤ HTML-kit: `www.chami.com/html-kit` (free)

And here are some alternative text editors that work with Mac OS X:

➤ TextWrangler: `www.barebones.com` (free)

➤ TextMate: `http://macromates.com/` (retail with 30 day free trial)

➤ You can find more text editors suitable for CSS and HTML at `http://en.wikipedia.org/wiki/List_of_HTML_editors`

In addition, there is the very popular Adobe Dreamweaver (`www.adobe.com/products/dreamweaver`), which combines a text editor with a WYSIWYG (or What You See Is What You Get) code generator, which lets you use a graphical interface to create web pages in HTML and CSS. To follow along with the code in this book, you must use the code view of Dreamweaver or similar application rather than the WYSIWYG view.

You must create HTML files with the `.html` extension. If you use Notepad or TextEdit, beware of your files being saved with a `.txt` extension, which will not result in a web browser interpreting your file as ordinary text rather than HTML.

To ensure that your files are saved properly on Windows, choose Start ➪ Run and type **Explorer** (or right-click Start and choose Explore from the pop-up menu) to open Windows Explorer. After

Windows Explorer is open, choose Tools ⇨ Folder Options to open the Folder Options window, click the View tab, and uncheck the Hide Extensions for Known File Types box. Then click OK.

On Mac OS X, open Finder, and go to Finder ⇨ Preferences. Select the Advanced tab, and check the box for Show All File Extensions.

YOUR FIRST CSS-ENABLED DOCUMENT

The following example is designed to introduce you to what CSS is capable of. It will help you get your feet wet and get straight down to the business of writing style sheets.

 NOTE *You can find the images and source code for the following example at* www.wrox.com. *While for this example you should obtain the source code from* www.wrox.com, *I recommend that for most chapters you type the example so that you can get used to writing the syntax and take in the different bits that come together in each example.*

TRY IT OUT Create a Web Page with HTML and CSS

Example 1-1

To write your first CSS-enabled document, follow these steps.

1. In your text editor of choice, enter the following markup:

```
<!DOCTYPE html PUBLIC "-//W3C//DTD HTML 4.01//EN"
    "http://www.w3.org/TR/html4/strict.dtd">
<html lang="en">
<head>
    <meta http-equiv="Content-Type" content="text/html; charset=utf-8">
    <title>Example 1-1</title>
    <link rel="stylesheet" type="text/css" href="example_1-1.css">
</head>
<body>

<h1>The gas giants</h1>

<div class="planet jupiter">

    <h2>Jupiter</h2>

    <p>Jupiter is the fifth planet from the Sun and the largest planet within the
        Solar System. The Romans named the planet after the god Jupiter. It is a gas
        giant with a mass two and a half times the mass of all the other planets in
        our Solar System combined.</p>

    <table>
        <caption>Jupiter Facts</caption>
        <tbody>
```

```html
        <tr>
            <th>Distance from the Sun</th>
            <td>78,412,020 km</td>
        </tr>
        <tr>
            <th>Equatorial Radius</th>
            <td>71,492 km</td>
        </tr>
        <tr>
            <th>Volume</th>
            <td>1,425,500,000,000,000 km<sup>3</sup></td>
        </tr>
        <tr>
            <th>Mass</th>
            <td>1,898,700,000,000,000,000,000,000 kg</td>
        </tr>
    </tbody>
</table>

<a href="http://solarsystem.jpl.nasa.gov/planets/profile.cfm?Object=Jupiter">
More Jupiter facts</a>

</div>

<div class="planet saturn">

<h2>Saturn</h2>

<p>Saturn is the sixth planet from the Sun and the second largest planet in the
    Solar System, after Jupiter. Saturn is named after the Roman god Saturn,
    equated to the Greek Cronus (the Titan father of Zeus), the Babylonian
    Ninurta, and the Hindu Shani.</p>

<table>
    <caption>Saturn Facts</caption>
    <tbody>
        <tr>
            <th>Distance from the Sun</th>
            <td>1,426,725,400 km</td>
        </tr>
        <tr>
            <th>Equatorial Radius</th>
            <td>60,268 km</td>
        </tr>
        <tr>
            <th>Volume</th>
            <td>827,130,000,000,000 km<sup>3</sup></td>
        </tr>
        <tr>
            <th>Mass</th>
            <td>568,510,000,000,000,000,000,000 kg</td>
        </tr>
    </tbody>
</table>

<a href="http://solarsystem.jpl.nasa.gov/planets/profile.cfm?Object=Saturn">
```

```
    More Saturn facts</a>

</div>

<div class="planet uranus">

    <h2>Uranus</h2>

    <p>Uranus is the seventh planet from the Sun, and the third-largest and
        fourth most massive planet in the Solar System. It is named after
        the ancient Greek deity of the sky Uranus the father of Cronus and
        grandfather of Zeus.</p>

    <table>
        <caption>Uranus Facts</caption>
        <tbody>
            <tr>
                <th>Distance from the Sun</th>
                <td>78,412,020 km</td>
            </tr>
            <tr>
                <th>Equatorial Radius</th>
                <td>25,559 km</td>
            </tr>
            <tr>
                <th>Volume</th>
                <td>69,142,000,000,000 km<sup>3</sup></td>
            </tr>
            <tr>
                <th>Mass</th>
                <td>86,849,000,000,000,000,000,000 kg</td>
            </tr>
        </tbody>
    </table>

    <a href="http://solarsystem.jpl.nasa.gov/planets/profile.cfm?Object=Uranus">
    More Uranus facts</a>

</div>

<div class="planet neptune">

    <h2>Neptune</h2>

    <p>Neptune is the eighth and farthest planet from the Sun in our Solar System.
        Named for the Roman god of the sea, it is the fourth-largest planet by
        diameter and the third-largest by mass.</p>

    <table>
        <caption>Neptune Facts</caption>
        <tbody>
            <tr>
                <th>Distance from the Sun</th>
                <td>4,498,252,900 km</td>
```

```
                </tr>
                <tr>
                    <th>Equatorial Radius</th>
                    <td>24,764 km</td>
                </tr>
                <tr>
                    <th>Volume</th>
                    <td>62,526,000,000,000 km<sup>3</sup></td>
                </tr>
                <tr>
                    <th>Mass</th>
                    <td>102,440,000,000,000,000,000,000,000 kg</td>
                </tr>
            </tbody>
        </table>

        <a href="http://solarsystem.jpl.nasa.gov/planets/profile.cfm?Object=Neptune">
        More Neptune facts</a>

    </div>

    </body>

    </html>
```

2. Save the preceding file in a new folder of its own as `example_1-1.html`.

3. Open `example_1-1.html` in your browser. You will see a page that looks something like the image in Figure 1-1.

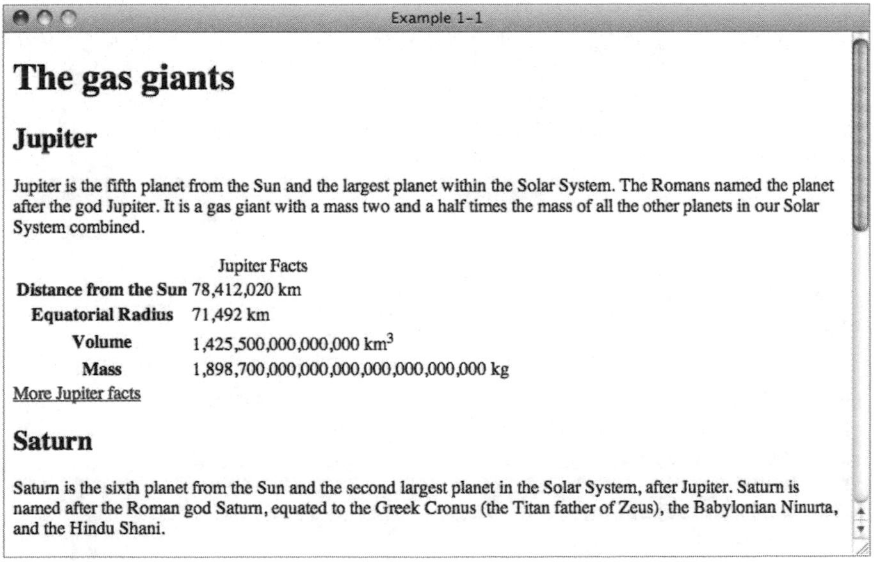

FIGURE 1-1

4. Create a new, blank document in your text editor, and enter the following CSS:

```css
body {
    width: 650px;
    margin: 0 auto;
    background: #000;
    color: #FFF;
    font: 12px sans-serif;
}

h1 {
    font-size: 24px;
}

h2 {
    font-size: 18px;
    margin-top: 0;
}

a {
    color: #FFF;
}

a:focus,
a:hover {
    text-decoration: none;
}

table {
    margin-bottom: 10px;
    border-spacing: 0;
}

caption {
    margin-bottom: 10px;
    font-size: 14px;
    font-weight: bold;
    text-align: left;
}

th,
td {
    padding: 0 10px 0 0;
    text-align: left;
}

.planet {
    margin: 10px 0;
    padding: 20px 20px 20px 200px;
    border: 1px solid #FFF;
    background-position: 20px 20px;
    background-repeat: no-repeat;
}

.jupiter {
```

```
    background-image: url(jupiter.jpg);
}

.saturn {
    background-image: url(saturn.jpg);
}

.uranus {
    background-image: url(uranus.jpg);
}

.neptune {
    background-image: url(neptune.jpg);
}
```

5. Save the preceding CSS in the same folder where you saved example_1-1.html, as
   example_1-1.css.

This code results in the image shown in Figure 1-2, when loaded into Safari on Mac OS X.

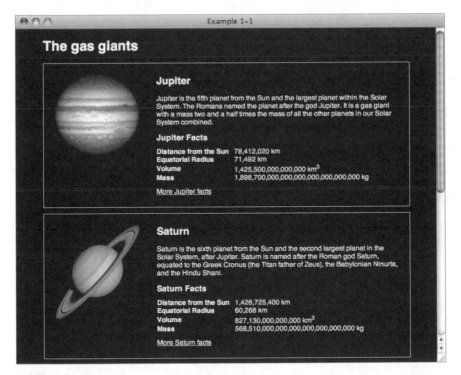

FIGURE 1-2

To see how example_1-1.html looks in other browsers, you can load it up by going to the File menu of
the browser you'd like to view it in, selecting Open or Open File, and locating example_1-1.html on
your hard disk.

How It Works

Example 1-1 is an introduction to a little of what CSS is capable of. This example is designed to get your hands dirty up front with CSS, as a preview of what you can expect throughout the rest of the book. With each new chapter, I introduce and explain the nuts and bolts that come together to make examples like the preceding one. In Figure 1-2, you see that CSS can be used to specify background images and other aesthetic aspects of an HTML document. I continue to revisit and explain the CSS that resulted in Figure 1-2 throughout the book.

If you are feeling adventurous, play around with the CSS used here — try changing some of the values to see what happens. Don't worry if things break, that's all part of learning.

Some times you might find that CSS requires some workarounds specifically to get older versions of Internet Explorer to display content in the same way as Safari, Firefox, Chrome, and Opera. Throughout this book, you also learn the hacks and workarounds that you need to make CSS-enabled web pages compatible with IE 6.

BROWSERS

Unlike with many traditional programming languages on the Web, we don't get to choose the environment in which CSS and HTML is run; your end users make this decision by selecting which web browser they use. Although CSS is a standard supported by all major browsers, there are often differences between them, so it is important to be aware of the top players and to be able to test in each of them before releasing professional code.

It is worth taking a look at Yahoo!'s Graded Browser Support page at `http://developer.yahoo .com/yui/articles/gbs/`, which is regularly updated to show the current range of browsers that Yahoo! recommends that developers test in. It is based on traffic analysis to the Yahoo! network and is quite representative of the Internet as a whole.

You can break down browsers into groups based on the engine that they use for rendering pages; this means browsers that share the same rendering engine are more likely to display things in the same way, which can cut down on testing.

Webkit

Webkit is the rendering engine used by the Apple Safari and Google Chrome browsers. It has good support for CSS 2.1 and supports many features of CSS3.

Safari

Safari is a browser based on the Webkit rendering engine from Apple. It is available for Windows and Mac OS X from `www.apple.com/safari`.

The current version of Safari is version 5 and has just under six percent market share.

Google Chrome

Google's Chrome is also based on the Webkit rendering engine. It is available for Windows and Mac OS X from www.google.com/chrome.

Chrome (the current version is 10) has just over fourteen percent market share. While Chrome is the newcomer to the browser market it is showing rapid rates of adoption and is under heavily active development from Google with new versions released regularly.

Trident

Trident is the engine used by Internet Explorer from Microsoft and comes with the Windows operating system. After many years of market dominance, there are four versions of Internet Explorer in wide use today. Overall, Internet Explorer has more than 46 percent market share. You can download all four versions from windows.microsoft.com/en-US/internet-explorer/downloads/ie.

Internet Explorer 9

Internet Explorer 9 is the latest version of Microsoft's browser; at the time of writing it hasn't even been released yet but will be available by the time this book is published.

Internet Explorer 9 will have good support for both CSS 2.1 and CSS3.

Internet Explorer 8

Internet Explorer 8 is currently the most widely used version with around a 27 percent market share.

Internet Explorer has decent support for CSS 2.1 but is lagging behind other major browsers in support for CSS 3.

Internet Explorer 7

While Internet Explorer 7 never built the market share of version 8 or that of its predecessor, version 6, it still has over 10 percent market share.

While Internet Explorer has decent support for CSS 2.1, it is lacking in support for CSS 3.

Internet Explorer 6

Even though it was released back in 2001, Internet Explorer 6 still has over 16 percent market share. This is thankfully dropping, but this browser will be around for a while and still needs to be tested in for good coverage of the market.

Internet Explorer 6 has support for much of CSS 2.1 but is missing parts that would otherwise make development much easier. It lacks support for CSS 3.

Installing Multiple Versions of Internet Explorer for Testing

At the time of this writing, you cannot install different versions of Internet Explorer on the same copy of Windows. For development, you need a way to test IE 6, IE 7, IE 8, and IE 9, since you'll have visitors to your website on all four browsers. The following are a few ways to do this.

➤ Use PC virtualization/emulation software such as Virtual PC or VirtualBox which allows you to install and run different versions of Windows (or other operating systems such as Linux) from within Windows or Mac OS X. You can load up a new instance of Windows from your Windows desktop and have that instance of Windows run in a window independently.

➤ Another option is setting up multiple different physical computers: one with each version of Internet Explorer installed. This is obviously a more costly option, but might be possible in a commercial environment.

Gecko

While there are many uncommon browsers that use the Gecko rendering engine for practical purposes, you only need to consider one: Mozilla Firefox.

Firefox

You can download Firefox for Windows, Mac OS X, and Linux at `www.firefox.com/`.

At the time of writing, the current version of Firefox is 3.6 and has just over 30 percent market share, making it the second most popular browser. By the time this book is published, Firefox 4 will have been released, which will have similar support for the CSS I cover.

Firefox has good support for CSS 2.1 and supports many features of CSS3.

Presto

The Presto rendering engine is developed by Opera Software for their own range of browsers.

Opera

Opera is a web browser from Opera Software, which has a small marker share of just over 2 percent. While commanding a small market share for desktop browsers, it is a major player in the rapidly expanding mobile market.

Opera has good support for CSS 2.1 and supports many features of CSS3.

The current version of the Opera browser is 11. You can download this browser for Windows, OS X, and Linux from `www.opera.com`.

EXERCISES

1. What are the key benefits of CSS?

2. Name the 5 main web browsers used today.

3. Which is the latest version of Internet Explorer?

► WHAT YOU LEARNED IN THIS CHAPTER

Cascading Style Sheets are the very necessary solution to a cry for more control over the presentation of a document. In this chapter, you learned the following:

TOPIC	KEY CONCEPTS
Why CSS is needed	CSS answers a need for a style sheet language capable of controlling the presentation of not only HTML documents but also several types of documents.
Benefits of CSS	CSS has many advantages. These include accessibility, applicability to more than one language, and applicability to more than one type of device. CSS also allows websites to be planned, produced, and maintained in much less time. CSS enables websites to take up significantly less bandwidth than formerly possible.
Browsers	Safari, Chrome, Internet Explorer, Firefox, and Opera make up the majority of browsers in use today, with Internet Explorer 8 being the world's most popular browser.

2

The Bits that Make Up a Style Sheet

WHAT YOU WILL LEARN IN THIS CHAPTER:

➤ The elements that make up a style sheet

➤ The type of values that are used in CSS

➤ How to include CSS in HTML documents

In Chapter 1 you received a taste of what CSS is capable of in Example 1-1, a web page that contains the four gas giant planets of our solar system and some facts about them. In this chapter, you look at the elements that you combine to make a style sheet.

RULES

A style sheet can be broken down into progressively smaller bits. From large to small, those pieces are:

➤ Style sheet

➤ Rule

➤ Selector

➤ Declaration

➤ Property

➤ Value

Special characters — curly braces, colons, and semi-colons — are used to mark the beginning and ending of each part, separating them from each other. The following rule shows the parts of a style sheet and the special characters that separate them.

```
body {
    width: 650px;
    margin: 0 auto;
    background: #000;
    color: #FFF;
    font: 12px sans-serif;
}
```

You can layout the rule according to your preferences; you can add line breaks and spacing to make CSS readable, sensible, and organized, or you can put everything on one line if you prefer.

Like HTML, CSS can use white space and line breaks to aid readability. In most cases the interpreter reading the CSS doesn't care how much white space appears in the style sheet or how many line breaks are used; provided you have spaces where they are required you can use one or 10. Humans, however, must often add some sort of structure to prevent eyestrain, and to increase maintainability and productivity.

The style used in this book is recommended for readability, but you may find that a different format makes more sense to you. The important thing is to be consistent — pick one style that suits you and stick to it.

Within a rule, *selectors* choose which elements to style in the HTML document. Your browser already applies a default style to most elements (for example, an h1 element is larger than regular text) and you only need to write CSS to change those default styles or to add styles.

SELECTORS

In CSS, a *selector* is the HTML element or elements to which a CSS rule is applied. Put simply, the selector tells the browser what to style. The simple selector that you saw in the previous section is called a *type selector*; it merely references a type of HTML element, and will style all that match. For example, a p type selector on its own will apply styles to all p elements.

As you saw in the example rule, body is written in the style sheet without the left and right angle brackets, < >, and the same applies when styling any element, just swap body with the element you wish to style. This rule applies the CSS properties: width, margin, background, color, and font to the <body> element. I talk more about what these properties do in later chapters, but you might be able to guess what they do just by their names.

Grouping Selectors

When more than one selector appears in the same rule, they are said to be *grouped*. You can group multiple selectors together in a single rule by providing a comma after each selector; the result is that a rule applies to more than one selector at a time, as shown in the following code.

```
th,
td {
    padding: 0 10px 0 0;
    text-align: left;
}
```

You group selectors so that you don't have to repeat the same declarations for each selector. Consider grouping if two or more selectors repeat all or the majority of their declarations.

For readability it is recommended that each selector goes on its own line.

DECLARATIONS

Declarations are enclosed within curly braces to separate them from selectors. In the rule shown previously, each line after body between the curly braces ({ and }) is a separate declaration. A *declaration* is composed of a property name, a colon, and, depending on the property, one or more values.

A colon is used to separate the property from the value, and the property appears before the colon. In our example selector (shown in the "Rules" section) width is a property and 650px is the value associated with it. A declaration always ends with a semi-colon.

VALUES

While the values for some properties can be quite simple, for example, just a single number in the case of the z-index property that you will learn about later, CSS can become quite complex in terms of what it allows a property's value to be. So far, you have only seen a small number of the potential types of values that you see in CSS. In the coming sections I discuss each of the different types of values used in CSS in greater detail, beginning with keyword values.

Keywords

A *keyword* value is a named value; for example, red, green, and blue are CSS keywords. Color keywords can be used on any property that accepts a color value.

The keywords in the following code are bold, and left. bold, when used with the font-weight property, provides the browser with instructions for how to render the text of a caption element, and left is a keyword that when used with the text-align property tells the browser how text is to be aligned.

```
caption {
    margin-bottom: 10px;
    font-size: 14px;
    font-weight: bold;
    text-align: left;
}
```

Many types of keywords are used in CSS, and sometimes a single keyword can apply different styles depending on the property or element on which it is used. The auto keyword, for example, is used by CSS to apply some default style or behavior, and although in both of the following examples its meaning is the same, the resulting effect is different. Try the auto keyword in the following Try It Out.

TRY IT OUT | **Adding Auto Width to a Table**

Example 2-1

To see the effects of the auto keyword as applied to a <table> element, follow these steps.

1.   Enter the following HTML-compliant markup.

```
<!DOCTYPE html PUBLIC "-//W3C//DTD HTML 4.01//EN"
    "http://www.w3.org/TR/html4/strict.dtd">
<html lang="en">
<head>
    <meta http-equiv="Content-Type" content="text/html; charset=utf-8">
    <title>Example 2-1</title>
    <style type="text/css">
        table {
            width: auto;
            background: black;
            color: white;
        }
    </style>
</head>
<body>

    <h1>How will this table react to auto width?</h1>

    <table>
        <caption>Jupiter Facts</caption>
        <tbody>
            <tr>
                <th>Distance from the Sun</th>
                <td>78,412,020 km</td>
            </tr>
            <tr>
                <th>Equatorial Radius</th>
                <td>71,492 km</td>
            </tr>
            <tr>
                <th>Volume</th>
                <td>1,425,500,000,000,000 km<sup>3</sup></td>
            </tr>
            <tr>
                <th>Mass</th>
                <td>1,898,700,000,000,000,000,000,000 kg</td>
            </tr>
```

```
        </tbody>
    </table>

</body>

</html>
```

2. Save the preceding markup as **example_2-1.html**, and then load it into a browser. Figure 2-1 shows width: auto; applied to the <table> element.

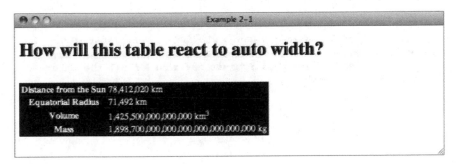

FIGURE 2-1

How It Works

In Figure 2-1, you can see that the table expands only enough to accommodate the text within it.

When width: auto; is applied to a <table> element, it invokes a different mechanism for width measurement than when it is applied to a <div> element. In the next Try It Out, see what happens when auto width is applied to a <div> element.

TRY IT OUT Applying Auto Width to a Div

Example 2-2

To see the effects of the auto keyword as applied to a <div> element, follow these steps.

1. Enter the following document:

```
<!DOCTYPE html PUBLIC "-//W3C//DTD HTML 4.01//EN"
    "http://www.w3.org/TR/html4/strict.dtd">
<html lang="en">
<head>
    <meta http-equiv="Content-Type" content="text/html; charset=utf-8">
    <title>Example 2-2</title>
    <style type="text/css">
        div {
            width: auto;
```

```
            background: black;
            color: white;
        }
    </style>
</head>
<body>

    <h1>How will this div react to auto width?</h1>

    <div>

        <h2>Jupiter</h2>

        <p>Jupiter is the fifth planet from the Sun and the largest planet within
        the Solar System. The Romans named the planet after the god Jupiter. It
        is a gas giant with a mass two and a half times the mass of all the other
        planets in our Solar System combined.</p>

    </div>

</body>

</html>
```

2. Save the preceding markup as **example_2-2.html**. Figure 2-2 shows width: auto; applied to the <div> element.

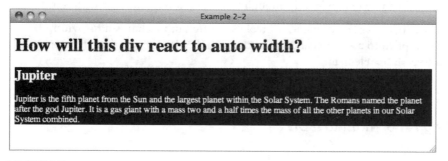

FIGURE 2-2

How It Works

All elements with a width property have an auto value by default, but not all elements behave the same way when auto width is applied. The <table> element, for instance, only expands horizontally to accommodate its data, which is a method called *shrink-to-fit*. A <div> element, on the other hand, expands horizontally as far as there is space, which is called *expand-to-fit*.

I've added a background for each element in Examples 2-1 and 2-2 so that you can see its width. The border outlines the edges of each element, showing exactly how much space each element occupies. You learn more about how width works in Chapter 8.

Keywords always invoke some special, predefined behavior. Another example I can present is with the CSS `border` property: A border may take three separate keywords that define how it appears when the browser renders it:

```
border: thin solid black;
```

This example defines a property with three keyword values: `thin`, `solid`, and `black`. Each value refers to a different characteristic of the border's appearance: `thin` refers to its measurement, `solid` to its style, and `black` to its color.

Sometimes you need to include content from a style sheet, or referencing a file path, or including a font name that has spaces in its name, or referencing an HTML element's attribute value. To accomplish these tasks, CSS supports a type of value called strings.

Strings

A *string* is any sequence of characters. For example, "Hello, World" is a string. As in most programming languages, strings in CSS are enclosed within either single or double quotation marks. Strings may contain text, numbers, symbols — any type of character.

 NOTE *A string is what is known as a data type. Other examples of data types are integers and real numbers. An integer can be a positive or negative number, but it can only be a whole number without decimal places. Real numbers are like integers, but they can have decimal places.*

The purpose of data types is to tell us where we can use different types of values. For example, we can't use a string or a real number if a property requires an integer as a value.

One use of strings in CSS is to specify a font that contains spaces in its name.

```
font-family: 'Times New Roman', Times, serif;
```

Font faces with spaces in the name are enclosed with quotations to keep the program that interprets CSS from getting confused. The quotes act as marking posts for where the font face's name begins and ends.

The following Try It Out shows the result of using a string as a value for the `font-family` property.

TRY IT OUT | **Change the Font of a Heading**

Example 2-3

1. Type in the following document:

```
<!DOCTYPE html PUBLIC "-//W3C//DTD HTML 4.01//EN"
    "http://www.w3.org/TR/html4/strict.dtd">
<html lang="en">
<head>
    <meta http-equiv="Content-Type" content="text/html; charset=utf-8">
    <title>Example 2-3</title>
    <style type="text/css">
        body {
            font: 12px sans-serif;
        }

        h1 {
            font-family: 'Times New Roman', Times, serif;
        }
    </style>
</head>
<body>

    <h1>Gas Giants</h1>

    <p>Information about the 4 gas planets in our solar system.</p>


</body>

</html>
```

2. Save the preceding markup as **example_2-3.html**. Figure 2-3 shows the output.

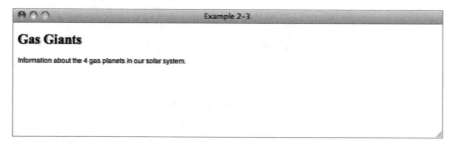

FIGURE 2-3

How It Works

The first rule in the CSS sets the font-family of all text in the <body> element to your browser's default sans-serif font. In the second rule you set the font of the <h1> element by setting the CSS font-family property to Times New Roman if that font is installed on your computer, falling back to Times if it is not, and finally to the browser's default serif font if neither Times New Roman or Times fonts are available.

Length and Measurement

There are two kinds of lengths used in CSS: relative and absolute. *Absolute lengths* are not dependent on any other measurement. An absolute measurement retains its length regardless of the environment (operating system, browser, or screen resolution of a computer monitor) in which it is applied. *Relative lengths*, on the other hand, depend on the environment in which they're used, such as the computer monitor's screen resolution or the size of a font.

Absolute measurements are defined based on real-world units such as inches, centimeters, points, and so on. These measurements have been used for centuries in the print industry, and one would be accustomed to finding them on a ruler.

Absolute Measurement

CSS supports a variety of real-world measurements. Each absolute length unit supported by CSS is defined in the following table.

UNIT ABBREVIATION	DESCRIPTION
in	Inches
cm	Centimeters
mm	Millimeters
pt	Points, 1 point is equal to 1/72nd of an inch
pc	Picas, 1 pica is equal to 12 points

Absolute lengths are not intended for the computer screen; they are intended for where a physical measurement is necessary. For example, printing a document requires real-word measurements. You cover print styles in Chapter 15. For now you will not be using absolute measurements.

Relative Measurement

Relative measurement is better suited for the purpose of onscreen layout. The following table defines the four types of relative measurement that CSS allows.

UNIT ABBREVIATION	DESCRIPTION
em	Length relevant to the nearest font size.
ex	The x-height of the relevant font (height of the letter x).
px	Pixels, relative to the viewing device, for example, a computer monitor.
%	Percentage measurement; how percentage length is calculated depends on what property it is being applied to.

The *em* and *ex* units are measured relative to the font size of a document, *pixels* use the real pixels of the monitor's screen resolution, and *percentage measurement* depends on what property it is being applied to. In the coming sections you explore each type of relative measurement in greater detail.

> **NOTE** *While pixels are defined in the CSS documentation as an absolute measurement, in reality the size of each pixel depends on a number of factors, most importantly the environment's screen resolution.*
>
> *For this reason I will treat pixels as a relative unit of measurement in this book.*

Pixel Measurements

As you may have guessed from the discussion in this chapter about absolute measurements, pixels, the *px* measurement, are measured relative to the computer monitor's settings. This measurement depends on the resolution of the user's monitor. For instance, a 1px measurement viewed at a resolution of 800 x 600 is larger than a 1px measurement viewed at a resolution of 1024 x 768.

Pixel measurements are most useful on the screen; for print it is often better to use absolute measurements or other relative units. I discuss this issue further in Chapter 15.

Try setting the size of text using pixel values yourself in the following Try It Out.

TRY IT OUT **Change the Size of a Heading with Pixels**

Example 2-4

To see how font sizes in absolute units work, follow these steps.

1. Enter the following markup into your text editor.

```
<!DOCTYPE html PUBLIC "-//W3C//DTD HTML 4.01//EN"
    "http://www.w3.org/TR/html4/strict.dtd">
<html lang="en">
<head>
    <meta http-equiv="Content-Type" content="text/html; charset=utf-8">
    <title>Example 2-4</title>
    <style type="text/css">
        body {
            font: 12px sans-serif;
        }

        h1 {
            font-family: 'Times New Roman', Times, serif;
            font-size: 46px;
        }
    </style>
```

```
</head>
<body>

    <h1>Gas Giants</h1>

    <p>Information about the 4 gas planets in our solar system.</p>

</body>

</html>
```

2. Save the document as **example_2-4.html**, and load it into your favorite browser. When you load Example 2-4 into a browser, you should see something like Figure 2-4.

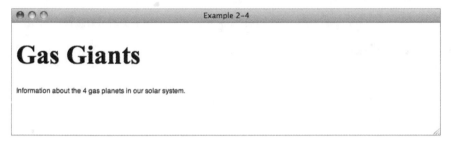

FIGURE 2-4

How It Works

In this example you set the font size of the <body> element and the <h1> element in pixel units by using the CSS font-size property.

Measurement Based on the Font Size

Measurement in *em* is one of three favored relative measurements for onscreen layout, for most measurements alongside pixels and percentages. A measurement that is relative to the font size allows for designs that scale up and down gracefully with the user's font size preferences.

All modern browsers provide a mechanism for scaling the font size up or down to the user's preference. This causes the size of an em to change as well, so any values based on em units will also change.

Try setting the size of text using em values yourself in the following Try It Out.

TRY IT OUT | Change the Size of a Heading with Em Values

Example 2-5

1. Type in the following document:

```
<!DOCTYPE html PUBLIC "-//W3C//DTD HTML 4.01//EN"
    "http://www.w3.org/TR/html4/strict.dtd">
<html lang="en">
<head>
    <meta http-equiv="Content-Type" content="text/html; charset=utf-8">
    <title>Example 2-5</title>
    <style type="text/css">
        body {
            font: 12px sans-serif;
        }

        h1 {
            font-family: 'Times New Roman', Times, serif;
            font-size: 2em;
        }
    </style>
</head>
<body>

    <h1>Gas Giants</h1>

    <p>Information about the 4 gas planets in our solar system.</p>

</body>

</html>
```

2. Save the preceding markup as **example_2-5.html**. Figure 2-5 shows the output.

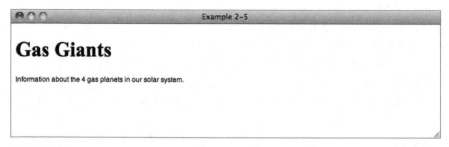

FIGURE 2-5

How It Works

The first rule is applied to the <body> element, and sets the default size of all text in the document to 12px. Then you set the font size of the <h1> element by using the CSS font-size property to 2em, or 2 times the size of regular text.

Percentage Measurements

Percentage measurements are always dependent on something else; therefore, percentage measurements are also a form of relative measurement. Specifically, they are relative to another element's measurement, whether it's an inherited font size or the width or height of a containing element. Exactly which element the percentage measurement is relative to depends on a number of factors, including the property and/or value you're using a percentage measurement for, as well as the other CSS applied to the document.

Measurements Based on the Height of the Lowercase Letter "x"

The *ex* measurement, also known as *x-height*, is (like the em) based on the font size. However, the ex measurement is relative to the height of the lowercase letter "x". The ex measurement is another unit of measurement derived from typography. This can be inconsistent across different fonts, so it is best avoided when designing for display on a computer monitor, and for print style sheets you will most commonly use em or pt values.

Because it's a presentational language, most of CSS is affected in some way by length and units of measurement. The fundamental unit for all measurements when you design for display on a computer monitor is the pixel, because computers display images in pixels. You can define lengths relative to font sizes, using em units as the most practical and consistent solution. Absolute lengths, on the other hand, are better suited for print because of the multitude of inconsistencies that occur when absolutes are used for presentations on a computer monitor. In the next section, I continue the discussion of CSS property values with a look at how CSS interprets numbers.

Numbers

CSS allows numbers as values for several properties. Two types of numbers are accepted by CSS: *integers* and *real numbers*. Like strings, integers and real numbers are data types and are often used in CSS for the measurement of length. Integers are whole numbers without a decimal value. Real numbers can have a decimal value which increases the precision of measurements in CSS. You can usually use either type of number anywhere a number is a valid value, but in some cases it doesn't make sense — pixel values cannot be more precise than an integer, for example, there is no such things as 0.5px.

In CSS, numbers may be preceded by a plus (+) or minus (-) to indicate that the number is positive or negative respectively. Although some properties, for example, font-size, do not accept negative values, many do. As you can see in the following example, one property that allows negative values is the margin property.

Setting a Negative Margin

Example 2-6

To see what happens when the margin property has a negative value, follow these steps.

1. Enter the following markup:

```
<!DOCTYPE html PUBLIC "-//W3C//DTD HTML 4.01//EN"
    "http://www.w3.org/TR/html4/strict.dtd">
<html lang="en">
<head>
    <meta http-equiv="Content-Type" content="text/html; charset=utf-8">
    <title>Example 2-6</title>
    <style type="text/css">
        body {
            font: 12px sans-serif;
        }

        h2 {
            margin-left: -20px;
        }

        div {
            padding-left: 20px;
        }
    </style>
</head>
<body>

    <h1>The gas giants</h1>

    <div class="planet jupiter">

        <h2>Jupiter</h2>

        <p>Jupiter is the fifth planet from the Sun and the largest planet within
        the Solar System. The Romans named the planet after the god Jupiter. It
        is a gas giant with a mass two and a half times the mass of all the other
        planets in our Solar System combined.</p>

    </div>

</body>

</html>
```

2. Save the markup that you entered as **example_2-6.html**, and load it into your favorite browser. You should see something similar to Figure 2-6.

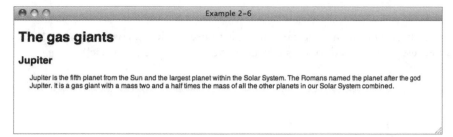

FIGURE 2-6

How It Works

From Figure 2-6, you can see that the text in the div has been shifted to the right by 20px by giving the `padding-left` property a value of `20px`, but the heading has been shifted back to the left by using a negative value for `margin-left`. You learn more about how the margin property works in Chapter 8.

Colors

CSS has a number of options for specifying colors, ranging from a 216-color, Web-safe palette to the full range of colors available in the RGB format, a total of 16,777,216 colors! More specifically, those options are as follows:

➤ **Color keywords:** These enable you to specify a color by its name. There are only a small number of keywords available compared to the millions that you can use with other color value types.

➤ **Hexadecimal:** This enables you to specify a color by a special hexadecimal number.

➤ **Shorthand hexadecimal:** This is a shortened representation of hexadecimal numbers; it is limited to a special 216-color, Web-safe palette.

➤ **RGB values:** These enable you to specify a color via a Red, Green, Blue representation, which provides access to millions of colors.

➤ **RGB percentage:** This option is the same as RGB but uses percentages.

➤ **RGBA (RGB with alpha channel):** The RGB palette is used with the addition of an alpha channel to specify transparency.

Each method is a means of accomplishing the same thing: specifying a color. You can use these methods to specify text color, border color, or background color. Next, you see what each of these methods looks like when used in the context of a style sheet rule.

Color Keywords

The first method for specifying color, mentioned previously, is to use a color keyword. This is the most intuitive method because all you need to do is reference the name of the color itself. Here are some examples:

```
div {
    color: black;
    background-color: red;
    border: thin solid orange;
}
```

This rule applies to any <div> element contained in the document. I have specified that each <div> element should have black text, a red background, and a thin, solid orange border around the element. In this example, black, red, and orange are color keywords, so a color keyword is simply the name of the color.

 NOTE A complete table of CSS-supported color keywords is available in Appendix D.

Hexadecimal Colors

Hexadecimal refers to a numbering scheme that uses 16 characters as its base, expressed in a combination of letters and numbers. A hexadecimal system uses 0-9 for the first 10 digits and A-F to represent the remaining 6 digits. Letter *A* corresponds to the decimal number 10, *B* to 11, *C* to 12, and so on up to 15, which is represented by *F*. Therefore 10 in hex is equivalent to 16 in decimal, and FFF in hex is the equivalent of 255 in decimal.

Hexadecimal values are another way of expressing an RGB value. For instance, #FFFFFF refers to white, which is expressed in RGB as 255, 255, 255.

In CSS, hexadecimal colors are included just as RGB or color keywords are, as shown in the following example.

```
div {
    color: #000000;
    background-color: #FF0000;
    border: thin solid #FFA500;
}
```

#000000 is the hexadecimal representation of black; the same as RGB 0, 0, 0 or simply the black color keyword. #FF0000 is a hexadecimal representation of red, or RGB 255, 0, 0, or the red color keyword. Finally, #FFA500 is a hexadecimal representation of orange, or RGB 255, 165, 0, or the orange color keyword.

Short Hexadecimal

When a hexadecimal value is made up of 3 pairs of duplicated values you can use a shorthand notation of the value which uses only a single value for each pair. For example, the hexadecimal value for white is #FFFFFF. This is 3 pairs of FF and can therefore be shortened to #FFF.

```
div {
    background-color: #FAB;
}
```

In this example, #FAB is equivalent to #FFAABB which fans of the 1960s British TV series *Thunderbirds* in particular may be interested to know is a rather vivid shade of pink!

RGB Colors

RGB stands for Red, Green, and Blue. These are the primary colors used to display the color of pixels on a computer monitor. When you use these three colors in various combinations, it is possible to create every color of the rainbow. Many computer monitors are capable of displaying millions of colors: 16,777,216 colors, in fact. CSS RGB color is specified using a special three-number syntax, with each one representing a color channel. This first number is red, the second green, and the third blue:

```
body {
    background-color: rgb(128, 128, 128);
}
```

This produces the same color as the CSS color keyword gray. Equal amounts of all three channels form a variation of gray, where 0, 0, 0 is black and 255, 255, 255 is white.

RGB values may also be represented using percentages:

```
body {
    background-color: rgb(50%, 50%, 50%);
}
```

This also produces the same color as the CSS color keyword gray.

The URI

CSS uses a special term — URI (Universal Resource Indicator) — when the location of a resource or data file must be specified. URIs are most often used in CSS for two purposes:

➤ The inclusion of style sheets

➤ The inclusion of background images

The URI is referenced using a special method, as shown in the following example:

```
.jupiter {
    background-image: url(jupiter.jpg);
}
```

The `url()` syntax is used to enclose the URI of the file being referenced. In this example, `jupiter .jpg` must exist in the same directory as the style sheet. If the style sheet is named `mystyle.css` and it's located at `www.example.com/styles/mystyle.css`, the `mypicture.jpg` file must also exist in the `styles` directory, where its path is `www.example.com/styles/mypicture.jpg`. The complete, absolute path or the shortened relative paths are both acceptable references to the file. I address this topic again in Chapter 7, where I discuss the `background` property and the syntax it allows.

INCLUDING CSS IN A DOCUMENT

CSS is very flexible regarding how you call it in a document. You can include CSS in a document in four ways:

➤ CSS can be included in a document by using embedded style sheets, which are included between `<style>` and `</style>` tags directly in an HTML document. These tags must appear between the `<head>` and `</head>` tags.

```
<style type="text/css">
    body {
        font: 12px sans-serif;
    }
</ style >
```

➤ CSS can be included in its own document and linked to an HTML document by using the `<link>` element. Note that as the link element can be used for more than just referencing CSS files, such as linking to RSS feeds for the current site, it is important to include `rel="stylesheet"` so that the browser knows what we want it to do.

```
<link rel="stylesheet" type="text/css" href="example_1-1.css">
```

➤ CSS can be imported from within either an embedded or linked style sheet by using an `@import` rule.

```
<style type="text/css">
        @import url(example_1-1.css);
</ style >
```

➤ CSS declarations can be applied directly to an element in an HTML document by using inline styles with the `style` attribute.

```
<body style="font: 12px sans-serif;">
```

So far, you have used embedded style sheets and linked style sheets. I recommend that you continue to use these unless you have a reason not to. There are benefits to the import method for more advanced authors of CSS, but disadvantages as well, which are beyond the scope of this book to discuss.

Under no circumstances can I recommend that you use `style` attributes directly on HTML elements. This approach removes many of the benefits of CSS, such as being able to style multiple elements with a single rule, and also makes your CSS harder to organize and manage as you will see in Chapter 4 when we discuss specificity.

Including an Embedded Style Sheet

To embed a style sheet in to your document simply add a `<style type="text/css"></style>` element to the `<head>` element of your document. Inside the `<style>` tags add CSS in the same way that you have done throughout this chapter.

Embedded style sheets are very useful for development and debugging. When you are working on a page, including CSS directly in the document removes browser cache issues, whereas a linked style sheet may be stored by your browser and not updated when you refresh the page.

They are not recommended when your site is live; however, there are benefits to linking to external style sheets, which we will discuss next.

Linking to External Style Sheets

External style sheets are the preferred method of CSS inclusion in a web document, as a single style sheet can be shared by multiple pages on a website and can be cached by the user's browser. Caching frees the user, who no longer needs to download the website's style sheet on every page, leading to faster page load times and less bandwidth used per page request.

Here's a demonstration of the `<link>` element method:

```
<link rel="stylesheet" type="text/css" href="example_1-1.css">
```

The following attributes are required to use the `<link>` element for linking to a CSS document:

➤ `rel`: Defines the relation between the external document and the current document. In this case, the relation is that the external document is the style sheet for the calling document.

➤ `type`: Refers to the MIME type of the external file. For CSS this is always `text/css`.

➤ `href`: Like the anchor tag, `<a>`, `href` stands for hyperlink reference. It accepts an absolute or relative path to the style sheet document.

An *absolute path* means the complete path to the file. For instance, www.example.com is an absolute path. A *relative path* triggers the application to find the CSS file relative to the requesting document. So if the example file's URL is www.example.com/example.html and the CSS document is stored in the `stylesheets` directory as `stylesheet.css`, the relative path included in `<link>` is `stylesheets/stylesheet.css` and the full absolute path to the document is www.example.com/stylesheets/stylesheet.css.

When you are serving your site from a web server rather than just a folder on your computer, it is recommended that you use an absolute path starting from after your domain name, i.e., `/stylesheets/stylesheet.css`.

THE IMPORTANCE OF GOOD HTML

Although this book is about CSS, we cannot ignore HTML. While all of the CSS in this book is used with HTML 4.01, they will also work without alteration with HTML written to other standards, for example, HTML5 or XHTML standards, such as XHTML 1.0.

Regardless of which flavor of HTML that you choose to use it cannot be stressed enough how important good, valid markup is to achieving consistent rendering across browsers. While valid markup is not an absolute guarantee that you will not encounter rendering problems, your markup is a good place to check first if you do. You can make use of the W3C markup validator at `http://validator.w3.org/` or your IDE may have validation tools built in.

Doctypes and Quirks Mode

The most important thing to ensure in HTML documents is that you have used a valid modern doctype. Any of the strict doctypes that are HTML 4.01 or above or any version of XHTML listed at `www.w3.org/QA/2002/04/valid-dtd-list.html` will be suitable.

The reason that you must use a valid doctype is that if you don't, modern browsers will use a rendering mode know as Quirks Mode. The reason for this is to allow for older code to render as it was intended, on the assumption that if the code author was following the recommended standards, then they would have included a valid doctype.

Quirks mode changes the way CSS works, for example, widths of elements are calculated differently, as are the styles applied to content in tables. This makes it difficult to write CSS that works as you expect in all browsers and greatly increases the amount of time you will need for testing.

EXERCISES

1. Name the different components that make up a CSS rule.

2. What's the difference between when `width: auto;` is applied to a `<table>` as opposed to a `<div>` element?

3. Complete the sequence: Declaration, Property, _____

4. Convert the color RGB(234, 123, 45) to hexadecimal.

5. What is the shortened hexadecimal notation of `#FFFFFF`?

6. If I have a style sheet located at `www.example.com/stylesheet.css`, and a web page located at `www.example.com/index.html`, what markup would I include in index.html to include `stylesheet.css` via a relative path?

▶ WHAT YOU LEARNED IN THIS CHAPTER

Throughout this chapter, you learned about the bits and pieces that make CSS work. To recap, in this chapter you learned the following:

TOPIC	KEY CONCEPTS
Elements of a style sheet	Style sheets are made up of rules; rules are made up of selectors and declarations; declarations are made up of properties and values.
Values	Can be keywords, lengths, colors, strings, integers, real numbers, or URIs.
Including CSS in documents	Style sheets can be embedded in documents, which is useful while developing, or linked to and included in external files, which is good practice in production.

3

Selectors

WHAT YOU WILL LEARN IN THIS CHAPTER:

➤ How to use class and ID selectors

➤ How to use the universal selector

➤ How descendant selectors can be used

➤ The pseudo selectors used to style links

In this chapter, you learn about the different types of selectors that CSS supports. In Chapter 2, you learned about the type selector, which applies style sheet declarations by using the HTML element's name. Selectors in CSS have spotty support with regard to IE 6; therefore, almost of the examples at this stage are designed to work in all of the browsers you reviewed in Chapter 1. Don't worry! Advanced selectors are discussed in Chapter 14 for those brave enough, or lucky enough , not to have to support IE 6.

We have already seen the *type selector* in use, that is a selector that references a type of HTML element, so let's continue our discussion of selectors with the most common and widely supported ones: *class* and *ID*.

CLASS AND ID SELECTORS

Class and *ID* selectors are the most widely supported. In fact, they are as widely supported as the type selector introduced in Chapter 2. There are two types of selectors. The `class` selector, which references the `class` attribute used on HTML elements, is the more generic of the two, meaning it may encompass many elements in a given document, even elements of different types or purposes. On the other hand, you can use the `id` attribute on only one element in an HTML document, so we use it in CSS to reference an element that is unique per page. Besides using it in CSS, you can also use an element's class or ID to access it via a scripting language such as JavaScript. You can also link to the location of the element with an ID name using fragment identifiers. Anchors are appended to URLs to force a browser to go to a specific place in a document. You can think of the id attribute as an element's address inside a document: No two addresses can be the same.

CLASS SELECTORS

The following code shows an example of a class name selector.

```
<style type="text/css">
    .planet {
        margin: 10px 0;
        padding: 20px 20px 20px 200px;
        border: 1px solid #FFF;
        background-position: 20px 20px;
        background-repeat: no-repeat;
    }
</style>

<div class="planet jupiter">
    <h2>Jupiter</h2>
</div>
```

The class name selector begins with a dot, followed by the class name itself, which you choose. In the preceding code, the class name selector is .planet. The class name should be comprised of letters, numbers, and hyphens only, to provide the best compatibility with older browsers. Class names must start with a letter and cannot include spaces.

The dot appearing before the class name in the CSS rule tells CSS that you are referencing a class selector. The dot does not need to appear in the class attribute value itself; in fact, it cannot, because the value of the class attribute is just the class name itself.

When used in this context, the type of element doesn't matter — in other words, you can also apply the class to other elements. What if you wanted to give both a <div> and an <img> element the same class name and have a style sheet rule that applies to <div> elements but not <img> elements? You can do that, too. Limiting a class selector to a type of element is demonstrated in the following code.

```
div.planet {
    margin: 10px 0;
    padding: 20px 20px 20px 200px;
    border: 1px solid #FFF;
    background-position: 20px 20px;
    background-repeat: no-repeat;
}
```

This code shows the combination of two types of selectors that you are already familiar with, the type selector you learned about in Chapter 2, and the class selector. When you append a type selector to a class selector, you limit the scope of the style sheet rule to only that type of element. In this example, the rule is limited so that it only applies to <div> elements and no other type of element. You can still create additional rules that reference other elements, such as a new rule that only applies to <img> elements with a class name of *planet*, such as img.planet, but the rule that you see in the preceding applies exclusively to <div> elements with a class name of *planet*.

NOTE *There must not be a space between the element name and the class selector. Including a space gives us a different type of selector, called a* descendant selector, *which we will look at later in this chapter.*

As you have seen, elements can also be assigned more than one class name, for example, class="planet jupiter". The value of this class attribute actually contains two class names: planet and jupiter. Each class name in the attribute is separated by a space. In the corresponding style sheet, the two classes may be referenced by two separate rules, as illustrated in the following code.

```
.planet {
    margin: 10px 0;
    padding: 20px 20px 20px 200px;
    border: 1px solid #FFF;
    background-position: 20px 20px;
    background-repeat: no-repeat;
}

.jupiter {
    background-image: url(jupiter.jpg);
}
```

The two style sheet rules in this code result in the <div> element, with both planet and jupiter class names receiving the declarations of both rules.

If you're thinking to yourself that jupiter looks like a good candidate to be an ID — there is only one Jupiter, but many planets — you're right. We'll revisit this in a few minutes when we look at ID selectors.

NOTE *It is considered best practice to use "semantic" class names in HTML and CSS — that is, class names that describe the function of an element, not its appearance. In the preceding example we could have used a class of* border-1px-solid-white *as follows:*

```
.border-1px-solid-white {
    border: 1px solid #FFF;
}
```

and it would be perfectly valid. However if we wanted to change the border to a different color we would either have to change our HTML to use a different class name, border-1px-solid-yellow *perhaps, or have class names that don't match the result of applying the style.*

By using a class name like planet *we describe what we want planet type elements to look like without tying ourselves to overly descriptive names that may later become out of date or plain wrong.*

You should apply the same principle to IDs — describe an elements function, not it's appearance.

The class names may also be chained together in the style sheet, as shown here:

```
.planet.jupiter {
    background-image: url(jupiter.jpg);
}
```

The preceding rule applies only to elements that reference both class names in their class attribute.

Unfortunately, IE 6 interprets chained class names per the CSS 1 specification, which did not allow chained class names in the style sheet. In IE 6, only the last class name in the chain is recognized. In the preceding example, IE 6 would interpret the .planet.jupiter selector as .jupiter only.

While this has been fixed in later versions of IE it makes the use of chained classes unreliable if you must support IE6, so while it is a powerful technique it is best avoided by beginners. The consequence is that all elements with a class of jupiter will be affected by .planet.jupiter even those that do not also have a class of planet.

Whereas classes are meant to reference more than one element, IDs are meant to reference only one element in a document.

ID Selectors

ID selectors are unique identifiers; an ID is meant to be unique, defined once per document. Like the class selectors discussed in the previous section, a special character precedes ID selectors in a style sheet. To reference an ID, you precede the ID name with a hash mark (or pound sign, #). Like class names, this name cannot contain spaces and must start with a letter. You should use names that only include letters, numbers, hyphens and undersores for compatibility with the older browsers. You see how this is done in the following code.

```
<style type="text/css">
    #jupiter {
        background-image: url(jupiter.jpg);
    }
</style>

<div class="planet" id="jupiter">
    <h2>Jupiter</h2>
</div>
```

Since there's only one Jupiter in the solar system, Jupiter lends itself as a good example of the concept of an ID selector. Just as there is only one Jupiter in the solar system, the ID name jupiter can be used only once in a document, on one element.

Browsers are forgiving of multiple ID names per document as far as style sheets are concerned. However, using an ID name more than once in a document can cause conflicts with other applications of unique ID names. For example, ID names can be used to link to a location within a document (as HTML anchors), or when referencing an element by ID name from JavaScript. When you have an ID name appearing more than once in the HTML document, on more than one element, the browser won't know which one you're linking to, or which one you want to refer to from JavaScript, and will generally select only the first element with the ID. Always use the ID name for its intended purpose, just once per document.

An ID name must be unique in so far as other ID names are concerned, but it may be repeated as a class name, should you want to do so. It's generally best to avoid this though as it's easy to get confused and use the wrong kind of selector, resulting in styling the wrong element(s).

Although only one element in a HTML document may have an ID of jupiter, the CSS may contain as many references to an ID as are necessary. The uniqueness rule only applies to naming the elements, not the references to them.

Now that you've had a proper introduction to the different types of things that ID and class name selectors are capable of, try the following proof-of-concept exercise that lets you see how ID and class selectors work.

TRY IT OUT Class and ID Selectors

Example 3-1

To see how class and ID selectors work, follow these steps.

1. Enter the following markup into your text editor:

```
<!DOCTYPE html PUBLIC "-//W3C//DTD HTML 4.01//EN"
    "http://www.w3.org/TR/html4/strict.dtd">
<html lang="en">
<head>
    <meta http-equiv="Content-Type" content="text/html; charset=utf-8">
    <title>Example 3-1</title>
    <style type="text/css">
        body {
            width: 650px;
            margin: 0 auto;
            background: #000;
            color: #FFF;
            font: 12px sans-serif;
        }

        h1 {
            font-size: 24px;
        }

        h2 {
            font-size: 18px;
            margin-top: 0;
        }

        a {
            color: #FFF;
        }

        a:focus,
        a:hover {
            text-decoration: none;
        }

        table {
```

```
            margin-bottom: 10px;
            border-spacing: 0;
        }

    caption {
        margin-bottom: 10px;
        font-size: 14px;
        font-weight: bold;
        text-align: left;
    }

    th,
    td {
        padding: 0 10px 0 0;
        text-align: left;
    }

    div.planet {
        margin: 10px 0;
        padding: 20px 20px 20px 200px;
        border: 1px solid #FFF;
        background-position: 20px 20px;
        background-repeat: no-repeat;
    }

    #jupiter {
        background-image: url(jupiter.jpg);
    }

    #saturn {
        background-image: url(saturn.jpg);
    }

    #uranus {
        background-image: url(uranus.jpg);
    }

    #neptune {
        background-image: url(neptune.jpg);
    }
    </style>
</head>
<body>

<h1>The gas giants</h1>

<div class="planet" id="jupiter">

    <h2>Jupiter</h2>

    <p>Jupiter is the fifth planet from the Sun and the largest planet within the
    Solar System. The Romans named the planet after the god Jupiter. It is a gas
    giant with a mass two and a half times the mass of all the other planets in
    our Solar System combined.</p>

    <table>
```

```
        <caption>Jupiter Facts</caption>
        <tbody>
            <tr>
                <th>Distance from the Sun</th>
                <td>78,412,020 km</td>
            </tr>
            <tr>
                <th>Equatorial Radius</th>
                <td>71,492 km</td>
            </tr>
            <tr>
                <th>Volume</th>
                <td>1,425,500,000,000,000 km<sup>3</sup></td>
            </tr>
            <tr>
                <th>Mass</th>
                <td>1,898,700,000,000,000,000,000,000 kg</td>
            </tr>
        </tbody>
    </table>

    <a href="http://solarsystem.jpl.nasa.gov/planets/profile.cfm?Object=Jupiter">
    More Jupiter facts</a>

</div>

<div class="planet" id="saturn">

    <h2>Saturn</h2>

    <p>Saturn is the sixth planet from the Sun and the second largest planet in the
    Solar System, after Jupiter. Saturn is named after the Roman god Saturn,
    equated to the Greek Cronus (the Titan father of Zeus), the Babylonian
    Ninurta, and the Hindu Shani.</p>

    <table>
        <caption>Saturn Facts</caption>
        <tbody>
            <tr>
                <th>Distance from the Sun</th>
                <td>1,426,725,400 km</td>
            </tr>
            <tr>
                <th>Equatorial Radius</th>
                <td>60,268 km</td>
            </tr>
            <tr>
                <th>Volume</th>
                <td>827,130,000,000,000 km<sup>3</sup></td>
            </tr>
            <tr>
                <th>Mass</th>
                <td>568,510,000,000,000,000,000,000 kg</td>
            </tr>
        </tr>
```

```
        </tbody>
    </table>

    <a href="http://solarsystem.jpl.nasa.gov/planets/profile.cfm?Object=Saturn">
    More Saturn facts</a>

</div>

<div class="planet" id="uranus">

    <h2>Uranus</h2>

    <p>Uranus is the seventh planet from the Sun, and the third-largest and fourth
    most massive planet in the Solar System. It is named after the ancient Greek
    deity of the sky Uranus the father of Cronus and grandfather of Zeus.</p>

    <table>
        <caption>Uranus Facts</caption>
        <tbody>
            <tr>
                <th>Distance from the Sun</th>
                <td>78,412,020 km</td>
            </tr>
            <tr>
                <th>Equatorial Radius</th>
                <td>25,559 km</td>
            </tr>
            <tr>
                <th>Volume</th>
                <td>69,142,000,000,000 km<sup>3</sup></td>
            </tr>
            <tr>
                <th>Mass</th>
                <td>86,849,000,000,000,000,000,000,000 kg</td>
            </tr>
        </tbody>
    </table>

    <a href="http://solarsystem.jpl.nasa.gov/planets/profile.cfm?Object=Uranus">
    More Uranus facts</a>

</div>

<div class="planet" id="neptune">

    <h2>Neptune</h2>

    <p>Neptune is the eighth and farthest planet from the Sun in our Solar System.
    Named for the Roman god of the sea, it is the fourth-largest planet by
    diameter and the third-largest by mass.</p>

    <table>
        <caption>Neptune Facts</caption>
        <tbody>
            <tr>
```

```
          <th>Distance from the Sun</th>
          <td>4,498,252,900 km</td>
      </tr>
      <tr>
          <th>Equatorial Radius</th>
          <td>24,764 km</td>
      </tr>
      <tr>
          <th>Volume</th>
          <td>62,526,000,000,000 km<sup>3</sup></td>
      </tr>
      <tr>
          <th>Mass</th>
          <td>102,440,000,000,000,000,000,000,000 kg</td>
      </tr>
  </tbody>
</table>

<a href="http://solarsystem.jpl.nasa.gov/planets/profile.cfm?Object=Neptune">
More Neptune facts</a>

</div>

</body>

</html>
```

2. Save the preceding document as **example_3-1.html**. Figure 3-1 shows what Example 3-1 looks like when rendered in Safari. You should see something similar in Firefox, IE, Chrome and Opera.

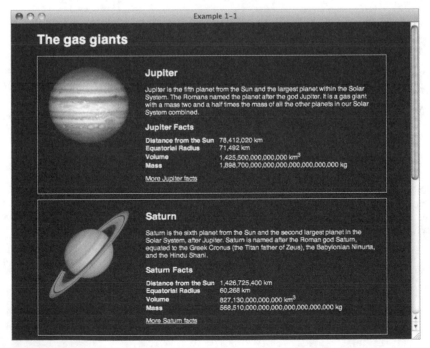

FIGURE 3-1

How It Works

In Example 3-1, you put your newly acquired class and ID selector skills to use by rewriting our example site from Chapter 1 to make use of ID selectors and class selectors qualified by a type selector.

Now that you have worked through this simple, proof-of-concept demonstration of class and ID selectors for yourself, continue to the next section, which discusses the universal, or wildcard selector.

THE UNIVERSAL SELECTOR

The *universal selector* is an asterisk. When used alone, the universal selector tells the CSS interpreter to apply the CSS rule to all elements in the document. The following code shows what a universal selector looks like.

```
* {
    font-family: Arial, Helvetica,sans-serif;
}
```

This rule is applied to all elements contained in the document. The universal selector applies to everything, including form input fields and tables of data. It applies style to any and every element present in a document. In this case all elements would have `font-family: Arial, Helvetica,sans-serif;` applied to them.

You probably won't use the universal selector very often because, as you will see later in this book, there are better ways of applying styles to the whole document.

DESCENDANT SELECTORS

In CSS, *descendant* means an element that is a child, grandchild, great grandchild, and so on, of another element. Descendant selectors apply style based on whether one element contains another. Take, for example, the following code.

```
<div class="planet" id="jupiter">

    <h2>Jupiter</h2>

    <p>Jupiter is the fifth planet from the Sun and the largest planet within the
    Solar System. The Romans named the planet after the god Jupiter. It is a gas
    giant with a mass two and a half times the mass of all the other planets in
    our Solar System combined.</p>

    <table>
        <caption>Jupiter Facts</caption>
        <tbody>
            <tr>
                <th>Distance from the Sun</th>
```

```
                    <td>78,412,020 km</td>
                </tr>
                <tr>
                    <th>Equatorial Radius</th>
                    <td>71,492 km</td>
                </tr>
                <tr>
                    <th>Volume</th>
                    <td>1,425,500,000,000,000 km<sup>3</sup></td>
                </tr>
                <tr>
                    <th>Mass</th>
                    <td>1,898,700,000,000,000,000,000,000 kg</td>
                </tr>
            </tbody>
        </table>

        <a href="http://solarsystem.jpl.nasa.gov/planets/profile.cfm?Object=Jupiter">
        More Jupiter facts</a>

    </div>
```

In this example the `<h2>`, `<p>`, `<a>` and `<table>` elements are child elements of the `<div>`; `<caption>` and `<tbody>` are child elements of the `<table>` but also descendants of `<div>` (in this case, grandchildren). The reverse is also true, `<h2>`, `<p>`, `<a>`, `<table>` and all the elements within the table have `<div>` as a common ancestor.

To target an element based on its ancestor we write the CSS that you see in the following code.

```
div.planet h2 {
    font-size: 18px;
    margin-top: 0;
}
```

Descendant selectors are used to select an element based on its context within the document. In the preceding code, you select a `<h2>` element but only if the `<h2>` element is a descendant of the `<div>` element with a `class` of planet.

Descendant selectors aren't limited to just two elements; you can include more elements in the ancestral lineage, if it suits your needs. Each selector in a descendant selector chain must be separated by a space. This is demonstrated in the following code.

```
div.planet table td {
    padding: 0 10px 0 0;
    text-align: left;
}
```

In fact, the entire lineage from the eldest ancestor, the `<html>` element, down through the generations to the element you want to select, can be included in a descendant selector chain.

In the next section, I present another type of selector, pseudo-class selectors.

PSEUDO-CLASSES

Pseudo-classes are used to represent dynamic events, a change in state, or a more general condition present in the document that is not easily accomplished through other means. This may be the user's mouse rolling over or clicking on an element. In more general terms, pseudo-classes style a specific state present in the target element, for example, a previously visited hyperlink. Pseudo-classes allow the author the freedom to dictate how the element should appear under different conditions. There are many more pseudo-classes than are listed here. I will cover more, such as the *nth-child* pseudo class which allows you to select an element based on its position within a document, later in the book.

Unlike normal classes, pseudo-classes have a single colon before the pseudo-class property.

Dynamic Pseudo-Classes

The following are considered *dynamic pseudo-classes*. They are a classification of elements only present after certain user actions have or have not occurred:

➤   `:link`: Signifies unvisited hyperlinks

➤   `:visited`: Indicates visited hyperlinks

➤   `:hover`: Signifies an element that currently has the user's mouse pointer hovering over it

➤   `:focus`: Signifies an element that currently has focus, for example if the user has used their keyboard to navigate to a link

➤   `:active`: Signifies an element on which the user is currently clicking

If you want to apply styles to an anchor regardless of its state you can, of course, still use the good old type selector without a pseudo class.

The first two dynamic pseudo-classes that I discuss are `:link` and `:visited`.

:link and :visited

The `:link` pseudo-class refers to an unvisited hyperlink, whereas `:visited`, of course, refers to visited hyperlinks. These two pseudo-classes are used to separate styles based on user actions. An unvisited hyperlink may be blue, whereas a visited hyperlink may be purple. Those are the default styles your browser applies. Using dynamic pseudo-classes it is possible to customize those styles.

In the following code, unvisited links are styled with the `:link` dynamic pseudo-class. They receive `meduimblue` text. Visited links, on the other hand, have `magenta` text.

There is one exception to this, however. Webkit browsers will apply `:link` pseudo class styles to all links, not just unvisited ones. Therefore it is a good idea to define the same properties in `:link` and `:visited` rules so that the correct styles are applied.

 NOTE *For obvious reasons, the* `:link` *and* `:visited` *pseudo-classes apply only to <a> elements.*

```
a:link {
    color: meduimblue;
}

a:visited {
    color: magenta;
}
```

The order in which dynamic pseudo-classes appear in the style sheet is important and has to do with the cascade, which I discuss in Chapter 4. If the `:link` pseudo-class is defined after the `:focus` pseudo-class in the style sheet, the `:link` pseudo-class takes precedence: The declarations with the `:link` pseudo-class override those defined for the `:focus` pseudo-class. As you see in Chapter 4, this has to do with how specific the selector is; in this example, the specificity is the same.

 WARNING *A mnemonic device used to remember the order in which dynamic pseudo-classes (as applied to links) must appear in style sheets is LoVe HAte, or* `:link`, `:visited`, `:hover` *and* `:active`. `:focus` *does not fit in this mnemonic, but as you will see you should always include a* `:focus` *style alongside* `:hover` *styles.*

:hover and :focus

The `:hover` pseudo-class refers to an element over which the user's mouse pointer is currently hovering. While the user's mouse pointer is over the element, the specified style is applied; when the user's mouse pointer leaves the element, it returns to the previously specified style. The `:focus` pseudo-class behaves in the same way, but for keyboard focus. To provide the same experience to keyboard and mouse users, it is good practice to include them both and is common for them to receive the same style.

The `:hover` and `:focus` pseudo-classes are applied in the same way that the `:link` and `:visited` pseudo-classes are applied. I like to put `:focus` first as it stops me forgetting it. An example appears in the following code.

When the user either hovers over the <a> element with their mouse or uses the keyboard to navigate to it, this code causes the text within the <a> element to be underlined.

```
a{
    text-decoration: none;
}

a:focus,
a:hover {
    text-decoration: underline;
}
```

 NOTE *In IE 6, the* `:hover` *pseudo-class applies only to hyperlinks (which is incorrect under the CSS 2 specification), whereas other browsers recognize the* `:hover` *pseudo-class on any rendered element, per the CSS 2 specification. This problem is fixed in IE 7 and later.*

:active

The :active pseudo-class refers to an element that the user is currently clicking and holding down the mouse button on. The specified style remains in place while the user holds down the mouse button, and the element does not return to its original state until the user releases the mouse button.

The following code shows the :active pseudo-class in use. When the user clicks an <a> element, while the mouse button is held down, and before it is released, the element is said to be *active*, in which case the styles in the :active pseudo-class rule are applied.

 NOTE *In IE 6 and IE 7,* :active *applies only to hyperlinks; whereas, other browsers allow it to be applied to any element.*

```
a:active {
    color: red;
}
```

Now that you have been introduced to dynamic pseudo-class selectors, you can try them out for yourself in the following example.

TRY IT OUT   **Dynamic Pseudo-Class Selectors**

Example 3-2

To try out dynamic pseudo-class selectors, follow these steps.

1.   Enter the following markup into your text editor:

```
<!DOCTYPE html PUBLIC "-//W3C//DTD HTML 4.01//EN"
    "http://www.w3.org/TR/html4/strict.dtd">
<html lang="en">
<head>
    <meta http-equiv="Content-Type" content="text/html; charset=utf-8">
    <title>Example 3-2</title>
    <style type="text/css">
        a:link {
            text-decoration: none;
            color: meduimblue;
        }

        a:visited {
            color: magenta;
        }

        a:focus,
        a:hover {
            text-decoration: underline;
        }

        a:active {
```

```
                    color: red;
                }
        </style>
</head>
<body>

    <h1>Links to useful sites</h1>

    <ul>
        <li><a href="http://www.wrox.com/">Wrox</a></li>
        <li><a href="http://p2p.wrox.com/">Wrox P2P</a></li>
        <li><a href="http://www.yahoo.cqm/">Yahoo</a></li>
        <li><a href="http://www.amazon.com/">Amazon</a></li>
    </ul>

</body>

</html>
```

2. Save the preceding markup as **example_3-2.html**. You should see output in your browser like that in Figure 3-2.

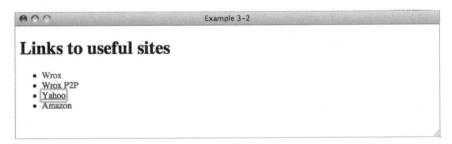

FIGURE 3-2

How It Works

In Example 3-2, you tried out the dynamic pseudo-classes for yourself. There were four dynamic pseudo-classes in use.

The first dynamic pseudo-class that you used styles unvisited links. Unvisited links receive the color meduimblue and have the underline removed.

```
a:link {
    text-decoration: none;
    color: meduimblue;
}
```

The second dynamic pseudo-class that you used styles visited links. Visited links receive the color magenta.

```
a:visited {
    color: magenta;
}
```

The third selector that you used, the :hover and :focus dynamic pseudo-classes, applies styles when the user's mouse cursor hovers over a link or when the link has keyboard focus. When a user's mouse cursor comes over a link or has the link has keyboard focus, the link is underlined.

```
a:focus,
a:hover {
    text-decoration: underline;
}
```

Last, you used the :active dynamic pseudo-class, which applies style when the user clicks and holds down the mouse button on a link. When the user clicks and holds down the mouse button, the link is red.

```
a:active {
    color: red;
}
```

EXERCISES

1. How would you apply a style to an element based on its class?

2. How many class names can one element have?

3. How would you apply a style to an element based on its ID?

4. How would you apply a style to an element based on its class and type?

5. If you wanted to style a link a different color when the user's mouse hovers over it, what might the selector look like?

▶ WHAT YOU LEARNED IN THIS CHAPTER

In this chapter, you learned about the basic selectors in CSS. To recap, you learned the following:

TOPIC	KEY CONCEPTS
Types of selector	Class, ID, Universal and Pseudo-classes can be used to target different elements in HTML.
Class Selectors	Classes can be applied to as many elements as you want, and CSS can be used to target them.
ID Selectors	An ID can only be applied to one element in a document, and can be combined with classes.
Descendant Selectors	Descendant selectors can be used to target elements based on the ancestors, for example a <h2> inside a <div> with a class of planet.
Pseudo-Classes	Pseudo-classes can be used to style elements based on user interaction, for example a link that has been visited.

The Cascade and Inheritance

WHAT YOU WILL LEARN IN THIS CHAPTER:

➤ The cascade and how style sheets and some selectors take precedence over others

➤ Inheritance and why the values of some properties are inherited and some are not

➤ The !important rule and how to force precedence

In Chapter 3, I discussed the various types of selectors that CSS supports. In this chapter, now that you have an understanding of some of the basic nuts and bolts that make up CSS, you continue along that path with the cascade and inheritance. In CSS, inheritance and the cascade are as fundamental as selectors, lengths, and properties. In fact, the importance of precedence is implied by the name of the language itself: Cascading Style Sheets. *Cascading* is a term used to describe precedence. Because a single element may be matched by multiple CSS declarations, the CSS specification includes a set of guidelines defining which declarations can take precedence over others and how this is decided.

THE CASCADE

Style sheets can come from more than one place. A style sheet can originate from any of the following sources:

➤ From the browser (the browser's default look and feel)

➤ From the user visiting the website (a user-defined style sheet)

➤ From the web page itself (a style sheet created by the website's author)

Because a style sheet can originate from more than one source, it is necessary to establish an order of precedence to determine in which order style sheets apply styles for the page the user is seeing. The first style sheet comes from the browser, and this style sheet applies some default styles for a web page, such as the default font and text color, how much space is applied between each line of text, and how much space is applied between each letter of text. In a nutshell, it controls the look and feel of the web page by controlling the behavior of each element when no styles are specified.

A style sheet can also be applied by a user visiting the website via a user-defined style sheet. This allows the user to specify his or her own look and feel. This aspect of CSS makes the Web more accessible: A user with visual disabilities can write a style sheet to accommodate his or her needs.

Finally, the author of the web page can specify a style sheet (of course). The precedence of each style sheet is as follows:

➤ The browser's style sheet is the weakest.

➤ The user's style sheet takes precedence over the browser's style sheet.

➤ The author's style sheet is the strongest and takes precedence over the user's and the browser's style sheets.

The HTML `style` attribute can also be used to apply styles directly to an element, and these styles are more important than styles defined in any style sheet. Because `style` attributes will override styles in style sheets, I do not recommend their use.

You might be wondering what kind of styles does the browser apply? The following code demonstrates this.

Available for download on Wrox.com

```
<!DOCTYPE html PUBLIC "-//W3C//DTD HTML 4.01//EN"
    "http://www.w3.org/TR/html4/strict.dtd">
<html lang="en">
<head>
    <meta http-equiv="Content-Type" content="text/html; charset=utf-8">
    <title>Figure 4-1</title>
</head>
<body>

<h1>The gas giants</h1>

<div class="planet jupiter">

    <h2>Jupiter</h2>

    <p>Jupiter is the fifth planet from the Sun and the largest planet
within the Solar System. The Romans named the planet after the god
Jupiter. It is a gas giant with a mass two and a half times the mass
of all the other planets in our Solar System combined.</p>

    <table>
        <caption>Jupiter Facts</caption>
        <tbody>
            <tr>
                <th>Distance from the Sun</th>
                <td>78,412,020 km</td>
```

```
        </tr>
        <tr>
            <th>Equatorial Radius</th>
            <td>71,492 km</td>
        </tr>
        <tr>
            <th>Volume</th>
            <td>1,425,500,000,000,000 km<sup>3</sup></td>
        </tr>
        <tr>
            <th>Mass</th>
            <td>1,898,700,000,000,000,000,000,000 kg</td>
        </tr>
    </tbody>
</table>

    <a href="http://solarsystem.jpl.nasa.gov/planets/profile.cfm?Object=Jupiter">
More Jupiter facts</a>

</div>

</body>

</html>
```

code snippet /chapter4/figure_4-1.html

This results in the output shown in Figure 4-1.

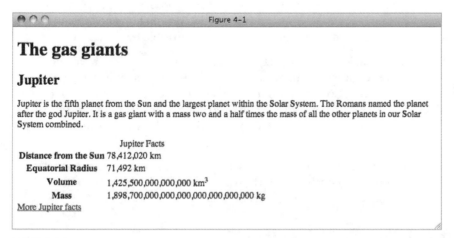

FIGURE 4-1

In Figure 4-1, you can see an example of some of the default styles that a browser applies. Examples include the spacing between styles applied to the heading and the text in the paragraph that follows, and the text alignment applied to the td elements.

The next code snippet demonstrates a style sheet that removes the default styles shown in Figure 4-1.

Available for
download on
Wrox.com

```
* {
    margin: 0;
    padding: 0;
    font-size: 16px;
    font-weight: normal;
}
```

code snippet /chapter4/figure_4-2.html

The style sheet in the preceding code is applied to the markup that produced Figure 4-1, which results in the output shown in Figure 4-2.

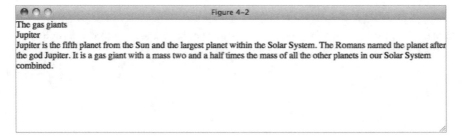

FIGURE 4-2

When you compare Figure 4-2 with Figure 4-1, you get an idea of what kinds of styles a browser applies by default. The browser applies spacing between elements and depending on the element, that spacing can be controlled by either the margin or the padding property. You learn more about those two properties in Chapter 8. Figure 4-2 demonstrates, however, that it is possible to override the browser's default styles. Overriding the default styles is made possible by the cascade.

The cascade sets the order of precedence, and in Figure 4-2, it says that my style sheet rules (the author's) have stronger precedence (are more important) than the browser's built-in style sheet rules. By and large, there are only two situations that a web designer will ever encounter in composing a style sheet: overriding the browser's default styles, and overriding styles set in other style sheets within the same website (that is, overriding the web designer's own styles set elsewhere in the same document).

In CSS, the precedence is determined by how specific a selector is. That is to say a vague selector has less precedence than a more specific selector. In the next section, I discuss how to find out how specific a selector is using a simple, easy-to-remember formula.

Calculating the Specificity of a Selector

In addition to style sheet precedence, an order of precedence exists for the selectors contained in each style sheet. This precedence is determined by how specific the selector is. For instance, an ID selector is the most specific, and the universal selector is the most general. Between these, the specificity of a selector is calculated using the following formula:

1. Count 1 if the styles are applied from the (X)HTML style attribute, and 0 otherwise; this becomes variable a.

2. Count the number of ID attributes in the selector; the sum is variable b.

3. Count the number of attributes, pseudo-classes, and class names in a selector; the sum is variable c.

4. Count the number of element names in the selector; this is variable d.

5. Ignore pseudo-elements.

Now take the four values and put them together in groups of four. In the following table I've demonstrated this, using commas to separate each value.

SELECTOR	SELECTOR TYPE	SPECIFICITY
`*`	Universal Selector	0,0,0,0, ($a = 0$, $b = 0$, $c = 0$, $d = 0$)
`li`	Element Name	0,0,0,1, ($a = 0$, $b = 0$, $c = 0$, $d = 1$)
`ul li`	Element Name	0,0,0,2, ($a = 0$, $b = 0$, $c = 0$, $d = 2$)
`div h1 + p`	Element Name	0,0,0,3, ($a = 0$, $b = 0$, $c = 0$, $d = 3$)
`input[type='text']`	Element Name + Attribute	0,0,1,1, ($a = 0$, $b = 0$, $c = 1$, $d = 1$)
`.someclass`	Class Name	0,0,1,0, ($a = 0$, $b = 0$, $c = 1$, $d = 0$)
`div.someclass`	Element Name + Class Name	0,0,1,1, ($a = 0$, $b = 0$, $c = 1$, $d = 1$)
`div.someclass.someother`	Element Name + Class Name + Class Name	0,0,2,1, ($a = 0$, $b = 0$, $c = 2$, $d = 1$)
`#someid`	ID Name	0,1,0,0, ($a = 0$, $b = 1$, $c = 0$, $d = 0$)
`div#someid`	Element Name + ID Name	0,1,0,1, ($a = 0$, $b = 1$, $c = 0$, $d = 1$)
`style` (attribute)	`style` (attribute)	1,0,0,0, ($a = 1$, $b = 0$, $c = 0$, $d = 0$)

Now compare each selector. The selector which has the highest left-most number has the highest specificity. In the case of a tie, move to the next number and compare once again.

If two selectors have the same specificity then they will be applied in the order in which they appear.

Eric Meyer, renowned CSS expert, has written about specificity, and explains it in a slightly different way at meyerweb.com/eric/css/link-specificity.html. I recommend you read this and choose whichever approach makes most sense to you.

In the following Try It Out, you experiment with specificity.

TRY IT OUT **Experimenting with Specificity**

Example 4-1

Follow these steps to experiment with specificity.

1. Enter the following markup into your text editor:

```
<!DOCTYPE html PUBLIC "-//W3C//DTD HTML 4.01//EN"
    "http://www.w3.org/TR/html4/strict.dtd">
<html lang="en">
<head>
    <meta http-equiv="Content-Type" content="text/html; charset=utf-8">
    <title>Example 3-1</title>
    <style type="text/css">
        body {
            width: 650px;
            margin: 0 auto;
            background: #000;
            color: #FFF;
            font: 12px sans-serif;
        }

        h1 {
            font-size: 24px;
        }

        h2 {
            font-size: 18px;
            margin-top: 0;
        }

        a {
            color: #FFF;
        }

        a:focus,
        a:hover {
            text-decoration: none;
        }

        table {
            margin-bottom: 10px;
            border-spacing: 0;
```

```
        }

        caption {
            margin-bottom: 10px;
            font-size: 14px;
            font-weight: bold;
            text-align: left;
        }

        th,
        td {
            padding: 0 10px 0 0;
            text-align: left;
        }

        tr.even {
            background: none;
        }

        tr {
            background: #666;
        }

        div.planet {
            background: none;
        }

        div.planet {
            margin: 10px 0;
            padding: 20px 20px 20px 200px;
            border: 1px solid #FFF;
            background-image: none;
            background-position: 20px 20px;
            background-repeat: no-repeat;
        }

        #jupiter {
            background-image: url(jupiter.jpg);
        }
    </style>
</head>
<body>

<h1>The gas giants</h1>

<div class="planet" id="jupiter">

    <h2>Jupiter</h2>

    <p>Jupiter is the fifth planet from the Sun and the largest planet within the
    Solar System. The Romans named the planet after the god Jupiter. It is a gas
    giant with a mass two and a half times the mass of all the other planets in
    our Solar System combined.</p>

    <table>
        <caption>Jupiter Facts</caption>
```

```
        <tbody>
            <tr>
                <th>Distance from the Sun</th>
                <td>78,412,020 km</td>
            </tr>
            <tr class="even">
                <th>Equatorial Radius</th>
                <td>71,492 km</td>
            </tr>
            <tr>
                <th>Volume</th>
                <td>1,425,500,000,000,000 km<sup>3</sup></td>
            </tr>
            <tr class="even">
                <th>Mass</th>
                <td>1,898,700,000,000,000,000,000,000,000 kg</td>
            </tr>
        </tbody>
    </table>

    <a href="http://solarsystem.jpl.nasa.gov/planets/profile.cfm?Object=Jupiter">
    More Jupiter facts</a>

</div>

</body>

</html>
```

2. Save the preceding document as `example_4-1.html`.

Example 4-1 results in the output you see in Figure 4-3.

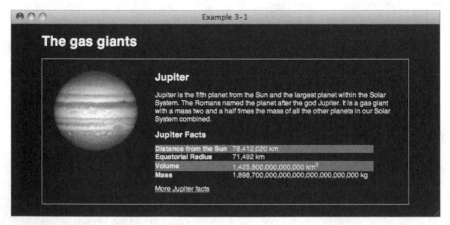

FIGURE 4-3

How It Works

In Example 4-1, you see an example of the cascade in action. Your HTML should be familiar to you by now, but there are changes to the CSS which demonstrate specificity.

Here you have two rules which apply to the background of table rows:

```css
tr.even {
    background: none;
}

tr {
    background: #666;
}
```

Even though the default style for each tr is to display background: #666; the preceding rule overrides it for table rows with a class of even because it has a specificity of 0,0,1,1 as it consists of both an element name and a class name, which is higher than the specificity of an element selector alone.

Your CSS also shows that order matters when selectors have equal specificity in the following snippet:

```css
div.planet {
    background: none;
}

div.planet {
    margin: 10px 0;
    padding: 20px 20px 20px 200px;
    border: 1px solid #FFF;
    background-image: none;
    background-position: 20px 20px;
    background-repeat: no-repeat;
}

#jupiter {
    background-image: url(jupiter.jpg);
}
```

You have two identical selectors, div.planet, but here only the second applies any styles. As you will learn in Chapter 7, background is a special property that combines the values for background-image, background-position, and background-repeat. If these two rules were reversed, all of these properties would be set to none.

However, you also have a rule that uses an ID selector #jupiter, which has a specificity of 100, higher than the specificity of div.planet, 10.

When an (X)HTML style attribute is applied, it is considered the most specific of any selector on the page. That's because according to the CSS specification, it is defined as having a specificity all of its own, that is higher than any other. The style attribute has a specificity of 1,0,0,0 therefore, the style attribute takes precedence over all other rules. It is not recommended that style attributes are used in your code, as they remove many of the benefits of CSS, for example the cascade itself and the ability to separate content and style.

> **NOTE** It is considered good practice to keep the specificity of each selector as low as possible. If you don't do this you, will find that you need to write more and more complex selectors with unnecessary IDs and classes in order to override other styles.

In the next section, I describe how you can override specificity by including special syntax within a CSS declaration.

!important Rules

Along with the need for the cascade in CSS is the need to override it. This is where !important rules come in. The !important syntax appears within a declaration, after the property value and before the semicolon that terminates the declaration. Two components make up this syntax: an exclamation mark, used here as a delimiter; and the important keyword. A *delimiter* marks the ending of one thing and the beginning of another. Here the exclamation mark signals the end of the declaration. The important keyword must appear next, followed by a semicolon to terminate the declaration; this is demonstrated in the following code.

```
body {
    background: #000 !important;
}
```

A declaration containing the !important rule, like the preceding one, takes precedence over any other declaration even the style attribute.

If more than one !important rule appears in a style sheet, and the style sheet has the same origin — that is, both rules come from the author's style sheet or both come from the user's style sheet — the latter rule wins out over any specified previously.

For this reason, it is strongly advised that you never use !important rules anywhere in your code. The only place that there could be a good reason for using one is in user defined style sheets when a specific style is required to make a site usable, for example specific foreground and background colors. Using !important rules in author style sheets makes it harder for users to define their own rules and makes site maintenance much more difficult as the only way to override an !important rule is to include another !important rule later in the author style sheet.

INHERITANCE

CSS is designed to simplify web document creation, enabling a property to be applied to all elements in a document. To put it another way, after a property has been applied to a particular element, its children retain those property values as well. This behavior is called *inheritance*. Not all properties are inherited, but many are, and you will learn which as you follow the examples in this book.

Many properties in CSS are inheritable; some are not. Where it is supported and appropriate, inheritance makes writing style sheets a snap. For the most part, two types of properties can be inherited: text and font properties. You have seen the code shown next in many of our examples so far.

```
body {
    width: 650px;
    margin: 0 auto;
    background: #000;
    color: #FFF;
    font: 12px sans-serif;
}
```

In each case, you have seen that the color of your text is white, or #FFFFFF in hexadecimal form (which can be shortened to #FFF). This is because all of our text has inherited its color from this style applied to the body element. The font and font sizes used has also been inherited from the same rule for most of our text, the exception being headings that have browser and author styles applied to them to change their size.

However, not all of these styles have been inherited; none of the other elements on the page have a width of 650px or have the same margins as our body element. This is because these properties are not inherited by other elements; they apply only to the element on which they are placed, not to its children.

This is a very good thing, as otherwise you would have to write additional rules to remove width and margin on every element that you didn't want these values to apply to!

 NOTE *Inheritance for each property is outlined in Appendix C.*

Now that you know the background of CSS, Part II will introduce many more CSS properties. In Chapter 5, you will learn about text manipulation properties.

EXERCISES

1. In the following style sheet, determine the specificity of each selector.

```
ul#hmenu ul.menu

ul#hmenu li li:hover

ul#hmenu ul.menu ul.menu

ul#hmenu li#menu-204 ul.menu ul.menu

ul#hmenu li#menu-848 ul.menu ul.menu ul.menu ul.menu

ul#hmenu li#menu-990 ul.menu ul.menu

ul#hmenu > li.menu.eas + li.menu.eas ul.menu ul.menu ul.menu
```

2. According to the following style sheet, what color is the link?

```
a.context:link {
    color: blue;
```

```
}

a.context:visited {
    color: purple;
}

a.context:focus,
a.context:hover {
    color: green;
}

a.context:active {
    color: red;
}
```

3. According to the following style sheet, what color is the link?

```
a.context:visited {
    color: purple;
}

a.context:focus,
a.context:hover {
    color: green;
}

a.context:active {
    color: red;
}

a.context:link {
    color: blue;
}
```

4. According to the following style sheet, what color is the link?

```
a.context:link {
    color: blue;
}

a.context:visited {
    color: purple !important;
}

a.context:focus,
a.context:hover {
    color: green;
}

a.context:active {
    color: red;
}
```

▶ **WHAT YOU LEARNED IN THIS CHAPTER**

Throughout this chapter, you learned about inheritance and the cascade, fundamental to CSS. To recap, in this chapter, you learned the following:

TOPIC	KEY CONCEPTS
Specificity	Specificity is how you calculate which styles are applied to an element when more than one rule could apply .
Inheritance	Some properties are inherited, which reduces redundancy in the document by eliminating the need for declarations to be written multiple times.
	Other properties are not inherited, which also reduces redundancy by preventing the effects of declarations from being applied to the element's descendants.
`!important`	You have learned to recognize `!important` rules and understand why they should not be used in author Style Sheets.

PART II
Properties

5

Applying Font Faces

WHAT YOU WILL LEARN IN THIS CHAPTER:

➤ The `font-family` property and how it is used to change the face of a font

➤ The `font-style` property and how it is used to make a font italic

➤ The `font-variant` property and how this property is used to create a small-caps effect

➤ The `font-weight` property and how it is used to increase or decrease how bold or light a font appears

➤ The `font-size` property and how it is used to increase or decrease the size of a font

➤ The `font` property and how it is used as shorthand to specify a number of other font properties

In Chapter 4, you learned how certain properties in CSS are inherited and how the cascade determines which style rules are the most important. In this and subsequent chapters, you begin an in-depth look at the individual properties of CSS and how these come together to style a document.

This chapter begins the discussion of text manipulation with CSS's font manipulation properties. CSS includes a variety of properties that change the face, size, and style of a font.

SETTING FONT FACES

The `font-family` property allows you to specify the typeface used to display a piece of text. You can specify more than one typeface, and the first one that the user has installed on their system will be the one used. You can make use of any of the fonts installed on the user's operating system, though in practice you'll generally stick to the set of *web safe* fonts that we discuss later in the chapter. There are also some so-called generic font families that browsers map to the most appropriate system font, as in the following table.

PROPERTY	VALUE
font-family	[[<family-name> | <generic-family>] [, <family-name>| <generic-family>]*] Initial value: Varies depending on the browser or user agent.

The following code is an example of the basic use of the font-family property.

Available for download on Wrox.com

```html
<!DOCTYPE html PUBLIC "-//W3C//DTD HTML 4.01//EN"
    "http://www.w3.org/TR/html4/strict.dtd">
<html lang="en">
<head>
    <meta http-equiv="Content-Type" content="text/html; charset=utf-8">
    <title>Figure 5-1</title>
    <style type="text/css">
        body {
            font-family: arial, helvetica, sans-serif;
        }

        h1 {
            font-family: "Times New Roman", Georgia, Serif;
        }
    </style>
</head>
<body>

<h1>Recipes for Cheese</h1>

<p>Cheese is a remarkably versatile food, available in literally hundreds
of varieties with different flavors and textures.</p>

</body>
</html>
```

code snippet /chapter5/figure_5-1.html

This results in the output shown in Figure 5-1.

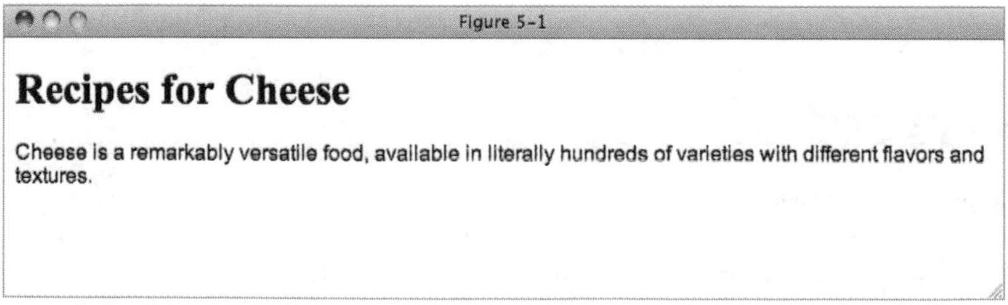

Recipes for Cheese

Cheese is a remarkably versatile food, available in literally hundreds of varieties with different flavors and textures.

FIGURE 5-1

The example is pretty straightforward, and hopefully by now you are sufficiently familiar with CSS to guess what it does. A set of font families, `arial`, `helvetica`, `sans-serif`, out of which the first installed font is applied to text within the body element, and a different set of font families `"Times New Roman"`, `Georgia`, `Serif` is applied to any h1 elements.

There are two things to note about the format. First, the names of each font are case insensitive (that is, they can be uppercase, lowercase, sentence case, or whatever mixture of cases you find most readable). Second, as you saw in Chapter 2, strings which contain spaces (for example, `"Times New Roman"` must be enclosed with quotation marks).

The `font-family` property can accept one or more fonts for its value, which is what is meant by the repetition of the syntax in the notation and the presence of the asterisk. The asterisk indicates that the syntax may be repeated one or more times, and a comma is used to separate each font name provided. You can specify two types of fonts. The first is documented as `<family-name>` in the preceding table. The `<family-name>` notation refers to fonts installed on the user's computer, which means that the available fonts depend on the user's operating system and the fonts available to that operating system. The `<generic-family>` notation refers to a small subset of predefined fonts that can be expected to always be available; this will be discussed shortly.

Don't worry if you find this syntax difficult to read. You will get used to it over the course of this book, and although it is not essential that you learn it, it will help you read the official CSS documentation if you do.

Font Families

The available font families that can be specified vary depending on the operating system. Using a default installation, Windows does not provide the same fonts as Mac OS X, for instance. Furthermore, the available fonts also vary depending on the programs installed on the user's computer. For instance, Microsoft Office installs a number of extra fonts in addition to those that ship with Mac OS X or Windows. In fact, with the exception of a few fonts, Mac OS X with Microsoft Office installed provides pretty much the same fonts as installed on Windows. Without Microsoft Office installed, however, many Windows fonts are not available on the Mac platform.

There is a huge number of fonts available across platforms, too many to list here. A great resource which lists many fonts and the likelihood of their being installed on each platform can be found at `www.codestyle.org/css/font-family/index.shtml`.

For this reason, there is the possibility of font inconsistencies, that the `font-family` property can accept more than one font as its value. The browser will use the first font provided that is installed and available on the end user's computer. The browser will fall back to the next font in the list in the event that previous fonts are not available. Subsequent fonts in the list are called *fallback fonts*. This capability is provided because it is difficult to foresee which fonts will be available on the user's computer.

The effect of specifying more than one font is that the browser goes through the list of comma-separated fonts until it finds one that it is capable of displaying.

CSS provides a couple of generic fonts that you can always rely on being installed and for this reason it is good practice to include a generic font as the last in the list.

The following table outlines the generic font family names defined in CSS.

GENERIC FONT	RESEMBLES
serif	Times, Times New Roman
sans-serif	Helvetica, Arial
cursive	Zapf-Chancery
fantasy	Western
monospace	Courier, Courier New

An example of each generic font family is shown in Figure 5-2.

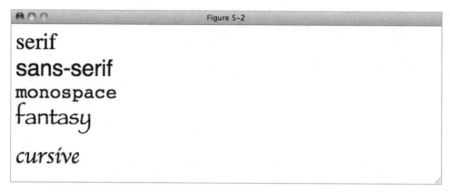

FIGURE 5-2

You will find that most text on the Web is displayed with a sans-serif font family. This is because sans-serif fonts tend to be easier to read on screen. Printed materials such as this book often use serif fonts because most people find them easier to read off screen. Serif fonts can also be used on the Web but usually only with text which is larger than average such as headings.

Use the following Try It Out to experiment with the `font-family` property for yourself.

TRY IT OUT **Applying the font-family Property**

Example 5-1

Follow these steps to experiment with the `font-family` property.

1. Write the following markup in your text editor:

```
<!DOCTYPE html PUBLIC "-//W3C//DTD HTML 4.01//EN"
    "http://www.w3.org/TR/html4/strict.dtd">
<html lang="en">
<head>
    <meta http-equiv="Content-Type" content="text/html; charset=utf-8">
    <title>Example 5-1</title>
```

```
    <style type="text/css">
        body {
            font-family: arial, helvetica, sans-serif;
        }

        h1 {
            font-family: "Times New Roman", Georgia, Serif;
        }

        ol {
            font-family: monospace;
        }
    </style>
</head>
<body>

<h1>Recipes for Cheese</h1>

<p>Cheese is a remarkably versatile food, available in literally hundreds of
varieties with different flavors and textures.</p>

<h2>Welsh Rarebit</h2>

<ol>
    <li>Lightly toast the bread</li>
    <li>Place on a baking tray, and spread with butter.</li>
    <li>Add the grated Cheddar cheese and 2 tablespoons of beer to a saucepan.
    Place the saucepan over a medium heat, and stir the cheese continuously until
    it has melted. Add a teaspoon of wholegrain mustard and grind in a little
    pepper. Keep stirring.</li>
    <li>When thick and smooth, pour over each piece of toast spreading it to the
    edges to stop the toast from burning.</li>
    <li>Place under the grill for a couple of minutes or until golden brown.</li>
</ol>

</body>
</html>
```

2. Save `example_5-1.html`. The results of these modifications are shown in Figure 5-3.

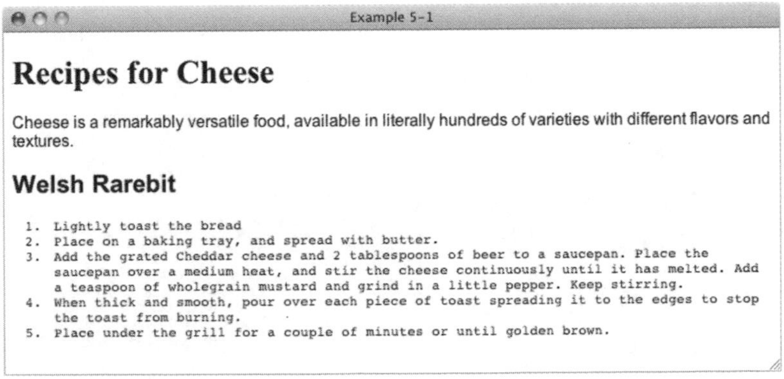

FIGURE 5-3

How It Works

In Example 5-1, you made use of several examples of the `font-family` property. Following is a review of each of the relevant rules.

The first example of the `font-family` property you used was `arial, helvetica, sans-serif` applied to the `body` element, setting default fonts for all text on the page.

```
body {
    font-family: arial, helvetica, sans-serif;
}
```

Next, you specify `"Times New Roman", Georgia, Serif` for all `h1` elements.

```
h1 {
    font-family: "Times New Roman", Georgia, Serif;
}
```

Finally, you specify the generic system `monospace` font for all `OL` (ordered list) elements.

```
ol {
    font-family: monospace;
}
```

In the next section, I discuss how to make text italic, bold, or small caps.

MAKING TEXT ITALIC, BOLD, OR SMALL CAPS

Making your text italic, bold, or displayed as small caps requires three different properties which all behave in a very similar way. We will cover them all in the following three sections.

Italic Text

The `font-style` property is used to switch between styles provided by a particular font; those styles are italic or oblique. For many fonts the information required to render text in an italic version of the font is included in the font file. The oblique style does not use this information, even if it is available, instead it simulates italicized text, not always to great effect.

The following table outlines the possible values for the `font-style` property.

PROPERTY	VALUE
font-style	normal | italic | oblique Initial value: normal

The italic and oblique values are, with most fonts, indistinguishable in how they render; however, I have never used or seen used the oblique style in real-world code, so we will limit our use of the font-style to italicizing text.

There is only one gotcha with font-style. Not all fonts have an italic style, and browsers differ in how they handle this case. IE will render the font in the normal style, whereas other browsers will fall back to the next specified font that has an italic version.

Bold Text

The font-weight property provides the functionality to specify how bold a font is. The following table outlines the font-weight property and the values that it allows.

PROPERTY	VALUE
font-weight	normal | bold | bolder | lighter | 100 | 200 | 300 | 400 | 500 | 600 | 700 | 800 | 900 Initial value: normal

As you can see in the preceding table, the font-weight property has several values. Despite all of these different values being available for the font-weight property, in real-world web design, a font is either bold or it isn't. That is to say, in real-world web design, the only two values that matter in the preceding table are the normal and bold values. This majority of fonts used on the Web do not support the variations that the font-weight property allows.

For those interested, normal text usually equates to a font-weight value of 400 and bold text to a value of 700.

Small Caps Text

The following table outlines the font-variant property and its possible values.

PROPERTY	VALUE
font-variant	normal | small-caps Initial value: normal

The font-variant: small-caps; declaration causes letters to appear in uppercase but scaled slightly smaller than capitalized letters. The capitalized letter maintains its case and size, but all lowercase letters are displayed as capital letters scaled slightly smaller than any *real* capital letters appearing in the markup's source code. It can be a nice effect to use in headings but can make long sections of text hard to read.

In the following Try It Out, you experiment with the font-style, font-weight, and font-variant properties.

TRY IT OUT | Applying the font-style, font-weight, and font-variant Properties

Example 5-2

Follow these steps to try out the font-style, font-weight, and font-variant properties.

1. Write the following markup in your text editor:

```
<!DOCTYPE html PUBLIC "-//W3C//DTD HTML 4.01//EN"
    "http://www.w3.org/TR/html4/strict.dtd">
<html lang="en">
<head>
    <meta http-equiv="Content-Type" content="text/html; charset=utf-8">
    <title>Example 5-2</title>
    <style type="text/css">
        body {
            font-family: arial, helvetica, sans-serif;
        }

        h1 {
            font-family: "Times New Roman", Georgia, Serif;
            font-variant: small-caps;
        }

        .intro {
            font-weight: bold;
        }

        .recipe .intro {
            font-weight: normal;
            font-style: italic;
        }
    </style>
</head>
<body>

<h1>Recipes for Cheese</h1>

<p class="intro">Cheese is a remarkably versatile food, available in literally
    hundreds of varieties with different flavors and textures.</p>

<div class="recipe">

    <h2>Welsh Rarebit</h2>

    <p class="intro">Cheese is a remarkably versatile food, available in literally
        hundreds of varieties with different flavors and textures.</p>

    <ol>
        <li>Lightly toast the bread</li>
        <li>Place on a baking tray, and spread with butter.</li>
        <li>Add the grated Cheddar cheese and 2 tablespoons of beer to a saucepan.
    Place the saucepan over a medium heat, and stir the cheese continuously until
    it has melted. Add a teaspoon of wholegrain mustard and grind in a little
```

```
    pepper. Keep stirring.</li>
        <li>When thick and smooth, pour over each piece of toast spreading it to
        the edges to stop the toast from burning.</li>
        <li>Place under the grill for a couple of minutes or until golden
        brown.</li>
    </ol>

</div>

</body>
</html>
```

2. Save the preceding markup as `example_5-2.html`. The example results in the output in Figure 5-4.

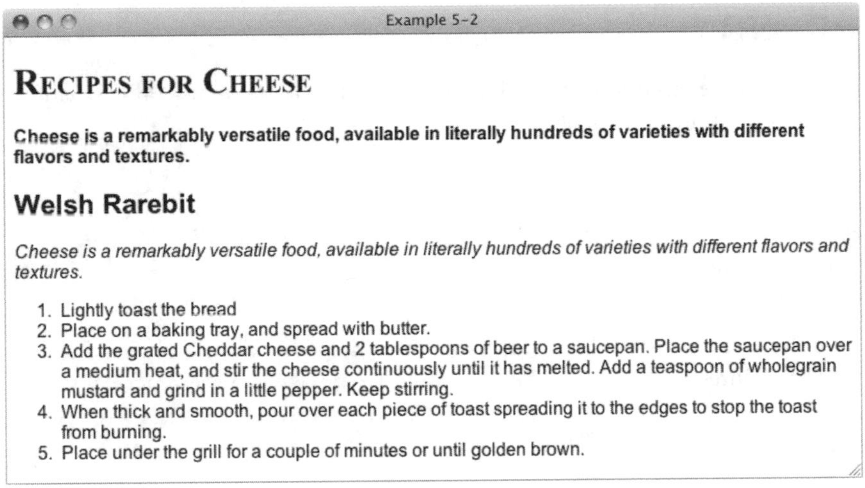

FIGURE 5-4

How It Works

In Example 5-2, you experimented a bit with the `font-style`, `font-weight`, and `font-variant` properties.

First, you applied the `small-caps` font variant to any h1 elements.

```
h1 {
    font-family: "Times New Roman", Georgia, Serif;
    font-variant: small-caps;
}
```

Then you applied the `bold` font weight to elements with class name `intro`.

```
.intro {
    font-weight: bold;
}
```

Finally, you applied the `normal` font weight and `italic` font variant to elements with the class name of `intro` with an ancestor element with a class name of `recipe`.

```
.recipe .intro {
    font-weight: normal;
    font-style: italic;
}
```

In the next section, I introduce the `font-size` property.

THE FONT-SIZE PROPERTY

The `font-size` property is, of course, used to control the size of fonts. The following table outlines the `font-size` property and its possible values.

PROPERTY	VALUE
font-size	`<absolute-size>` | `<relative-size>` | `<length>` | `<percentage>` Initial value: medium

Of these, you will rarely find any values other than length and percentage in use in real world code, so let's briefly take a look at absolute-size and relative-size before we move on to the practical stuff.

Absolute Font Sizes

The `<absolute-size>` value notation of the `font-size` property refers to one of seven keyword values. Absolute values for the `font-size` property are defined using keywords that range from `xx-large` to `xx-small`. The following table outlines the absolute values and their relation to HTML heading sizes.

ABSOLUTE KEYWORD	XX-SMALL	X-SMALL	SMALL	MEDIUM	LARGE	X-LARGE	XX-LARGE
HTML	n/a	`<h6>`	`<h5>`	`<h4>`	`<h3>`	`<h2>`	`<h1>`Heading

These keywords specify the font size based on a scaling factor of 1.2. *Scaling factor* is the ratio between two shapes. The scaling factor is determined by multiplying the font size by 1.2 to determine the next font size relative to the previous one. For instance, if a font size of 16 pixels is assumed for the `medium` keyword value, the `large` keyword would be approximately 20 pixels, rounding up from 19.2, because 16 multiplied by 1.2 equals 19.2.

Relative Font Sizes

The `<relative-size>` notation of the `font-size` property refers to two values: `larger` and `smaller`. When either of these two values is used, the font size is determined by the values appearing in the table for absolute size. If the value is specified with a length unit — say, for instance, as pixels — the browser simply applies a 1.2 scaling factor to that size to get the larger size.

Length and Percentage Font Sizes

Length and percentage font sizes are what you will most commonly see and use, and both work in the same way.

Font sizes can be set in any of the absolute (inches, centimeters, millimeters, points, and picas) or relative (em, ex, pixels and percentage) measurements that we saw in the "Length and Measurement" section in Chapter 2. Of these you will rarely see absolute measurements used for text outside of print style sheets (see Chapter 15) and will rarely see ex used in any context.

Let's start with the easiest to understand, pixels, demonstrated in the following code.

Available for download on Wrox.com

```
<!DOCTYPE html PUBLIC "-//W3C//DTD HTML 4.01//EN"
    "http://www.w3.org/TR/html4/strict.dtd">
<html lang="en">
<head>
    <meta http-equiv="Content-Type" content="text/html; charset=utf-8">
    <title>Figure 5-5</title>
    <style type="text/css">
        body {
            font-family: arial, helvetica, sans-serif;
            font-size: 12px;
        }

        h1 {
            font-family: "Times New Roman", Georgia, Serif;
            font-size: 30px;
        }
    </style>
</head>
<body>

<h1>Recipes for Cheese</h1>

<p>Cheese is a remarkably versatile food, available in literally hundreds
of varieties with different flavors and textures.</p>

</body>
</html>
```

code snippet /chapter5/figure_5-5.html

This results in the output shown in Figure 5-5.

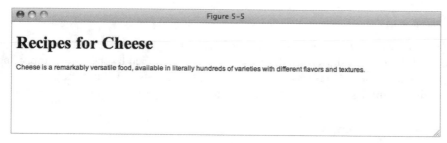

FIGURE 5-5

If you compare this to previous examples, you will see that the paragraph text is smaller and the heading text is larger than before. This is very simple and easy to implement and would probably the most common method of setting font sizes on the Web if it wasn't for one small wrinkle: Internet Explorer. All browsers provide a mechanism for users to resize text in their browser. This is an important accessibility feature, in particular helping those with poor vision to read text in a size comfortable for them.

Unfortunately, IE does not resize text if the font size is set in pixels or for that matter in any absolute units. It won't even resize text if you override the default font size on a child element with a relative measurement such as a percentage if the initial value is set with pixels. If you want your sites to be accessible (and you do!), you must look to other measurements, namely percentages and ems.

Percentage font sizes work much like the em units discussed in Chapter 2. Consider this example:

Available for download on Wrox.com

```
<!DOCTYPE html PUBLIC "-//W3C//DTD HTML 4.01//EN"
    "http://www.w3.org/TR/html4/strict.dtd">
<html lang="en">
<head>
    <meta http-equiv="Content-Type" content="text/html; charset=utf-8">
    <title>Figure 5-6</title>
    <style type="text/css">
        body {
            font-family: arial, helvetica, sans-serif;
        }

        h1 {
            font-size: 1.5em;
            font-weight: normal;
        }

        p {
            font-size: 150%;
        }
    </style>
</head>
<body>

<h1>Recipes for Cheese</h1>

<p>Cheese is a remarkably versatile food, available in literally hundreds
```

```
of varieties with different flavors and textures.</p>

</body>
</html>
```

code snippet /chapter5/figure_5-6.html

This results in the output shown in Figure 5-6.

Recipes for Cheese

Cheese is a remarkably versatile food, available in literally hundreds of varieties with different flavors and textures.

FIGURE 5-6

Figure 5-6 shows that percentage values are based on the element's ancestry. The font size for the h1 element is 1.5em, which means 1.5 times the default font size. The font size of the p element is made 150% larger than the default font, and you can see that they are both the same size. This means that 1em is interchangeable with 100%, with 2em being the same as 200% etc.

As long as you set your font sizes with ems or percentages, all browsers, including IE, will allow your users to resize text. It is therefore common to see styles such as the one in the following code.

```
body {
    font-size: 62.5%;
}
```

Based on the default font size of 16px, common to all modern web browsers, this sets the size of 1em to 10px, making it much easier to calculate the value required to set font sizes of other values (for cxample, 13px would be 1.3em or 130%).

There is one gotcha with relative measurements: They are cumulative. In other words, if you nest two elements that both have styles changing the font size of the text, both changes will be applied. The following code shows this.

Available for
download on
Wrox.com

```
<!DOCTYPE html PUBLIC "-//W3C//DTD HTML 4.01//EN"
    "http://www.w3.org/TR/html4/strict.dtd">
<html lang="en">
<head>
    <meta http-equiv="Content-Type" content="text/html; charset=utf-8">
    <title>Figure 5-7</title>
    <style type="text/css">
        .intro {
            font-size: 1.2em;
```

```
            }

            .recipe {
                font-size: 1.1em;
            }
        </style>
    </head>
    <body>

    <p class="intro">Cheese is a remarkably versatile food, available in
    literally hundreds of varieties with different flavors and textures.</p>

    <div class="recipe">

        <h2>Welsh Rarebit</h2>

        <p class="intro">Cheese is a remarkably versatile food, available in
    literally hundreds of varieties with different flavors and textures.</p>

    </div>

    </body>
    </html>
```

code snippet /chapter5/figure_5-7.html

This results in the output shown in Figure 5-7.

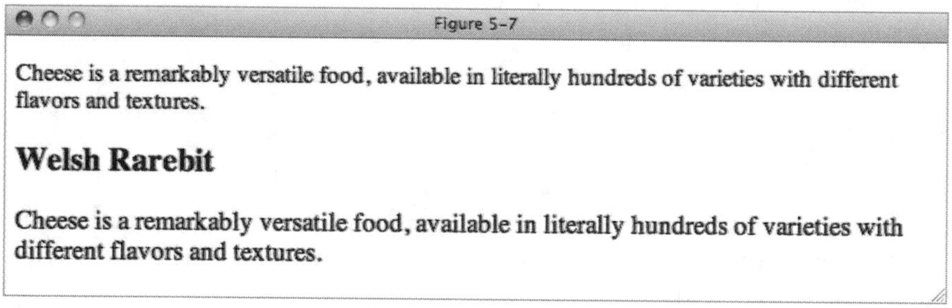

Cheese is a remarkably versatile food, available in literally hundreds of varieties with different flavors and textures.

Welsh Rarebit

Cheese is a remarkably versatile food, available in literally hundreds of varieties with different flavors and textures.

FIGURE 5-7

The result in Figure 5-7 is that the p element inside the div with class name of recipe has been increased in size by 10% because it is of the .recipe selector and by a further 20% on top of the 10% because of the .intro selector! This makes the text much bigger than expected.

The next section examines a special shorthand property used to specify several font properties in one.

THE FONT SHORTHAND PROPERTY

font is a shorthand property that allows you to write several font-related properties in a single property. The following table outlines the font property and the values that it allows.

PROPERTY	VALUE
font	[<'font-style'> || <'font-variant'> || <'font-weight'>]? <'font-size'> [/ <'line-height'>]? <'font-family'>] caption | icon | menu | message-box | small-caption | status-bar

The notation for the font property is somewhat more complicated than that presented in previous examples. For now, just ignore the caption, icon, menu, message-box, small-caption, and status-bar values — these are called system fonts, and you will rarely see them used in real-world code.

The font Properties

As for the first part of the notation, here's a breakdown of each portion:

    [<'font-style'> || <'font-variant'> || <'font-weight'>]?

This indicates that a font-style, font-variant, or font-weight value can be provided. The question mark indicates that this part is optional; you don't have to include a font-style, font-variant, or a font-weight. The double vertical bars in the notation indicate that each value is optional, and they also indicate that any combination of the three can appear. You can include just a font-style, just a font-variant, just a font-weight, all three, or any combination of the three. The next part indicates that a font size must be specified:

    <'font-size'>

The font size is not optional, so a font-size value must always be provided.

The next part indicates that a line-height (discussed in Chapter 6) may be specified, but because a question mark follows it, the line height is optional:

    [/ <'line-height'>]?

The forward slash in the notation indicates that if a line height is specified, a forward slash must separate the font-size and line-height properties. The question mark after the closing square bracket indicates that this portion of the syntax is optional.

 NOTE *Line height controls the spacing between lines of text, and is covered in detail in the next chapter.*

The last portion indicates that a font-family must be specified:

    <'font-family'>

So at the very least, a font-size value and a font-family value must be specified.

It's important to note that using shorthand properties of any kind resets to their default the values of any of the individual properties that haven't been specified in the shorthand property. The following code gives an example:

Available for download on Wrox.com

```
<!DOCTYPE html PUBLIC "-//W3C//DTD HTML 4.01//EN"
    "http://www.w3.org/TR/html4/strict.dtd">
<html lang="en">
<head>
    <meta http-equiv="Content-Type" content="text/html; charset=utf-8">
    <title>Figure 5-8</title>
    <style type="text/css">
        body {
            font-weight: bold;
        }

        p {
            font: 100% arial, helvetica, sans-serif;
        }
    </style>
</head>
<body>

<h1>Recipes for Cheese</h1>

<p>Cheese is a remarkably versatile food, available in literally hundreds
of varieties with different flavors and textures.</p>

</body>
</html>
```

code snippet /chapter5/figure_5-8.html

In Figure 5-8 you can see that although the first rule applied to the body sets all text on the page to be bold, the rule targeting the paragraph does not specify a `font-weight` and therefore the default `font-weight` style of `normal` has been applied.

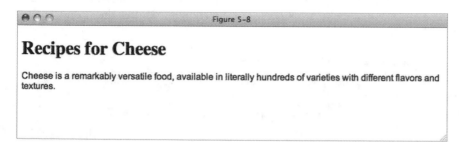

FIGURE 5-8

Now that you understand the notation (I hope!), you can try the `font` property for yourself in the following Try It Out.

TRY IT OUT   Applying the font Property

Example 5-3

Follow these steps to try out the font property.

1.   In your text editor, type the following markup:

```
<!DOCTYPE html PUBLIC "-//W3C//DTD HTML 4.01//EN"
    "http://www.w3.org/TR/html4/strict.dtd">
<html lang="en">
<head>
    <meta http-equiv="Content-Type" content="text/html; charset=utf-8">
    <title>Example 5-3</title>
    <style type="text/css">
        body {
            font: 62.5% arial, helvetica, sans-serif;
        }

        h1 {
            font: small-caps 1.6em "Times New Roman", Georgia, Serif;
        }

        .recipe .intro {
            font: italic 1em arial, helvetica, sans-serif;
        }
    </style>
</head>
<body>

<h1>Recipes for Cheese</h1>

<p class="intro">Cheese is a remarkably versatile food, available in literally
    hundreds of varieties with different flavors and textures.</p>

<div class="recipe">

    <h2>Welsh Rarebit</h2>

    <p class="intro">Cheese is a remarkably versatile food, available in literally
    hundreds of varieties with different flavors and textures.</p>

    <ol>
        <li>Lightly toast the bread</li>
        <li>Place on a baking tray, and spread with butter.</li>
        <li>Add the grated Cheddar cheese and 2 tablespoons of beer to a saucepan.
Place the saucepan over a medium heat, and stir the cheese continuously until
it has melted. Add a teaspoon of wholegrain mustard and grind in a little
pepper. Keep stirring.</li>
        <li>When thick and smooth, pour over each piece of toast spreading it to
the edges to stop the toast from burning.</li>
        <li>Place under the grill for a couple of minutes or until golden
        brown.</li>
```

```
        </ol>

    </div>

  </body>
</html>
```

2. Save the markup as `example_5-3.html`. The results of these modifications are shown in Figure 5-9.

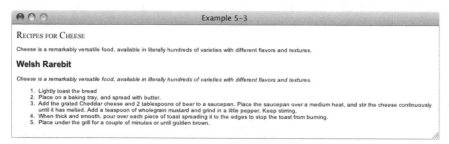

FIGURE 5-9

How It Works

In Example 5-3, you saw three examples of the font shorthand property. The first example sets the font for the whole document. Because the `font` property is inherited, the font will stay 16px and sans-serif unless specified otherwise for a child element.

```
body {
    font: 62.5% arial, helvetica, sans-serif;
}
```

You then set the font of all h1 elements to be small caps, 1.6em (which is equivalent to 16px thanks to the rule on the body element), and with a font family of `"Times New Roman", Georgia, Serif`.

```
h1 {
    font: small-caps 1.6em "Times New Roman", Georgia, Serif;
}
```

Finally, you set the font style to italic, the font size to 1em, and the font family to arial, helvetica, sans-serif for all elements with a class of `intro` that are also ancestors of an element with class of recipe.

```
.recipe .intro {
    font: italic 1em arial, helvetica, sans-serif;
}
```

You may think that the last rule is pointlessly complicated, and you would be right. All you are really changing here is the `font-syle` property, all other values are duplicating the style on the body element. This shows that short hand properties are not always the right choice, but in many cases can reduce the amount of code that you have to write. Ultimately I would advise you to write CSS in the style that is most comfortable for you — use short hand notation where appropriate if you want to, but don't feel that you have to.

EXERCISES

1. Why aren't the values of the `font-weight` property `100` through `900`, `bolder`, and `lighter` used in real-world web design?

2. How could the following rules be better written?

```
p {
    font-family: Arial, sans-serif;
    font-weight: bold;
    font-size: 24px;
    color: crimson;
}
p.copy {
    font-style: italic;
    font-weight: bold;
    line-height: 2em;
}
p#footer {
    font-size: 12px;
    line-height: 2em;
    font-family: Helvetica, Arial, sans-serif;
}
```

3. What's wrong with the following rule?

```
p {
    font-size: 24;
}
```

4. Would the declaration `font-size: 75%;` make the font size larger or smaller?

▶ **WHAT YOU LEARNED IN THIS CHAPTER**

Throughout this chapter, you learned about inheritance and the cascade, fundamental to CSS. To recap, in this chapter you learned the following:

TOPIC	KEY CONCEPTS
font-family	Setting font faces with the `font-family` property
Font styles	How to make text italic with `font-style`, bold with `font-weight` and small-caps with `font-variant`
Font sizes	The various ways of setting the size of text with `font-size` and the problems each unit of measurement has
Font shorthand	How to use the `font` shorthand and when it is appropriate to do so

Manipulating the Display of Text

WHAT YOU WILL LEARN IN THIS CHAPTER:

➤ The `line-height` property and how it is used control the space between lines of text

➤ The `letter-spacing` property and how it is used to add or subtract space between the letters that make up a word

➤ The `word-spacing` property and how it is used to add or subtract space between the words of a sentence

➤ The `text-indent` property and how it is used to indent the text of a paragraph

➤ The `text-align` property and how it is used to align the text of a document

➤ The `text-decoration` property and how it is used to underline, overline, and strikethrough text

➤ The `text-transform` property and how it is used to capitalize text or convert text to uppercase or lowercase letters

➤ The `white-space` property and how it is used to control the flow and formatting of text

In this chapter, I look specifically at properties that manipulate the presentation of text. You can manipulate text in a variety of ways, from the length of space between letters in words of text, to the length of space between the words of a sentence, to the spacing between sentences in a paragraph, to how much space is used to indent the text contained in a paragraph.

The text manipulation properties of CSS allow you to design the layout of a document in much the same way as you use a word processing application.

LINE HEIGHT

The `line-height` property refers to the height of the line on which each line of text appears. The `line-height` property and its values are outlined in the following table.

PROPERTY	VALUE
line-height	normal | \<number\> | \<length\> | \<percentage\> | inherit
	initial value: normal

No matter which value type is used, line-height works in the same way: The value refers to the height of a line of text, from which the vertical space that the charters in the text take up is deducted. The remainder is then split in two, with half added to the top of the line of text and half to the bottom.

The best way to specify line-height is with the number value type as you see in the following code.

Available for download on Wrox.com

```
<!DOCTYPE html PUBLIC "-//W3C//DTD HTML 4.01//EN"
    "http://www.w3.org/TR/html4/strict.dtd">
<html lang="en">
<head>
    <meta http-equiv="Content-Type" content="text/html; charset=utf-8">
    <title>Figure 6-1</title>
    <style type="text/css">
        .intro {
            line-height: 3;
        }
    </style>
</head>
<body>

<p class="intro">Welsh Rarebit is a savory dish made from melted cheese, often
Cheddar, on toasted bread, and a variety of other ingredients such as mustard,
 egg, or bacon. Here is one take on this classic.</p>

</body>
</html>
```

code snippet /chapter6/figure_6-1.html

Figure 6-1 shows that each line of text is contained in a `line-height` of 3, which means each line is 3 times the height of the text.

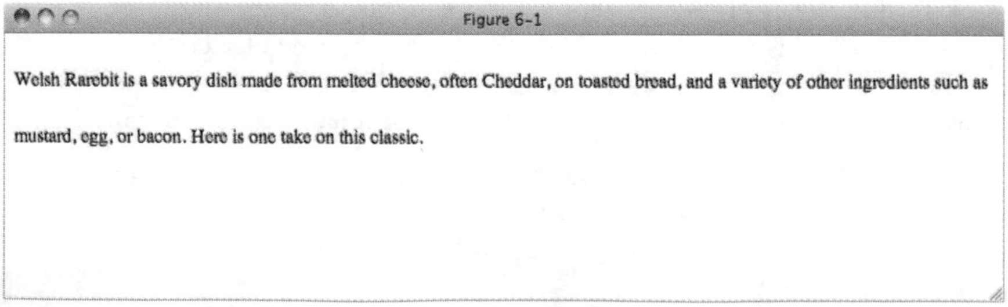

![Figure 6-1 browser window showing text: Welsh Rarebit is a savory dish made from melted cheese, often Cheddar, on toasted bread, and a variety of other ingredients such as mustard, egg, or bacon. Here is one take on this classic.]

FIGURE 6-1

Length and percentage values work in the same way (for example, a `line-height` of 3em is equivalent to a line-height of 3, as is a `line-height` of 30px on text that has a `font-size` of 10px). However, the way the value is inherited is different because it is only calculated once. If you were to set a `line-height` of 1.5em at a `font-size` of 10px on the body element, the inherited `line-height` of all text in the document would be 15px, even if the `font-size` was different. For this reason, it is a good idea to use only the number value option.

In the following example, you try the `line-height` property out for yourself.

TRY IT OUT Change the Spacing Between Lines of Text

Example 6-1

To see the `line-height` property in action, follow these steps.

1.   Enter the following markup:

```
<!DOCTYPE html PUBLIC "-//W3C//DTD HTML 4.01//EN"
    "http://www.w3.org/TR/html4/strict.dtd">
<html lang="en">
<head>
    <meta http-equiv="Content-Type" content="text/html; charset=utf-8">
    <title>Example 6-1</title>
    <style type="text/css">
        body {
            font: 13px arial,helvetica,clean,sans-serif;
        }

        .recipe .intro {
            font-style: italic;
            line-height: 3;
        }
    </style>
</head>
<body>

<h1>Recipes for Cheese</h1>

<p class="intro">Cheese is a remarkably versatile food, available in literally
hundreds of varieties with different flavors and textures.</p>

<div class="recipe">

    <h2>Welsh Rarebit</h2>

    <p class="intro">Welsh Rarebit is a savory dish made from melted cheese, often
    Cheddar, on toasted bread, and a variety of other ingredients such as mustard,
    egg, or bacon. Here is one take on this classic.</p>

    <ol>
        <li>Lightly toast the bread</li>
        <li>Place on a baking tray, and spread with butter.</li>
        <li>Add the grated Cheddar cheese and 2 tablespoons of beer to a saucepan.
```

```
        Place the saucepan over a medium heat, and stir the cheese continuously
        until it has melted. Add a teaspoon of wholegrain mustard and grind in a
        little pepper. Keep stirring.</li>
        <li>When thick and smooth, pour over each piece of toast spreading it to
        the edges to stop the toast from burning.</li>
        <li>Place under the grill for a couple of minutes or until golden
        brown.</li>
    </ol>

</div>

</body>
</html>
```

2. Save the preceding CSS as `example_6-1.html`. The preceding example results in the output in Figure 6-2.

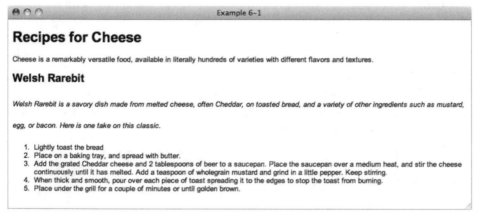

FIGURE 6-2

How It Works

In this Try It Out, you typed an example of the `line-height` property so that you could see it work in a browser for yourself. You applied two relevant style sheet rules. The second rule refers to elements with the class name of `recipe` inside an element with the class name of `intro`. Text in these elements will have a `line-height` three times the height of the `font-size`.

The first rule is on the body element and looks like:

```
font: 13px/1.231 arial,helvetica,clean,sans-serif;
```

So the calculated line height of the targeted element is 3 x 13px, or 39px.

As mentioned in Chapter 5, `line-height` can follow the setting of the font size on the shorthand `font` property.

CONTROLLING THE SPACING BETWEEN LETTERS

The letter-spacing property, as demonstrated briefly in previous chapters, controls the amount of space between letters. The following table shows its values.

PROPERTY	VALUE
letter-spacing	normal | <length> | inherit Initial value: normal

letter-spacing is a simple property that accepts a length as its value. A <length> value is any length value supported by CSS, as discussed in Chapter 2. normal is the default value and is determined by the font being used. This is equal to a zero length value.

The following code shows an example of the letter-spacing property.

Available for download on Wrox.com

```
<!DOCTYPE html PUBLIC "-//W3C//DTD HTML 4.01//EN"
    "http://www.w3.org/TR/html4/strict.dtd">
<html lang="en">
<head>
    <meta http-equiv="Content-Type" content="text/html; charset=utf-8">
    <title>Figure 6-3</title>
    <style type="text/css">
        .intro {
            letter-spacing: 0.2em;
        }
    </style>
</head>
<body>

<p class="intro">Welsh Rarebit is a savory dish made from melted cheese, often
Cheddar, on toasted bread, and a variety of other ingredients such as mustard,
egg, or bacon. Here is one take on this classic.</p>

</body>
</html>
```

code snippet /chapter6/figure_6-3.html

This code shows how the letter-spacing property would be specified.

Figure 6-3 shows the output of the code in the Safari browser.

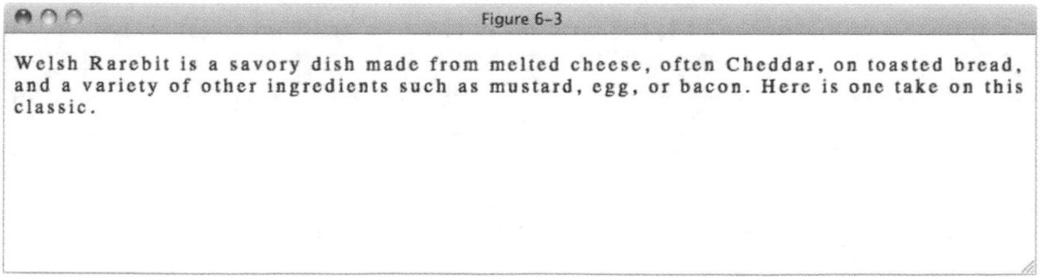

Welsh Rarebit is a savory dish made from melted cheese, often Cheddar, on toasted bread, and a variety of other ingredients such as mustard, egg, or bacon. Here is one take on this classic.

FIGURE 6-3

The `letter-spacing` property may have either a positive or negative value. When given a negative value, letters are rendered closer together.

In the next section, I present a property similar to `letter-spacing`: `word-spacing`.

CONTROLLING THE SPACING BETWEEN WORDS

The `word-spacing` property functions identically to the `letter-spacing` property. However, instead of controlling the space between letters, the `word-spacing` property controls the space between words. The following table shows its values.

PROPERTY	VALUE
word-spacing	normal | <length> | inherit
	Initial value: normal

To demonstrate the effect of the `word-spacing` property, consider the following code.

Available for download on Wrox.com

```
<!DOCTYPE html PUBLIC "-//W3C//DTD HTML 4.01//EN"
    "http://www.w3.org/TR/html4/strict.dtd">
<html lang="en">
<head>
    <meta http-equiv="Content-Type" content="text/html; charset=utf-8">
    <title>Figure 6-4</title>
    <style type="text/css">
        .intro {
            word-spacing: 0.2em;
        }
    </style>
</head>
<body>

<p class="intro">Welsh Rarebit is a savory dish made from melted cheese, often
Cheddar, on toasted bread, and a variety of other ingredients such as mustard,
egg, or bacon. Here is one take on this classic.</p>

</body>
</html>
```

code snippet /chapter6/figure_6-4.html

This results in the output shown in Figure 6-4; the spacing between words has been increased.

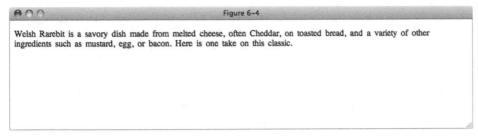

FIGURE 6-4

Additionally, like the letter-spacing property, the word-spacing property can contain a negative value. If given a negative value, the effect is less space between each word.

As you did with the letter-spacing property in Example 6-1, in the following Try It Out, you experiment with the word-spacing property for yourself.

TRY IT OUT | The Letter-Spacing and Word-Spacing Properties

Example 6-2

To see the letter-spacing and word-spacing properties in action, follow these steps.

1. Enter the following markup into your text editor:

```
<!DOCTYPE html PUBLIC "-//W3C//DTD HTML 4.01//EN"
    "http://www.w3.org/TR/html4/strict.dtd">
<html lang="en">
<head>
    <meta http-equiv="Content-Type" content="text/html; charset=utf-8">
    <title>Example 6-2</title>
    <style type="text/css">
        body {
            font: 13px/1.231 arial,helvetica,clean,sans-serif;
        }

        h1 {
            font-family: "Times New Roman", Georgia, Serif;
            font-variant: small-caps;
            letter-spacing: -0.1em;
        }

        .intro {
            font-weight: bold;
            word-spacing: 0.2em;
        }

        .recipe .intro {
            font-weight: normal;
            font-style: italic;
            word-spacing: normal;
        }
```

```
        </style>
    </head>
    <body>

    <h1>Recipes for Cheese</h1>

    <p class="intro">Cheese is a remarkably versatile food, available in literally
    hundreds of varieties with different flavors and textures.</p>

    <div class="recipe">

        <h2>Welsh Rarebit</h2>

        <p class="intro">Welsh Rarebit is a savory dish made from melted cheese, often
        Cheddar, on toasted bread, and a variety of other ingredients such as mustard,
        egg, or bacon. Here is one take on this classic.</p>

        <ol>
            <li>Lightly toast the bread</li>
            <li>Place on a baking tray, and spread with butter.</li>
            <li>Add the grated Cheddar cheese and 2 tablespoons of beer to a saucepan.
            Place the saucepan over a medium heat, and stir the cheese continuously
            until it has melted. Add a teaspoon of wholegrain mustard and grind in a
            little pepper. Keep stirring.</li>
            <li>When thick and smooth, pour over each piece of toast spreading it to
            the edges to stop the toast from burning.</li>
            <li>Place under the grill for a couple of minutes or until golden
            brown.</li>
        </ol>

    </div>

    </body>
    </html>
```

2. Save the preceding CSS as `example_6-2.html`. The preceding markup and CSS result in the output shown in Figure 6-5.

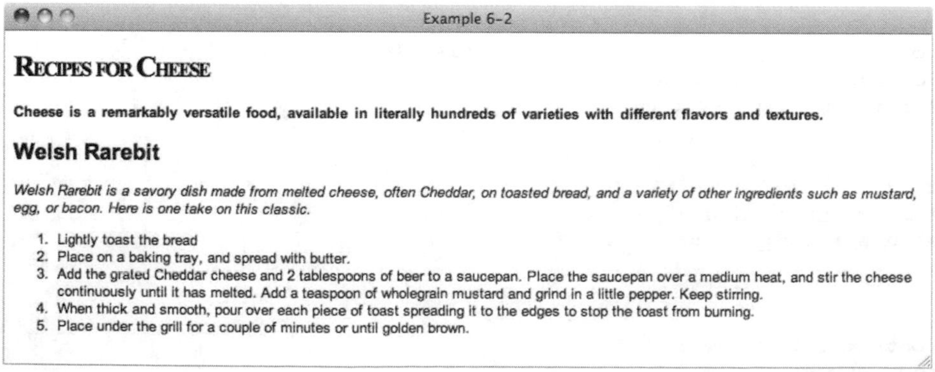

FIGURE 6-5

How It Works

In Example 6-2, you experimented with the `letter-spacing` and `word-spacing` properties. Following is a recap of the relevant rules.

The first rule you applied to `h1` elements applying the `letter-spacing` property with a value of -0.1em, meaning that each letter in the heading will be slightly closer together.

Then, in a subsequent rule, you applied a `word-spacing` value of 0.2em to elements with an `intro` class name. This time, the space between words is slightly increased.

Now that you have seen how to control the space between letters and words, the next section describes how to indent text within a paragraph.

INDENTING TEXT

Indenting text in CSS is done using the `text-indent` property. The `text-indent` property applied to a paragraph or any other element inserts the specified length before the first line of text, thus indenting the text. The following table shows this property's values.

PROPERTY	VALUE
text-indent	`<length>` | `<percentage>` | `inherit` Initial value: 0

The `text-indent` property accepts either a normal length value or a percentage value. The following code demonstrates the text-indent property with a normal length value in ems applied.

Available for
download on
Wrox.com

```html
<!DOCTYPE html PUBLIC "-//W3C//DTD HTML 4.01//EN"
    "http://www.w3.org/TR/html4/strict.dtd">
<html lang="en">
<head>
    <meta http-equiv="Content-Type" content="text/html; charset=utf-8">
    <title>Figure 6-6</title>
    <style type="text/css">
        .intro {
            text-indent: 2em;
        }
    </style>
</head>
<body>

<p class="intro">Welsh Rarebit is a savory dish made from melted cheese, often
Cheddar, on toasted bread, and a variety of other ingredients such as mustard,
egg, or bacon. Here is one take on this classic.</p>

</body>
</html>
```

code snippet /chapter6/figure_6-6.html

Figure 6-6 shows the result of the preceding rule and markup.

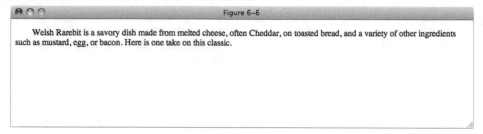

Welsh Rarebit is a savory dish made from melted cheese, often Cheddar, on toasted bread, and a variety of other ingredients such as mustard, egg, or bacon. Here is one take on this classic.

FIGURE 6-6

Figure 6-6 demonstrates the most common use of the `text-indent` property, with a normal length value, used to indent the text of the target element.

The `text-indent` property can also accept a percentage width. The percentage width assigned by the `text-indent` property depends on the width of the element's parent. For instance, if a `<p>` element were to be assigned a fixed width of 200 pixels and is inside a `<div>` with a width of 800px, the indention of the first line of the `<p>` element would be 80 pixels. It is rare to use percentage values because, as you can see, they are harder to control.

Like the `letter-spacing` and `word-spacing` properties, the `text-indent` property can accept a negative value. In that case, the text will be shifted to the outside of the text, to the left in left-to-right languages such as English.

In the next section, I discuss the `text-align` property.

HORIZONTALLY ALIGNING TEXT

The purpose of the `text-align` property is simple: It aligns text! The following table outlines each of the values for the `text-align` property.

PROPERTY	VALUE
text-align	left | right | center | justify Initial value: left

The `text-align` property has a number of keyword values that align text left or right or center it or justify it.

The following code demonstrates what the `center` and `justify` keyword values of the `text-align` property do.

Available for
download on
Wrox.com

```
<!DOCTYPE html PUBLIC "-//W3C//DTD HTML 4.01//EN"
    "http://www.w3.org/TR/html4/strict.dtd">
<html lang="en">
<head>
    <meta http-equiv="Content-Type" content="text/html; charset=utf-8">
    <title>Figure 6-7</title>
    <style type="text/css">
        h2 {
            text-align: center;
        }

        .intro {
            text-align: justify;
        }
    </style>
</head>
<body>

<h2>Welsh Rarebit</h2>

<p class="intro">Welsh Rarebit is a savory dish made from melted cheese, often
Cheddar, on toasted bread, and a variety of other ingredients such as mustard,
egg, or bacon. Here is one take on this classic.</p>

</body>
</html>
```

code snippet /chapter6/figure_6-7.html

The CSS and markup from this code results in the output displayed in Figure 6-7. You see that center has aligned the heading text in the center.

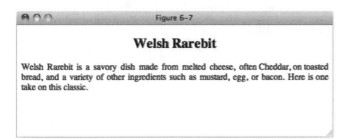

FIGURE 6-7

You may not be familiar with the justify keyword. As you see in Figure 6-7, padding has been added to the text so that the right hand edge lines up. This is commonly seen in newspapers, but on websites it can make text hard to read and can produce uncertain results; it's best to avoid it.

Vertically aligning content, including text, is a little more complicated. You will learn how to do this in Chapter 9.

DECORATING TEXT WITH UNDERLINES, OVERLINES, OR STRIKETHROUGH

The `text-decoration` property applies underlining, overlining, and strikethrough to text. The following table outlines the `text-decoration` property and the values it allows.

PROPERTY	VALUE
text-decoration	none | [underline || overline || line-through || blink] Initial value: none

The `text-decoration` property is quite straightforward, so let's go through the three values you might want to use.

The following code shows the CSS for underlining text as shown in Figure 6-8.

Available for download on Wrox.com

```
<!DOCTYPE html PUBLIC "-//W3C//DTD HTML 4.01//EN"
    "http://www.w3.org/TR/html4/strict.dtd">
<html lang="en">
<head>
    <meta http-equiv="Content-Type" content="text/html; charset=utf-8">
    <title>Figure 6-8</title>
    <style type="text/css">
        .intro {
            text-decoration: underline;
        }
    </style>
</head>
<body>

<p class="intro">Welsh Rarebit is a savory dish made from melted cheese, often
Cheddar, on toasted bread, and a variety of other ingredients such as mustard,
egg, or bacon. Here is one take on this classic.</p>

</body>
</html>
```

code snippet /chapter6/figure_6-8.html

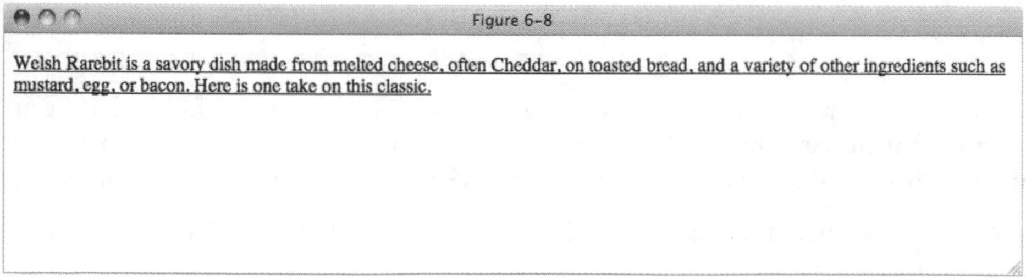

Figure 6-8

Welsh Rarebit is a savory dish made from melted cheese, often Cheddar, on toasted bread, and a variety of other ingredients such as mustard, egg, or bacon. Here is one take on this classic.

FIGURE 6-8

The next code shows the CSS for adding a line over the text as shown in Figure 6-9.

Available for download on Wrox.com

```
<!DOCTYPE html PUBLIC "-//W3C//DTD HTML 4.01//EN"
    "http://www.w3.org/TR/html4/strict.dtd">
<html lang="en">
<head>
    <meta http-equiv="Content-Type" content="text/html; charset=utf-8">
    <title>Figure 6-9</title>
    <style type="text/css">
        .intro {
            text-decoration: overline;
        }
    </style>
</head>
<body>

<p class="intro">Welsh Rarebit is a savory dish made from melted cheese, often
Cheddar, on toasted bread, and a variety of other ingredients such as mustard,
egg, or bacon. Here is one take on this classic.</p>

</body>
</html>
```

code snippet /chapter6/figure_6-9.html

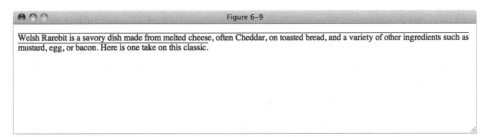

FIGURE 6-9

The following code shows the CSS for adding a strikethrough to the text as shown in Figure 6-10.

Available for download on Wrox.com

```
<!DOCTYPE html PUBLIC "-//W3C//DTD HTML 4.01//EN"
    "http://www.w3.org/TR/html4/strict.dtd">
<html lang="en">
<head>
    <meta http-equiv="Content-Type" content="text/html; charset=utf-8">
    <title>Figure 6-10</title>
    <style type="text/css">
        .intro {
            text-decoration: line-through;
        }
    </style>
</head>
```

```
<body>

<p class="intro">Welsh Rarebit is a savory dish made from melted cheese, often
Cheddar, on toasted bread, and a variety of other ingredients such as mustard,
egg, or bacon. Here is one take on this classic.</p>

</body>
</html>
```

code snippet /chapter6/figure_6-10.html

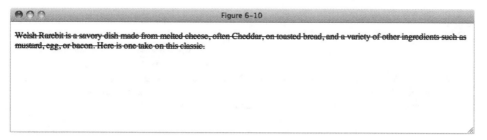

FIGURE 6-10

The last value is `blink`, the usage of which has thankfully died out on most of the Web. Its purpose is to make text flash on and off. As you can imagine, this can be very annoying, not to mention an accessibility problem. Support for `blink` is poor in modern browsers and long may it stay that way!

It is possible to apply more than one `text-decoration` value; simply list them with a space between each (for example, `text-decoration: underline line-through;`). I strongly advise careful use of `text-decoration`; however, too much decoration makes text hard to read, and you should be careful not to confuse your website's users. It is common for underlined text to be a link, so making non-link text underlined can be frustrating when users try to click it.

The following Try It Out gives an example of how you may use `text-decoration` to style links.

TRY IT OUT   **Decorate Links**

Example 6-3

To experiment with the `text-decoration` property, follow these steps.

1.   Enter the following into your text editor:

```
<!DOCTYPE html PUBLIC "-//W3C//DTD HTML 4.01//EN"
    "http://www.w3.org/TR/html4/strict.dtd">
<html lang="en">
<head>
    <meta http-equiv="Content-Type" content="text/html; charset=utf-8">
    <title>Example 6-3</title>
    <style type="text/css">
```

```
        body {
            font: 13px/1.231 arial,helvetica,clean,sans-serif;
        }

        a:link {
            text-decoration: none;
        }

        a:focus,
        a:hover {
            text-decoration: underline;
        }
    </style>
</head>
<body>

<h1>Recipes for Cheese</h1>

<p class="intro">Cheese is a remarkably versatile food, available in literally
hundreds of varieties with different flavors and textures.</p>

<div class="recipe">

    <h2>Welsh Rarebit</h2>

    <p class="intro">Welsh Rarebit is a savory dish made from melted cheese, often
    Cheddar, on toasted bread, and a variety of other ingredients such as mustard,
    egg, or bacon. Here is one take on this classic.</p>

    <p><a href="#">More Welsh Rarebit recipes</a></p>

    <ol>
        <li>Lightly toast the bread</li>
        <li>Place on a baking tray, and spread with butter.</li>
        <li>Add the grated Cheddar cheese and 2 tablespoons of beer to a saucepan.
        Place the saucepan over a medium heat, and stir the cheese continuously
        until it has melted. Add a teaspoon of wholegrain mustard and grind in a
        little pepper. Keep stirring.</li>
        <li>When thick and smooth, pour over each piece of toast spreading it to
        the edges to stop the toast from burning.</li>
        <li>Place under the grill for a couple of minutes or until golden
        brown.</li>
    </ol>

</div>

</body>
</html>
```

2. Save the preceding code as `example_6-3.html`. The aforementioned CSS and markup result in the output in Figure 6-11.

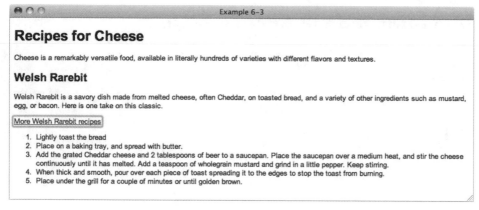

FIGURE 6-11

How It Works

In Example 6-3, you removed the underline from links in their default state, but on `hover` or `focus` added it back. You will see styles like this on many websites.

In the next section, I discuss the `text-transform` property, which allows you to control the case of text via CSS.

TRANSFORMING LETTER-CASE TO LOWERCASE OR UPPERCASE OR CAPITALIZING THE INITIAL CHARACTERS OF WORDS

The `text-transform` property exists purely to manipulate the case of text (for instance, to capitalize or make all characters uppercase or lowercase). The following table shows the `text-transform` property and its values.

PROPERTY	VALUE
text-transform	capitalize | uppercase | lowercase | none Initial value: none

The `text-transform` property is also quite straightforward, so again we'll go through each value in turn.

The next code snippet shows the CSS for capitalizing text (that is the first letter of each word is capitalized, as shown in Figure 6-12).

Available for download on Wrox.com

```
<!DOCTYPE html PUBLIC "-//W3C//DTD HTML 4.01//EN"
    "http://www.w3.org/TR/html4/strict.dtd">
<html lang="en">
<head>
    <meta http-equiv="Content-Type" content="text/html; charset=utf-8">
    <title>Figure 6-12</title>
    <style type="text/css">
        h1 {
            text-transform: capitalize;
        }
    </style>
</head>
<body>

<h1>Recipes for Cheese</h1>

</body>
</html>
```

code snippet /chapter6/figure_6-12.html

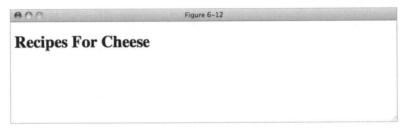

FIGURE 6-12

The following code shows the CSS for making text uppercase, as shown in Figure 6-13.

Available for download on Wrox.com

```
<!DOCTYPE html PUBLIC "-//W3C//DTD HTML 4.01//EN"
    "http://www.w3.org/TR/html4/strict.dtd">
<html lang="en">
<head>
    <meta http-equiv="Content-Type" content="text/html; charset=utf-8">
    <title>Figure 6-13</title>
    <style type="text/css">
        h1 {
            text-transform: uppercase;
        }
    </style>
</head>
<body>

<h1>Recipes for Cheese</h1>

</body>
</html>
```

code snippet /chapter6/figure_6-13.html

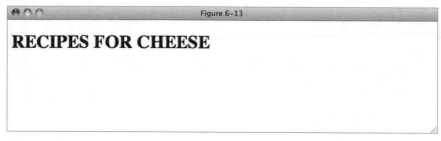

FIGURE 6-13

The next code shows the CSS for making text lowercase, as shown in Figure 6-14.

Available for
download on
Wrox.com

```html
<!DOCTYPE html PUBLIC "-//W3C//DTD HTML 4.01//EN"
    "http://www.w3.org/TR/html4/strict.dtd">
<html lang="en">
<head>
    <meta http-equiv="Content-Type" content="text/html; charset=utf-8">
    <title>Figure 6-14</title>
    <style type="text/css">
        h1 {
            text-transform: lowercase;
        }
    </style>
</head>
<body>

<h1>Recipes for Cheese</h1>

</body>
</html>
```

code snippet /chapter6/figure_6-14.html

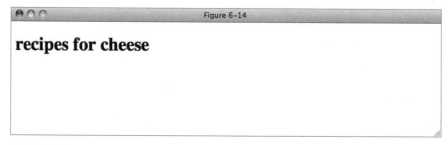

FIGURE 6-14

It is good practice to write all text in markup in the way you normally would if you were ignoring whatever typographical style your design demands. This way if the design changes it is a simple matter to change the CSS rather than having to change content, which could be spread throughout your site.

In the next section, I present CSS's white-space property, which controls whether or not spaces and line breaks in the source code are recognized and whether or not text wraps automatically.

CONTROLLING HOW WHITE SPACE IS HANDLED

The white-space property allows you to control text formatting in the source code of the web document. The following table outlines the keyword values of the white-space property as of CSS 2.

PROPERTY	VALUE
white-space	normal | pre | nowrap Initial value: normal

The white-space property is mainly used with the pre keyword value, and it used to output content exactly as it appears in your markup.

The following code snippet is an example of the white-space: pre; declaration applied to a <code> element.

Available for
download on
Wrox.com

```
<!DOCTYPE html PUBLIC "-//W3C//DTD HTML 4.01//EN"
    "http://www.w3.org/TR/html4/strict.dtd">
<html lang="en">
<head>
    <meta http-equiv="Content-Type" content="text/html; charset=utf-8">
    <title>Figure 6-15</title>
    <style type="text/css">
        code {
            white-space: pre;
        }
    </style>
</head>
<body>

<code>
&lt;script type="text/javascript"&gt;
    document.documentElement.className = 'js';
&lt;/script&gt;
</code>

</body>
</html>
```

code snippet /chapter6/figure_6-15.html

The result looks like Figure 6-15.

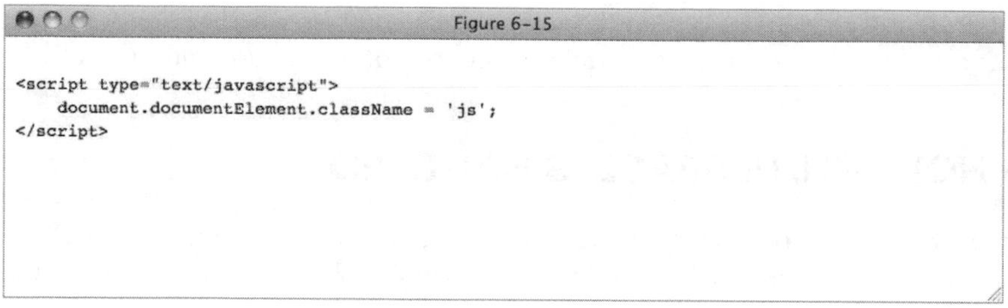

```
<script type="text/javascript">
    document.documentElement.className = 'js';
</script>
```

FIGURE 6-15

With the `white-space: pre;` declaration, spaces and line breaks are preserved in the browser's rendered output.

By default, the browser will collapse the extra spaces between words and ignore the line breaks, which is the behavior of the `white-space: normal;` declaration. The `white-space: pre;` declaration preserves that extra space and keeps the line breaks where they appear in the source code.

Under normal circumstances, if there is too much text to appear on a single line, the extra text overflows onto the following line or lines. The `white-space: nowrap;` declaration prevents that overflow from happening and forces the text to stay on one line, unless an HTML line break `<br>` element is encountered. While it is not unheard of to see this declaration used, it is advisable that you don't use it, as it can cause layout problems when your text overlaps or pushes other content out of the way!

EXERCISES

1. If you want to reduce the spacing between letters, how will you do so? Provide an example declaration.

2. How do you remove the underlines from links but restore the underlines when the links are focused on or hovered over?

3. When indenting text in a paragraph, how is a percentage value calculated?

4. What are the keywords that CSS offers for changing the case of text within an element?

5. If you want to preserve line breaks and spacing as formatted in the source code, what CSS declaration will you use?

▶ WHAT YOU LEARNED IN THIS CHAPTER

In this chapter, I discussed a variety of CSS text-manipulation properties. To recap, in this chapter you learned the following:

TOPIC	KEY CONCEPTS
`line-height`	Controlling the spacing between lines of text
`letter-spacing` and `word-spacing`	Controlling the spacing between letters and words
`text-indent`	How to indent the first line of a block of text
`text-align`	How to horizontally align text
`text-decoration`	How to apply underlines, overlines, and strikethrough styles
`text-transform`	How to control the case of text, making it uppercase, lowercase or sentence case
`white-space`	How to control how white space is handled in text, allowing it to be displayed according to the source format

7

Background Colors and Images

WHAT YOU WILL LEARN IN THIS CHAPTER:

➤ How to use the `background-color` property to set a background color

➤ How to use the `background-image` property to specify a background image

➤ How to use the `background-repeat` property to control background tiling

➤ How to use the `background-position` property to control how the background is positioned

➤ How to use the `background-attachment` property to control whether the background scrolls with the page or remains fixed in place with respect to the view port

➤ How to use the `background` shorthand property to combine all the separate background properties into a single property

Backgrounds play a large role in CSS design and are often the bread and butter of the overall aesthetic presentation of a web page. This chapter begins the discussion of background properties by exploring the `background-color` property.

BACKGROUND COLORS

The `background-color` property is used to specify a solid background color. The following table shows the possible values for the `background-color` property.

PROPERTY	VALUE
background-color	`<color>`	`transparent` Initial value: `transparent`

The `background-color` property allows any of the color values supported by CSS that I covered in chapter 2, such as a color keyword, an RGB value, or a hexadecimal, or short hexadecimal value. It may also be given the `transparent` keyword, which indicates that no color should be used. This is straightforward, so let's Try It Out right away. The following exercise applies the `background-color` property to a style sheet.

TRY IT OUT   Applying a Background Color

Example 7-1

To see the `background-color` property in action, follow these steps.

1.   Enter the following markup:

```
<!DOCTYPE html PUBLIC "-//W3C//DTD HTML 4.01//EN"
    "http://www.w3.org/TR/html4/strict.dtd">
<html lang="en">
<head>
    <meta http-equiv="Content-Type" content="text/html; charset=utf-8">
    <title>Example 7-1</title>
    <style type="text/css">
        body {
            background-color: #000;
            color: #FFF;
        }
    </style>
</head>
<body>

<h1>Recipes for Cheese</h1>

<p class="intro">Cheese is a remarkably versatile food, available in literally
hundreds of varieties with different flavors and textures.</p>

</body>
</html>
```

2.   Save the preceding CSS and markup as `example_7-1.html`. This example results in the rendered output in Figure 7-1.

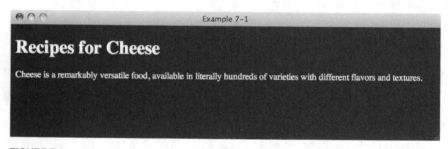

FIGURE 7-1

How It Works

In Example 7-1, you applied the `background-color` property to the body element, with a short hexadecimal value of #000, making the background black. A `color` of #FFF, which represents white, is also specified, to ensure that the text is readable against the background color.

> **NOTE** *It is good practice to specify a `color` when you set a `background-color` as it helps to ensure that any text within the element you're applying the styles to will be readable. You should also always set a background and text color, even if they are white and black, on the body element of documents, to ensure that your text will display as you expect—don't rely on browser defaults.*

In the next section I discuss the `background-image` property.

BACKGROUND IMAGES

As you probably guessed, the `background-image` property enables you to provide an image for the background. The following table outlines the values available for the `background-image` property.

PROPERTY	VALUE
background-image	<uri> | none Initial value: none

The `background-image` property allows you to reference a URL, which is indicated by the <uri> notation in the preceding table, or a keyword of none. When you specify a background image, by default the image tiles across the entire area available to it, that is the area encompassing the content and padding of the element being styled. In the following Try It Out, you try the `background-image` property for yourself. The images and source code for this and all the other examples in this book can be found online at www.wrox.com.

TRY IT OUT Applying a Background Image

Example 7-2

To see the `background-image` property in action, follow these steps.

1. Enter the following markup:

```
<!DOCTYPE html PUBLIC "-//W3C//DTD HTML 4.01//EN"
    "http://www.w3.org/TR/html4/strict.dtd">
<html lang="en">
<head>
    <meta http-equiv="Content-Type" content="text/html; charset=utf-8">
    <title>Example 7-2</title>
    <style type="text/css">
        body {
            background-image: url(bg-page.png);
        }
    </style>
</head>
<body>

<h1>Recipes for Cheese</h1>

<p class="intro">Cheese is a remarkably versatile food, available in literally
hundreds of varieties with different flavors and textures.</p>

<div class="recipe">

    <h2>Welsh Rarebit</h2>

    <p class="intro">Welsh Rarebit is a savory dish made from melted cheese, often
    Cheddar, on toasted bread, and a variety of other ingredients such as mustard,
    egg, or bacon. Here is one take on this classic.</p>

    <ol>
        <li>Lightly toast the bread</li>
        <li>Place on a baking tray, and spread with butter.</li>
        <li>Add the grated Cheddar cheese and 2 tablespoons of beer to a saucepan.
        Place the saucepan over a medium heat, and stir the cheese continuously
        until it has melted. Add a teaspoon of wholegrain mustard and grind in
        a little pepper. Keep stirring.</li>
        <li>When thick and smooth, pour over each piece of toast spreading it to
        the edges to stop the toast from burning.</li>
        <li>Place under the grill for a couple of minutes or until golden
        brown.</li>
    </ol>

</div>

</body>
</html>
```

2. Save the preceding CSS and markup as `example_7-2.html`. This example results in the output in Figure 7-2.

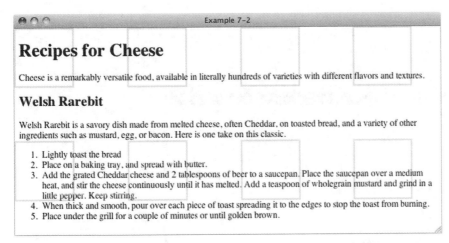

FIGURE 7-2

How It Works

In Example 7-2, you applied the `background-image` property with a `<uri>` value, which outputs the tiled background of a light grey square.

Interestingly, the background image is applied to the entire document, not just the area that the `<body>` element takes up, as you can see in Figure 7-3.

Recipes for Cheese

Cheese is a remarkably versatile food, available in literally hundreds of varieties with different flavors and textures.

Welsh Rarebit

Welsh Rarebit is a savory dish made from melted cheese, often Cheddar, on toasted bread, and a variety of other ingredients such as mustard, egg, or bacon. Here is one take on this classic.

1. Lightly toast the bread
2. Place on a baking tray, and spread with butter.
3. Add the grated Cheddar cheese and 2 tablespoons of beer to a saucepan. Place the saucepan over a medium heat, and stir the cheese continuously until it has melted. Add a teaspoon of wholegrain mustard and grind in a little pepper. Keep stirring.
4. When thick and smooth, pour over each piece of toast spreading it to the edges to stop the toast from burning.
5. Place under the grill for a couple of minutes or until golden brown.

FIGURE 7-3

This is because all background properties applied to the `body` element are considered to be applied to the `html` element, unless the `<html>` element also has a background property of any type set. This can allow some interesting effects, as you can see in Figure 7-4.

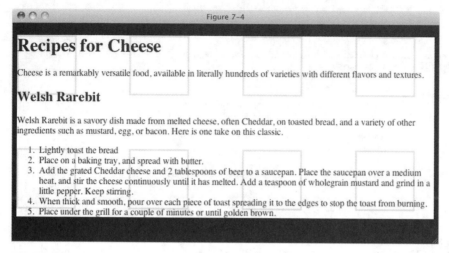

FIGURE 7-4

 NOTE One good use for background images is for sprites. If your site used several small icons (for example, a magnifying glass icon next to a search field or the appropriate flag next to each item in a list of countries), you can combine them into one image with plenty of empty space between each one. You can then use the `background-image` property in combination with the `background-repeat` and `background-position` properties, which you will look at next, to show the icon that you need in each circumstance.

Done right, this can have the benefit of making your site load faster for your users, as they will only have to download one image instead of many.

For a great article on using sprites see `www.alistapart.com/articles/sprites`.

As you saw with the `background-image` property, the image is tiled by default. In the next section, I describe how to control tiling with the `background-repeat` property.

CONTROLLING HOW BACKGROUND IMAGES REPEAT

The `background-repeat` property is used to control how an image is tiled, or if it is tiled at all. The following table shows the values for the `background-repeat` property.

PROPERTY	VALUE
background-repeat	repeat | repeat-x | repeat-y | no-repeat Initial value: repeat

As you saw in the last section, by default, a background is tiled vertically and horizontally. The `background-repeat` property offers control over this. The `repeat-x` keyword limits tiling to the horizontal or x-axis, and the `repeat-y` keyword limits tiling to the vertical or y-axis. As you have already seen, the default keyword of `repeat` tiles the image in both the x-axis and the y-axis. The `no-repeat` keyword turns off tiling altogether, and the background image will be displayed only once, as demonstrated in the following code.

Available for download on Wrox.com

```
<!DOCTYPE html PUBLIC "-//W3C//DTD HTML 4.01//EN"
    "http://www.w3.org/TR/html4/strict.dtd">
<html lang="en">
<head>
    <meta http-equiv="Content-Type" content="text/html; charset=utf-8">
    <title>Figure 7-5</title>
    <style type="text/css">
        body {
            background-image: url(bg-page.png);
            background-repeat: no-repeat;
        }
    </style>
</head>
<body>

<h1>Recipes for Cheese</h1>

<p class="intro">Cheese is a remarkably versatile food, available in literally
hundreds of varieties with different flavors and textures.</p>

<div class="recipe">

    <h2>Welsh Rarebit</h2>

    <p class="intro">Welsh Rarebit is a savory dish made from melted cheese, often
    Cheddar, on toasted bread, and a variety of other ingredients such as mustard,
    egg, or bacon. Here is one take on this classic.</p>

    <ol>
        <li>Lightly toast the bread</li>
        <li>Place on a baking tray, and spread with butter.</li>
        <li>Add the grated Cheddar cheese and 2 tablespoons of beer to a saucepan.
        Place the saucepan over a medium heat, and stir the cheese continuously
        until it has melted. Add a teaspoon of wholegrain mustard and grind in
        a little pepper. Keep stirring.</li>
        <li>When thick and smooth, pour over each piece of toast spreading it to
```

```
        the edges to stop the toast from burning.</li>
        <li>Place under the grill for a couple of minutes or until golden
        brown.</li>
      </ol>

  </div>

  </body>
</html>
```

code snippet /chapter7/figure_7-5.html

This CSS and markup results in the output you see in Figure 7-5.

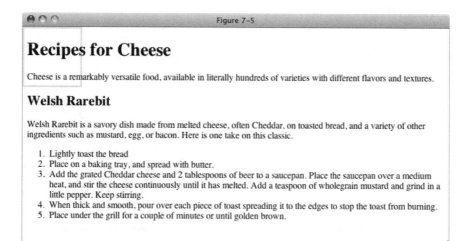

FIGURE 7-5

Now let's see how the `background-repeat` property is used to tile a background image in one direction only.

TRY IT OUT   Controlling Background Repetition

Example 7-3

To see the `background-repeat` property in action, follow these steps.

1.   Enter the following markup:

```
<!DOCTYPE html PUBLIC "-//W3C//DTD HTML 4.01//EN"
    "http://www.w3.org/TR/html4/strict.dtd">
<html lang="en">
<head>
    <meta http-equiv="Content-Type" content="text/html; charset=utf-8">
    <title>Example 7-3</title>
    <style type="text/css">
        body {
            background-image: url(bg-page.png);
            background-repeat: repeat-x;
        }
    </style>
</head>
<body>

<h1>Recipes for Cheese</h1>

<p class="intro">Cheese is a remarkably versatile food, available in literally
hundreds of varieties with different flavors and textures.</p>

<div class="recipe">

    <h2>Welsh Rarebit</h2>

    <p class="intro">Welsh Rarebit is a savory dish made from melted cheese, often
    Cheddar, on toasted bread, and a variety of other ingredients such as mustard,
     egg, or bacon. Here is one take on this classic.</p>

    <ol>
        <li>Lightly toast the bread</li>
        <li>Place on a baking tray, and spread with butter.</li>
        <li>Add the grated Cheddar cheese and 2 tablespoons of beer to a saucepan.
        Place the saucepan over a medium heat, and stir the cheese continuously
        until it has melted. Add a teaspoon of wholegrain mustard and grind in
        a little pepper. Keep stirring.</li>
        <li>When thick and smooth, pour over each piece of toast spreading it to
        the edges to stop the toast from burning.</li>
        <li>Place under the grill for a couple of minutes or until golden
        brown.</li>
    </ol>

</div>

</body>
</html>
```

2. Save the preceding CSS and markup as example_7-3.html. This example results in the rendered output in Figure 7-6.

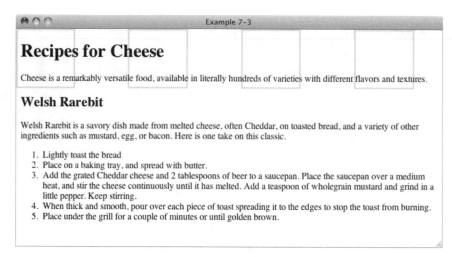

FIGURE 7-6

How It Works

In Example 7-3, you used the `background-repeat` property to tile the background image in only the horizontal, or x-axis. The image no longer tiles in the vertical, or y-axis, so it appears as a single 'row' of images.

In the next section, I discuss the `background-position` property.

POSITIONING BACKGROUND IMAGES

The `background-position` property, as its name implies, allows you to control the placement of the background. The following table shows the values for the `background-position` property.

PROPERTY	VALUE
background-position	`[ [ <percentage> | <length> | left | center | right ] [ <percentage> | <length> | top | center | bottom ]? ] | [ [ left | center | right ] || [ top | center | bottom ] ] | inherit` Initial value: `0% 0%`

At first glance, this property looks a little complicated; in truth, it isn't all that complex. The notation boils down to this: The property allows one value that applies the same value to both the horizontal and vertical background position, or two values that express the horizontal and vertical position of the background separately. Square brackets are used to group the values. The following is the first subgrouping of values within the first grouping:

```
[<percentage> | <length> ]{1,2}
```

The first grouping indicates that the value may be a percentage or length value. Either one or two values may be provided.

The second subgrouping is preceded by a vertical bar, which indicates another possibility for the value:

```
| [ [top | center | bottom] || [left | center | right] ]
```

The second grouping indicates that either one or two keyword values may be provided. If two values are provided, it may be any keyword from the first grouping combined with any of the keywords from the second grouping. In addition, any of the keyword values can be mixed with either a `<length>` or `<percentage>` value.

The following code demonstrates some possible values for the `background-position` property.

Available for
download on
Wrox.com

```
<!DOCTYPE html PUBLIC "-//W3C//DTD HTML 4.01//EN"
    "http://www.w3.org/TR/html4/strict.dtd">
<html lang="en">
<head>
    <meta http-equiv="Content-Type" content="text/html; charset=utf-8">
    <title>Figure 7-7</title>
    <style type="text/css">
        body {
            background-image: url(bg-page.png);
            background-repeat: no-repeat;
            background-position: bottom right;
        }
    </style>
</head>
<body>

<h1>Recipes for Cheese</h1>

<p class="intro">Cheese is a remarkably versatile food, available in literally
hundreds of varieties with different flavors and textures.</p>

<div class="recipe">

    <h2>Welsh Rarebit</h2>

    <p class="intro">Welsh Rarebit is a savory dish made from melted cheese, often
    Cheddar, on toasted bread, and a variety of other ingredients such as mustard,
    egg, or bacon. Here is one take on this classic.</p>

    <ol>
        <li>Lightly toast the bread</li>
        <li>Place on a baking tray, and spread with butter.</li>
        <li>Add the grated Cheddar cheese and 2 tablespoons of beer to a saucepan.
        Place the saucepan over a medium heat, and stir the cheese continuously
        until it has melted. Add a teaspoon of wholegrain mustard and grind in
        a little pepper. Keep stirring.</li>
        <li>When thick and smooth, pour over each piece of toast spreading it to
        the edges to stop the toast from burning.</li>
        <li>Place under the grill for a couple of minutes or until golden
        brown.</li>
```

```
        </ol>

    </div>

    </body>
    </html>
```

code snippet /chapter7/figure_7-7.html

This CSS and markup results in the output you see in Figure 7-7.

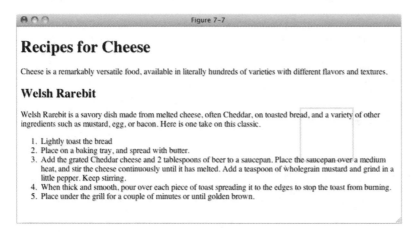

FIGURE 7-7

In Figure 7-7, you see what the `background-position` property with two values looks like. In this case, the background image (including the white space that is part of the image that allows for the spacing between the tiles) is positioned to the bottom right of the document. This figure shows what happens when both values are of the same ilk (that is, both length values both percentage values, or both keyword values).

Mixing Background Position Values

What happens when you mix length with percentage or percentage with a keyword? This question is answered by the example in the following code.

Available for download on Wrox.com

```
<!DOCTYPE html PUBLIC "-//W3C//DTD HTML 4.01//EN"
    "http://www.w3.org/TR/html4/strict.dtd">
<html lang="en">
<head>
    <meta http-equiv="Content-Type" content="text/html; charset=utf-8">
    <title>Figure 7-8</title>
    <style type="text/css">
        body {
            background-image: url(bg-page.png);
            background-repeat: no-repeat;
            background-position: right 100%;
        }
    </style>
```

```
</head>
<body>

<h1>Recipes for Cheese</h1>

<p class="intro">Cheese is a remarkably versatile food, available in literally
hundreds of varieties with different flavors and textures.</p>

<div class="recipe">

    <h2>Welsh Rarebit</h2>

    <p class="intro">Welsh Rarebit is a savory dish made from melted cheese, often
    Cheddar, on toasted bread, and a variety of other ingredients such as mustard,
    egg, or bacon. Here is one take on this classic.</p>

    <ol>
        <li>Lightly toast the bread</li>
        <li>Place on a baking tray, and spread with butter.</li>
        <li>Add the grated Cheddar cheese and 2 tablespoons of beer to a saucepan.
        Place the saucepan over a medium heat, and stir the cheese continuously
        until it has melted. Add a teaspoon of wholegrain mustard and grind in
        a little pepper. Keep stirring.</li>
        <li>When thick and smooth, pour over each piece of toast spreading it to
        the edges to stop the toast from burning.</li>
        <li>Place under the grill for a couple of minutes or until golden
        brown.</li>
    </ol>

</div>

</body>
</html>
```

code snippet /chapter7/figure_7-8.html

This CSS and markup results in the output you see in Figure 7-8.

FIGURE 7-8

> **WARNING** *If at least one value is not a keyword, then the first value represents the horizontal position and the second represents the vertical position*
>
> *That is to say, when you use two keywords it's obvious which one applies to the horizontal positioning and which one applies to the vertical positioning based on the keyword name (left and right are horizontal, top and bottom are vertical) so they can be specified in any order and the browser will understand what that means. However, this is not necessarily the case when using one or two length/ percentage values, so you have to specify them in order.*

Repeating a Background Image and Controlling Its Position

What happens when the background is tiled and a position is set? You see an example of positioning a tiled background with a length measurement in the following example.

Available for
download on
Wrox.com

```
<!DOCTYPE html PUBLIC "-//W3C//DTD HTML 4.01//EN"
    "http://www.w3.org/TR/html4/strict.dtd">
<html lang="en">
<head>
    <meta http-equiv="Content-Type" content="text/html; charset=utf-8">
    <title>Figure 7-9</title>
    <style type="text/css">
        body {
            background-image: url(bg-page.png);
            background-repeat: repeat-x;
            background-position: bottom right;
        }
    </style>
</head>
<body>

<h1>Recipes for Cheese</h1>

<p class="intro">Cheese is a remarkably versatile food, available in literally
hundreds of varieties with different flavors and textures.</p>

<div class="recipe">

    <h2>Welsh Rarebit</h2>

    <p class="intro">Welsh Rarebit is a savory dish made from melted cheese, often
    Cheddar, on toasted bread, and a variety of other ingredients such as mustard,
    egg, or bacon. Here is one take on this classic.</p>

    <ol>
        <li>Lightly toast the bread</li>
        <li>Place on a baking tray, and spread with butter.</li>
        <li>Add the grated Cheddar cheese and 2 tablespoons of beer to a saucepan.
        Place the saucepan over a medium heat, and stir the cheese continuously
```

```
    until it has melted. Add a teaspoon of wholegrain mustard and grind in
    a little pepper. Keep stirring.</li>
    <li>When thick and smooth, pour over each piece of toast spreading it to
    the edges to stop the toast from burning.</li>
    <li>Place under the grill for a couple of minutes or until golden
    brown.</li>
  </ol>

</div>

</body>
</html>
```

code snippet /chapter7/figure_7-9.html

This CSS and markup results in the output you see in Figure 7-9.

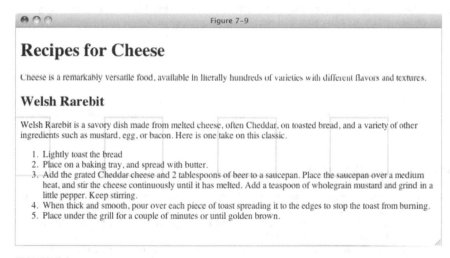

FIGURE 7-9

In Figure 7-9, you see how specifying a background position affects the tiling of a background image. When both axes are tiled, the position that you specify determines where the image tiling begins. Note that tiling happens in both directions: left to right and right to left, top to bottom and bottom to top.

Controlling Position with the Center Keyword

The `center` keyword has an interesting side effect. Background images are positioned at the center point of the container from the center of point of the image, not the edge of the image as we have seen previously. This means that our background image, with its white space to add a space between tiles, will actually be positioned slightly to the right rather than slightly to the left as would be the case if it had been positioned relative to the left hand edge. The following code illustrates this effect.

Available for download on Wrox.com

```
<!DOCTYPE html PUBLIC "-//W3C//DTD HTML 4.01//EN"
    "http://www.w3.org/TR/html4/strict.dtd">
<html lang="en">
<head>
    <meta http-equiv="Content-Type" content="text/html; charset=utf-8">
    <title>Figure 7-10</title>
    <style type="text/css">
        body {
            background-image: url(bg-page.png);
            background-repeat: no-repeat;
            background-position: center center;
        }
    </style>
</head>
<body>

<h1>Recipes for Cheese</h1>

<p class="intro">Cheese is a remarkably versatile food, available in literally
hundreds of varieties with different flavors and textures.</p>

<div class="recipe">

    <h2>Welsh Rarebit</h2>

    <p class="intro">Welsh Rarebit is a savory dish made from melted cheese, often
    Cheddar, on toasted bread, and a variety of other ingredients such as mustard,
    egg, or bacon. Here is one take on this classic.</p>

    <ol>
        <li>Lightly toast the bread</li>
        <li>Place on a baking tray, and spread with butter.</li>
        <li>Add the grated Cheddar cheese and 2 tablespoons of beer to a saucepan.
        Place the saucepan over a medium heat, and stir the cheese continuously
        until it has melted. Add a teaspoon of wholegrain mustard and grind in
        a little pepper. Keep stirring.</li>
        <li>When thick and smooth, pour over each piece of toast spreading it to
        the edges to stop the toast from burning.</li>
        <li>Place under the grill for a couple of minutes or until golden
        brown.</li>
    </ol>

</div>

</body>
</html>
```

code snippet /chapter7/figure_7-10.html

This CSS and markup results in the output you see in Figure 7-10.

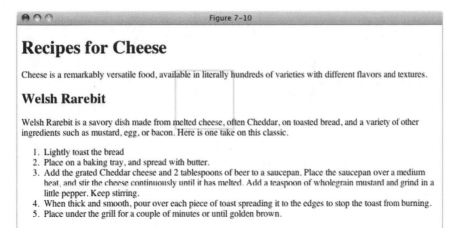

FIGURE 7-10

In Figure 7-10 you used the `center` keyword instead of a length measurement. When the tiling is along the x-axis, one `center` keyword centers the tiled images along the y-axis, and the other `center` keyword causes the tiling of each image to begin with the center of the image, rather than the left border of the image. This result is the same in every browser.

In the next section, I describe how to control the `background-position` when the page is scrolled with the `background-attachment` property.

FIXING A BACKGROUND IMAGE IN PLACE

You can use the `background-attachment` property to control whether a background image scrolls with the content of a web page (when scroll bars are activated because that content is larger than the browser window). The following table outlines the possible values for the `background-attachment` property.

PROPERTY	VALUE
background-attachment	scroll | fixed Initial value: scroll

 NOTE *IE 6 supports the* `fixed` *keyword only if applied to the* `<body>` *element; all other browsers support the* `fixed` *keyword as applied to any element.*

The `background-attachment` property provides one very cool effect. By default, the background image scrolls with the content of the web page; this is the behavior of the `background-attachment: scroll;` declaration, as you can see in Figure 7-11.

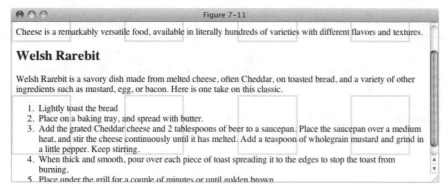

FIGURE 7-11

If the `fixed` keyword is provided, the background image remains in place while the page scrolls. The following code shows an example of this scenario.

Available for download on Wrox.com

```
<!DOCTYPE html PUBLIC "-//W3C//DTD HTML 4.01//EN"
    "http://www.w3.org/TR/html4/strict.dtd">
<html lang="en">
<head>
    <meta http-equiv="Content-Type" content="text/html; charset=utf-8">
    <title>Figure 7-12</title>
    <style type="text/css">
        body {
            background-image: url(bg-page.png);
            background-attachment: fixed;
        }
    </style>
</head>
<body>

<h1>Recipes for Cheese</h1>

<p class="intro">Cheese is a remarkably versatile food, available in literally
hundreds of varieties with different flavors and textures.</p>

<div class="recipe">

    <h2>Welsh Rarebit</h2>

    <p class="intro">Welsh Rarebit is a savory dish made from melted cheese, often
    Cheddar, on toasted bread, and a variety of other ingredients such as mustard,
    egg, or bacon. Here is one take on this classic.</p>

    <ol>
        <li>Lightly toast the bread</li>
        <li>Place on a baking tray, and spread with butter.</li>
        <li>Add the grated Cheddar cheese and 2 tablespoons of beer to a saucepan.
        Place the saucepan over a medium heat, and stir the cheese continuously
        until it has melted. Add a teaspoon of wholegrain mustard and grind in
        a little pepper. Keep stirring.</li>
        <li>When thick and smooth, pour over each piece of toast spreading it to
```

```
        the edges to stop the toast from burning.</li>
        <li>Place under the grill for a couple of minutes or until golden
        brown.</li>
    </ol>

</div>

</body>
</html>
```

code snippet /chapter7/figure_7-12.html

This CSS and markup results in the output you see in Figure 7-12.

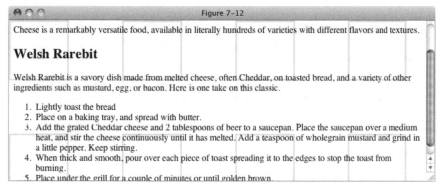

FIGURE 7-12

 NOTE *When the* `fixed` *keyword is provided, the background image's position is offset relative to the viewport, no matter what element the background image is applied to.*

In the next section, I describe how to simplify the plethora of separate background properties into just one property using the `background` shorthand property.

BACKGROUND SHORTHAND

Like the shorthand properties I introduced in previous chapters, the `background` property combines each of the individual background properties into a single property. The following table outlines the values allowed by the `background` property.

PROPERTY	VALUE
background	<'background-color'> || <'background-image'> || <'background-repeat'> || <'background-attachment'> || <'background-position'> Initial value: n/a

With the `background` property, you can specify anywhere from one to five separate background properties. An example of how the background property combines different background properties appears in the following code.

Available for download on Wrox.com

```
<!DOCTYPE html PUBLIC "-//W3C//DTD HTML 4.01//EN"
    "http://www.w3.org/TR/html4/strict.dtd">
<html lang="en">
<head>
    <meta http-equiv="Content-Type" content="text/html; charset=utf-8">
    <title>Figure 7-13</title>
    <style type="text/css">
        body {
            background: #CCC url(bg-page.png) repeat-x fixed top right;
        }
    </style>
</head>
<body>

<h1>Recipes for Cheese</h1>

<p class="intro">Cheese is a remarkably versatile food, available in literally
hundreds of varieties with different flavors and textures.</p>

<div class="recipe">

    <h2>Welsh Rarebit</h2>

    <p class="intro">Welsh Rarebit is a savory dish made from melted cheese, often
    Cheddar, on toasted bread, and a variety of other ingredients such as mustard,
    egg, or bacon. Here is one take on this classic.</p>

    <ol>
        <li>Lightly toast the bread</li>
        <li>Place on a baking tray, and spread with butter.</li>
        <li>Add the grated Cheddar cheese and 2 tablespoons of beer to a saucepan.
        Place the saucepan over a medium heat, and stir the cheese continuously
        until it has melted. Add a teaspoon of wholegrain mustard and grind in
        a little pepper. Keep stirring.</li>
        <li>When thick and smooth, pour over each piece of toast spreading it to
        the edges to stop the toast from burning.</li>
        <li>Place under the grill for a couple of minutes or until golden
        brown.</li>
    </ol>

</div>

</body>
</html>
```

code snippet /chapter7/figure_7-13.html

This CSS and markup results in the output you see in Figure 7-13.

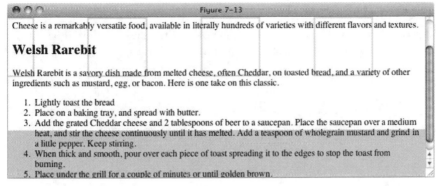

FIGURE 7-13

In Figure 7-13, you see how to use the `background` shorthand property to combine the five separate background properties, `background-color`, `background-image`, `background-repeat`, `background-attachment`, and `background-position` into just one single `background` property. Using the `background` property, you can include all five properties, or any combination of the other properties, in any order.

EXERCISES

1. What are two properties that you can use to specify a background color in a web page?

2. What declaration causes a background image to be tiled only along the x-axis?

3. What keyword value can you use to turn off tiling of a background image?

4. If you wanted to offset an image ten pixels from the left and ten pixels from the top, what declaration would you use?

5. If you wanted a background image to scroll with the document, what declaration would you use?

6. When a background image is said to be "fixed," what HTML element is the background image position relative to?

7. Write a declaration that contains all five background properties in one.

▶ **WHAT YOU LEARNED IN THIS CHAPTER**

The CSS background properties provide a fine-grained control over the presentation of backgrounds in a web document, which allows interesting aesthetic possibilities. To recap, in this chapter you learned the following:

TOPIC	KEY CONCEPTS
background-color	Specifying a solid background color using the `background-color` property
gradient	Creating gradient color effects with the `gradient` property
background-image	How to use an image as a background with the `background-image` property
background-repeat	Controlling how background images repeat with the `background-repeat` property
background-position	How to offset the position of a background image using the `background-position` property
background-attachment	How to fix a background image to the browser window instead of scrolling with the page using the `background-attachment` property
background	How the `background` shorthand property can be used to write more concise CSS by combining background properties into one declaration

The Box Model: Controlling Margins, Borders, Padding, Width, and Height

WHAT YOU WILL LEARN IN THIS CHAPTER:

➤ The box model

➤ Setting margins

➤ Setting padding

➤ Setting borders

➤ Setting width and height

➤ Specifying minimum and maximum width and height

➤ Determining how overflowing content behaves

In this chapter, I discuss one of the most important concepts in CSS-based web design, the box model. The box model is a set of rules that dictate how width, height, padding, borders, and margin are measured on HTML elements. We'll start with an overview of what the box model is.

OVERVIEW

The CSS box model is a collection of properties that define the amount of space around an element, its dimensions, its margins, its borders, and padding between the content of the element and the borders. In Figure 8-1, you see a diagram of the box model.

In Figure 8-1 you see what the different components that come together to make the box model look like. Around the outside of an element is space called the *margin*, inside of the margin is the *border*, inside of the border is the *padding*, and inside of padding is the content of the element.

In the coming sections, I pick apart the various properties that comprise the box model in CSS, beginning with margin.

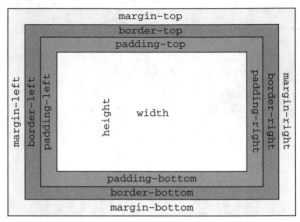

FIGURE 8-1

MARGINS

The margin property applies space outside the box, between the box and the browser window, or between the box and the other elements in the document. The following table shows the various margin properties.

PROPERTY	VALUE
margin	[<length> | <percentage> | auto] {1,4}
margin-top margin-right margin-bottom margin-left	<length> | <percentage> | auto

The margin property is a shorthand property for the four individual margin properties, margin-top, margin-right, margin-bottom, and margin-left.

 NOTE *Box model shorthand properties are always specified in a clockwise order, from the top: top, right, bottom, and left.*

margin Property with Four Values

The following code shows a comparison between individual margin properties.

Available for download on Wrox.com

```
<!DOCTYPE html PUBLIC "-//W3C//DTD HTML 4.01//EN"
    "http://www.w3.org/TR/html4/strict.dtd">
<html lang="en">
<head>
    <meta http-equiv="Content-Type" content="text/html; charset=utf-8">
    <title>Figure 8-2</title>
    <style type="text/css">
        .intro {
            margin-top: 70px;
            margin-left: 100px;
            margin-bottom: 50px;
            margin-right: 100px;
        }
    </style>
</head>
<body>

<h1>Recipes for Cheese</h1>

<p class="intro">Cheese is a remarkably versatile food, available in literally
hundreds of varieties with different flavors and textures.</p>

<div class="recipe">

    <h2>Welsh Rarebit</h2>

    <p class="intro">Welsh Rarebit is a savory dish made from melted cheese, often
    Cheddar, on toasted bread, and a variety of other ingredients such as mustard,
    egg, or bacon. Here is one take on this classic.</p>

    <ol>
        <li>Lightly toast the bread</li>
        <li>Place on a baking tray, and spread with butter.</li>
        <li>Add the grated Cheddar cheese and 2 tablespoons of beer to a saucepan.
        Place the saucepan over a medium heat, and stir the cheese continuously
        until it has melted. Add a teaspoon of wholegrain mustard and grind in
        a little pepper. Keep stirring.</li>
        <li>When thick and smooth, pour over each piece of toast spreading it to
        the edges to stop the toast from burning.</li>
        <li>Place under the grill for a couple of minutes or until golden
        brown.</li>
    </ol>

</div>

</body>
</html>
```

code snippet /chapter8/figure_8-2.html

This CSS and markup results in the output you see in Figure 8-2.

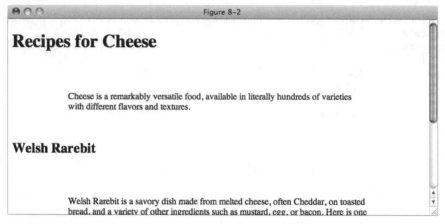

FIGURE 8-2

As you can see, there is a 70px margin above the intro paragraph, 100px left and right margins, and there is a 50px margin between the intro paragraph and the next heading.

The four declarations in the `.intro` rule could be combined into one as follows:

```
margin: 70px 100px 50px 100px;
```

margin Property with Three Values

In Figure 8-2, you saw an example of specifying margin using four values, but because the left and right margin values are the same, you can also specify only three values for the `margin` shorthand property. The same declaration can be written as:

```
margin: 70px 100px 50px;
```

 WARNING *Box model shorthand properties with three values always follow the convention top, right and left, bottom.*

The first value is the top value as usual, the second is the value for both left *and* right margins, and the third is the value for the bottom margin. It is common to want equal left and right margins, and this makes it easy to do, especially if you need to change the value later as you won't forget the other.

WARNING *Because it can be easy to confuse the order in which values in the three value form should come, you won't see it used as much as the four or two value versions.*

Although, as mentioned, there is a benefit to using the three value form, I recommend against its use for this reason.

margin Property with Two Values

The margin shorthand property also supports two values. When two values are specified, the first value refers to the top and bottom sides, and the second value refers to the right and left sides. This is demonstrated in Figure 8-3.

Available for
download on
Wrox.com

```
<!DOCTYPE html PUBLIC "-//W3C//DTD HTML 4.01//EN"
    "http://www.w3.org/TR/html4/strict.dtd">
<html lang="en">
<head>
    <meta http-equiv="Content-Type" content="text/html; charset=utf-8">
    <title>Figure 8-3</title>
    <style type="text/css">
        .intro {
            margin: 50px 100px;
        }
    </style>
</head>
<body>

<h1>Recipes for Cheese</h1>

<p class="intro">Cheese is a remarkably versatile food, available in literally
hundreds of varieties with different flavors and textures.</p>

<div class="recipe">

    <h2>Welsh Rarebit</h2>

    <p class="intro">Welsh Rarebit is a savory dish made from melted cheese, often
    Cheddar, on toasted bread, and a variety of other ingredients such as mustard,
    egg, or bacon. Here is one take on this classic.</p>

    <ol>
        <li>Lightly toast the bread</li>
        <li>Place on a baking tray, and spread with butter.</li>
        <li>Add the grated Cheddar cheese and 2 tablespoons of beer to a saucepan.
        Place the saucepan over a medium heat, and stir the cheese continuously
        until it has melted. Add a teaspoon of wholegrain mustard and grind in
        a little pepper. Keep stirring.</li>
        <li>When thick and smooth, pour over each piece of toast spreading it to
```

```
            the edges to stop the toast from burning.</li>
            <li>Place under the grill for a couple of minutes or until golden
            brown.</li>
        </ol>

    </div>

    </body>
    </html>
```

code snippet /chapter8/figure_8-3.html

This CSS and markup results in the output you see in Figure 8-3.

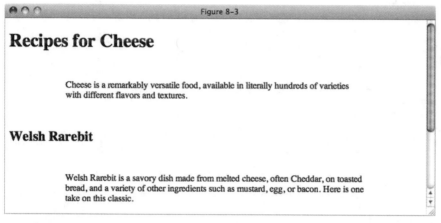

FIGURE 8-3

 NOTE *Box model shorthand properties with two values always follow the convention top and bottom, right and left — for example,* margin: 15px 10px;.

margin Property with One Value

You can specify just one value for the margin property, which simultaneously sets all four sides of an element's margin to the same value.

```
margin: 50px;
```

Margin Collapsing

In CSS, *margin collapsing* occurs when the top or bottom margin of one element comes into contact with the top or bottom margin of another element. Only vertical margins collapse, horizontal margins do not. The concept is simple: When two margins are collapsed, the distance between the two boxes will use whichever margin value is greater. Margin collapsing is demonstrated in the following code.

Available for download on Wrox.com

```
<!DOCTYPE html PUBLIC "-//W3C//DTD HTML 4.01//EN"
    "http://www.w3.org/TR/html4/strict.dtd">
<html lang="en">
<head>
    <meta http-equiv="Content-Type" content="text/html; charset=utf-8">
    <title>Figure 8-4</title>
    <style type="text/css">
        .h1 {
            margin-bottom: 100px;
        }

        .intro {
            margin-top: 100px;
        }
    </style>
</head>
<body>

<h1>Recipes for Cheese</h1>

<p class="intro">Cheese is a remarkably versatile food, available in literally
hundreds of varieties with different flavors and textures.</p>

</body>
</html>
```

code snippet /chapter8/figure_8-4.html

This CSS and markup results in the output you see in Figure 8-4.

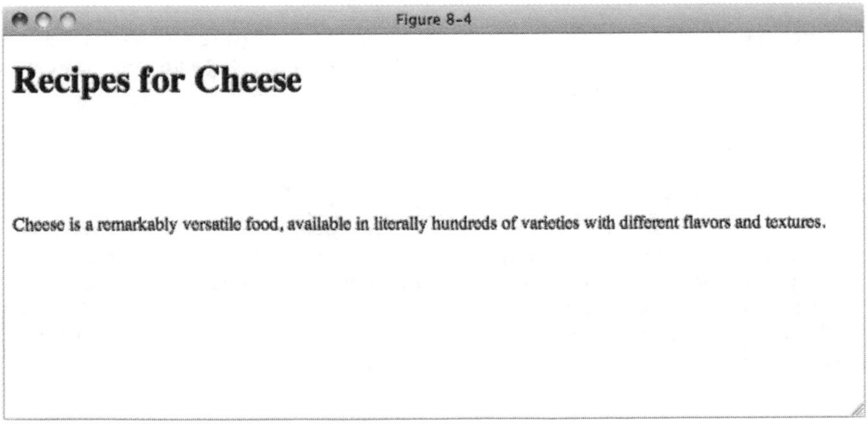

FIGURE 8-4

In Figure 8-4, you see the most common form of margin collapsing; the top margin of one element comes into contact with the bottom margin of another element. When this happens, the element with the bigger margin wins.

Margin collapsing also happens when an element is contained inside of another element. It doesn't matter where the two margins come into contact, even an element inside of another element will margin collapse with its parent if the two margins come into contact. An example of this appears in the following code.

Available for download on Wrox.com

```
<!DOCTYPE html PUBLIC "-//W3C//DTD HTML 4.01//EN"
    "http://www.w3.org/TR/html4/strict.dtd">
<html lang="en">
<head>
    <meta http-equiv="Content-Type" content="text/html; charset=utf-8">
    <title>Figure 8-5</title>
    <style type="text/css">
        h2 {
            margin-top: 50px;
        }

        .recipe {
            margin-top: 50px;
        }
    </style>
</head>
<body>

<h1>Recipes for Cheese</h1>

<p class="intro">Cheese is a remarkably versatile food, available in literally
hundreds of varieties with different flavors and textures.</p>

<div class="recipe">

    <h2>Welsh Rarebit</h2>

    <p class="intro">Welsh Rarebit is a savory dish made from melted cheese, often
    Cheddar, on toasted bread, and a variety of other ingredients such as mustard,
    egg, or bacon. Here is one take on this classic.</p>

    <ol>
        <li>Lightly toast the bread</li>
        <li>Place on a baking tray, and spread with butter.</li>
        <li>Add the grated Cheddar cheese and 2 tablespoons of beer to a saucepan.
        Place the saucepan over a medium heat, and stir the cheese continuously
        until it has melted. Add a teaspoon of wholegrain mustard and grind in
        a little pepper. Keep stirring.</li>
        <li>When thick and smooth, pour over each piece of toast spreading it to
        the edges to stop the toast from burning.</li>
```

```
        <li>Place under the grill for a couple of minutes or until golden
        brown.</li>
    </ol>

</div>

</body>
</html>
```

code snippet /chapter8/figure_8-5.html

This CSS and markup results in the output you see in Figure 8-5.

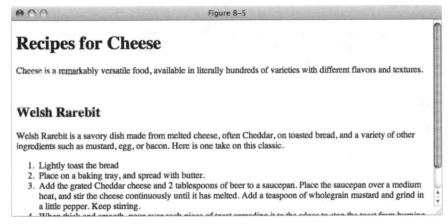

FIGURE 8-5

In Figure 8-5, you see how margin collapsing works between a parent and child element. If a child's margin comes into direct contact with the margin of a parent, the margins collapse. Like the example in Figure 8-4 that contained adjacent sibling margins collapsing, the larger margin is the winning margin. The winning margin is always applied to the parent element, and the child element's margin always collapses. In this scenario, margin collapsing can be stopped if you prevent the two margins from coming into contact with one another. You can prevent the two margins from coming into contact with one another by applying padding or a border to the parent element. An example of this appears in the following snippet.

Available for download on Wrox.com

```
<!DOCTYPE html PUBLIC "-//W3C//DTD HTML 4.01//EN"
    "http://www.w3.org/TR/html4/strict.dtd">
<html lang="en">
<head>
    <meta http-equiv="Content-Type" content="text/html; charset=utf-8">
```

```
        <title>Figure 8-6</title>
        <style type="text/css">
            h2 {
                margin-top: 50px;
            }

            .recipe {
                margin-top: 50px;
                border-top: 1px solid #000;
            }
        </style>
    </head>
    <body>

    <h1>Recipes for Cheese</h1>

    <p class="intro">Cheese is a remarkable versatile food, available in literally
    hundreds of varieties with different flavors and textures.</p>

    <div class="recipe">

        <h2>Welsh Rarebit</h2>

        <p class="intro">Welsh Rarebit is a savory dish made from melted cheese, often
        Cheddar, on toasted bread, and a variety of other ingredients such as mustard,
        egg, or bacon. Here is one take on this classic.</p>

        <ol>
            <li>Lightly toast the bread</li>
            <li>Place on a baking tray, and spread with butter.</li>
            <li>Add the grated Cheddar cheese and 2 tablespoons of beer to a saucepan.
            Place the saucepan over a medium heat, and stir the cheese continuously
            until it has melted. Add a teaspoon of wholegrain mustard and grind in
            a little pepper. Keep stirring.</li>
            <li>When thick and smooth, pour over each piece of toast spreading it to
            the edges to stop the toast from burning.</li>
            <li>Place under the grill for a couple of minutes or until golden
            brown.</li>
        </ol>

    </div>

    </body>
    </html>
```

code snippet /chapter8/figure_8-6.html

This CSS and markup results in the output you see in Figure 8-6.

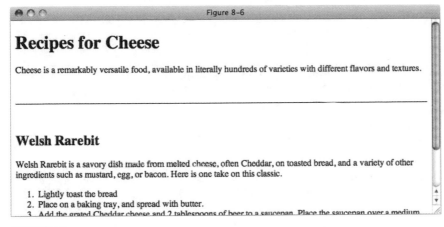

FIGURE 8-6

In Figure 8-6, you see how to stop margin collapsing from happening. You must give the parent element a border or padding to prevent the top and bottom margin of the child element from coming into contact with the top and bottom margin of the parent element.

Horizontally Aligning Elements with the margin Property

The margin property has one other useful function: It can be used to center or align elements. An example of this concept appears in the following code.

Available for download on Wrox.com

```
<!DOCTYPE html PUBLIC "-//W3C//DTD HTML 4.01//EN"
    "http://www.w3.org/TR/html4/strict.dtd">
<html lang="en">
<head>
    <meta http-equiv="Content-Type" content="text/html; charset=utf-8">
    <title>Figure 8-7</title>
    <style type="text/css">
        h1 {
            width: 200px;
            margin-right: auto;
        }

        .intro {
            width: 200px;
            margin-right: auto;
            margin-left: auto;
        }

        .recipe {
            width: 200px;
            margin-left: auto;
        }
    </style>
```

```
</head>
<body>

<h1>Recipes for Cheese</h1>

<p class="intro">Cheese is a remarkably versatile food, available in literally
hundreds of varieties with different flavors and textures.</p>

<div class="recipe">

    <h2>Welsh Rarebit</h2>

    <p class="intro">Welsh Rarebit is a savory dish made from melted cheese, often
    Cheddar, on toasted bread, and a variety of other ingredients such as mustard,
    egg, or bacon. Here is one take on this classic.</p>

    <ol>
        <li>Lightly toast the bread</li>
        <li>Place on a baking tray, and spread with butter.</li>
        <li>Add the grated Cheddar cheese and 2 tablespoons of beer to a saucepan.
        Place the saucepan over a medium heat, and stir the cheese continuously
        until it has melted. Add a teaspoon of wholegrain mustard and grind in
        a little pepper. Keep stirring.</li>
        <li>When thick and smooth, pour over each piece of toast spreading it to
        the edges to stop the toast from burning.</li>
        <li>Place under the grill for a couple of minutes or until golden
        brown.</li>
    </ol>

</div>

</body>
</html>
```

code snippet /chapter8/figure_8-7.html

This CSS and markup results in the output you see in Figure 8-7.

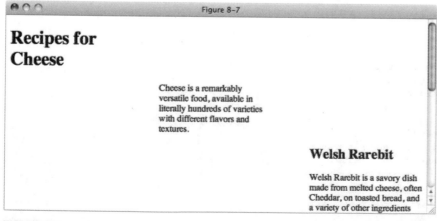

FIGURE 8-7

In Figure 8-7, you see a technique used to align elements in a document via the combination of the `auto` keyword with the left or right margin of an element. The margin that is specified must be either the left or the right margin, because the `auto` keyword is ignored when applied to the top or bottom margin.

ALIGNING ELEMENTS IN IE QUIRKS RENDERING MODE

Every modern browser today supports the DOCTYPE switch, a method of selecting the rendering mode of your browser based on the Document Type Declaration that appears at the top of an HTML document. If you structure your documents like the examples you see here in this book, you'll never encounter *quirks rendering mode*, but if you are working with legacy websites that must maintain backward compatibility with the Web of yesterday, chances are you'll encounter a quirks mode site sooner or later.

If you encounter quirks mode, you'll also discover that some CSS features don't work in quirks mode, but do work in standards mode. Aligning an element using the `auto` keyword in conjunction with the `margin` property is one such quirks mode incompatibility. In IE, this feature is only implemented in standards mode.

There is a workaround due to a bug in IE, using the `text-align` property on an element with values of left, center and right as appropriate.

The following Try It Out shows you how to center a page with the `margin` property.

TRY IT OUT   **Center a Page with the margin Property**

Example 8-1

To see the `margin` property in action, follow these steps.

1.   Enter the following markup:

```
<!DOCTYPE html PUBLIC "-//W3C//DTD HTML 4.01//EN"
    "http://www.w3.org/TR/html4/strict.dtd">
<html lang="en">
<head>
    <meta http-equiv="Content-Type" content="text/html; charset=utf-8">
    <title>Example 8-1</title>
    <style type="text/css">
        body {
            width: 600px;
            margin: 1em auto;
        }
    </style>
```

```
</head>
<body>

<h1>Recipes for Cheese</h1>

<p class="intro">Cheese is a remarkably versatile food, available in literally
hundreds of varieties with different flavors and textures.</p>

<div class="recipe">

    <h2>Welsh Rarebit</h2>

    <p class="intro">Welsh Rarebit is a savory dish made from melted cheese, often
    cheddar, on toasted bread, and a variety of other ingredients such as mustard,
    egg, or bacon. Here is one take on this classic.</p>

    <ol>
        <li>Lightly toast the bread</li>
        <li>Place on a baking tray, and spread with butter.</li>
        <li>Add the grated cheddar cheese and 2 tablespoons of beer to a saucepan.
        Place the saucepan over a medium heat, and stir the cheese continuously
        until it has melted. Add a teaspoon of wholegrain mustard and grind in
        a little pepper. Keep stirring.</li>
        <li>When thick and smooth, pour over each piece of toast spreading it to
        the edges to stop the toast from burning.</li>
        <li>Place under the grill for a couple of minutes or until golden
        brown.</li>
    </ol>

</div>

</body>
</html>
```

2. Save the preceding CSS and markup as `example_8-1.html`. This example results in the output in Figure 8-8.

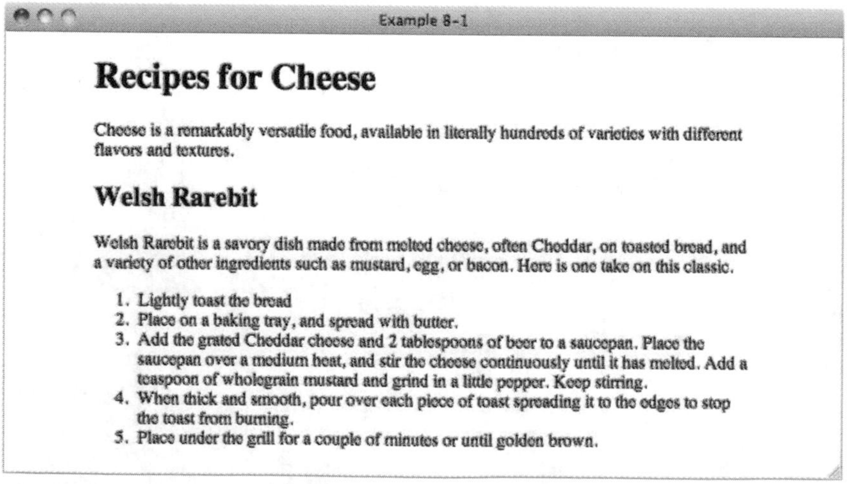

FIGURE 8-8

How It Works

In Example 8-1, you set the `margin` of the body element to have values of `1em` for top and bottom and `auto` for left and right. Combined with a width this has the consequence of centering the body with the document.

In the next section I discuss the box model properties that control borders.

BORDERS

Borders appear between the `margin` and `padding` in the box model depicted in Figure 8-1. Borders put lines around boxes. Applying borders usually makes the other box model properties easier to see. The following sections examine each border property.

border-width

The `border-width` properties all control the width of a box border in some fashion. The following table outlines each `border-width` property.

PROPERTY	VALUE
border-top-width border-right-width border-bottom-width border-left-width	\<border-width\> Initial value: medium
border-width	\<border-width\> {1,4} Initial value: medium

A \<border-width\> value refers to one of the following: thin | medium | thick | \<length\>

The individual `border-top-width`, `border-right-width`, `border-bottom-width`, and `border-left-width` properties exist for setting the width of the individual sides of a box. Each of these properties can be combined into the single `border-width` shorthand property.

Borders aren't allowed to have percentage values; however, they are capable of accepting any length measurement supported by CSS (em, pixel, centimeter, and so on). In addition to length units, the border width may also be specified using one of three keywords: `thin`, `medium`, and `thick`. These are rarely (if ever) used in professional code, however.

Most commonly the `border-width` properties will be given a length value in pixels. An example of this concept appears in the following snippet.

Available for download on Wrox.com

```
<!DOCTYPE html PUBLIC "-//W3C//DTD HTML 4.01//EN"
    "http://www.w3.org/TR/html4/strict.dtd">
<html lang="en">
<head>
    <meta http-equiv="Content-Type" content="text/html; charset=utf-8">
    <title>Figure 8-9</title>
    <style type="text/css">
        .intro {
            border-top-width: 1px;
            border-right-width: 3px;
            border-bottom-width: 5px;
            border-left-width: 7px;
            border-style: solid;
        }
    </style>
</head>
<body>

<h1>Recipes for Cheese</h1>

<p class="intro">Cheese is a remarkably versatile food, available in literally
hundreds of varieties with different flavors and textures.</p>

</body>
</html>
```

code snippet /chapter8/figure_8-9.html

This CSS and markup results in the output you see in Figure 8-9.

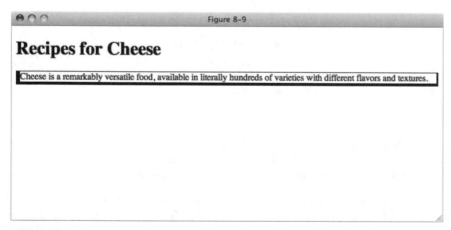

FIGURE 8-9

This could also be expressed as:

```
border-width: 1px 3px 5px 7px;
```

Three-value, two-value, and one-value shorthand syntax is also supported.

In the next section I discuss the `border-style` property, and how it is used to change the style of border.

border-style

You use the `border-style` property to specify the style of border to be used. The `border-style` property is very similar to the `border-width` property presented in the previous section in that it uses an identical syntax to specify the style of border to be used for each side of the box. The following table outlines the `border-style` family of properties.

PROPERTY	VALUE
border-style A <border-style> value refers to one of the following: none | hidden | dotted | dashed | solid | double | groove | ridge | inset | outset	<border-style> {1,4} Initial value: none
border-top-style border-right-style border-bottom-style border-left-style	<border-style> Initial value: none

Like the `border-width` property, the `border-style` property is also a shorthand property, which combines the individual `border-top-style`, `border-right-style`, `border-bottom-style`, and `border-left-style` properties into the single `border-style` property. The following code shows the rendered representation of some of the `border-style` keywords.

Available for download on Wrox.com

```
<!DOCTYPE html PUBLIC "-//W3C//DTD HTML 4.01//EN"
    "http://www.w3.org/TR/html4/strict.dtd">
<html lang="en">
<head>
    <meta http-equiv="Content-Type" content="text/html; charset=utf-8">
    <title>Figure 8-10</title>
    <style type="text/css">
        body {
            border-width: 3px;
            border-top-style: ridge;
            border-right-style: dashed;
            border-bottom-style: dotted;
            border-left-style: double;
        }
    </style>
</head>
```

```
<body>

<h1>Recipes for Cheese</h1>

<p class="intro">Cheese is a remarkably versatile food, available in literally
hundreds of varieties with different flavors and textures.</p>

</body>
</html>
```

code snippet /chapter8/figure_8-10.html

This CSS and markup results in the output you see in Figure 8-10.

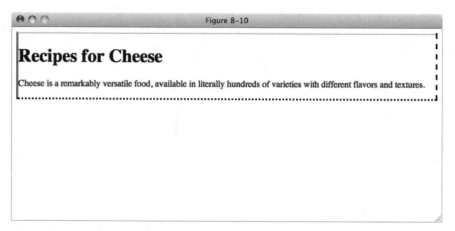

FIGURE 8-10

Like the `border-width` property, the `border-style` property can accept up to four values to specify the style for each side of the box:

```
border-style: ridge dashed dotted double;
```

As is the case for the `margin` and `border-width` properties, the shorthand is specified as top, right, bottom, and left, and `border-style` also supports the three-value, two-value, and one-value shorthand syntax as the `border-width` and `margin` properties.

border-color

The `border-color` property is yet another shorthand property. Like the `border-style` and `border-width` properties, you can use `border-color` to control how a border is styled. The `border-color` property, as you may have guessed, specifies the border color for each side of the box. The following table outlines the `border-color` family of properties.

PROPERTY	VALUE
border-color	[<color> | transparent] {1,4} Initial value: the value of the 'color' property
border-top-color border-right-color border-bottom-color border-left-color	<color> | transparent Initial value: the value of the 'color' property

 NOTE *IE 6 and IE 7 do not support the* transparent *keyword as applied to border color; in IE, the* transparent *keyword is rendered black.*

Like border-style, margin, and border-width, the border-color property can accept up to four values. This property accepts a <color> value, meaning that it can accept a color keyword, a hexadecimal value, a short hexadecimal value, or an RGB value; any color value accepted by the color property is also acceptable to the border-color properties.

 WARNING *When the* border-color *property is not specified, the* border-color *is the same color as specified for the* color *property, i.e., the text color.*

The following code shows an example of the border-color keywords.

Available for
download on
Wrox.com

```
<!DOCTYPE html PUBLIC "-//W3C//DTD HTML 4.01//EN"
    "http://www.w3.org/TR/html4/strict.dtd">
<html lang="en">
<head>
    <meta http-equiv="Content-Type" content="text/html; charset=utf-8">
    <title>Figure 8-11</title>
    <style type="text/css">
        body {
            border-width: 3px;
            border-style: dashed;
            border-top-color: red;
            border-right-color: blue;
            border-bottom-color: green;
            border-left-color: purple;
        }
    </style>
</head>
```

```
<body>

<h1>Recipes for Cheese</h1>

<p class="intro">Cheese is a remarkably versatile food, available in literally
hundreds of varieties with different flavors and textures.</p>

</body>
</html>
```

code snippet /chapter8/figure_8-11.html

This CSS and markup results in the output you see in Figure 8-11.

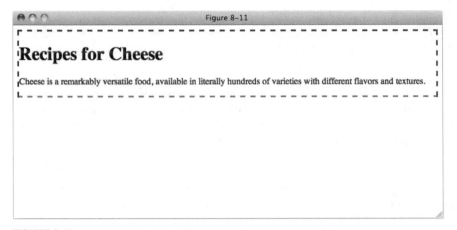

FIGURE 8-11

Now that you've seen an overview of what is possible with borders, the upcoming sections discuss the border shorthand properties.

Border Shorthand Properties

The `border-top`, `border-right`, `border-bottom`, `border-left`, and `border` properties combine the `border-width`, `border-style`, and `border-color` properties into single properties for each side of the box, or all sides of the box. The following table outlines the possible values for these five properties.

PROPERTY	VALUE
border-top border-right border-bottom border-left	\<border-width\> || \<border-style\> || \<color\>border-right
border	\<border-width\> || \<border-style\> || \<color\>

The notation for the `border-top`, `border-right`, `border-bottom`, `border-left`, and `border` properties indicates that one to three values are possible; each value refers to a `border-width` value, a `border-style` value, and a `border-color` value. The following code demonstrates the border shorthand property.

```
<!DOCTYPE html PUBLIC "-//W3C//DTD HTML 4.01//EN"
    "http://www.w3.org/TR/html4/strict.dtd">
<html lang="en">
<head>
    <meta http-equiv="Content-Type" content="text/html; charset=utf-8">
    <title>Figure 8-12</title>
    <style type="text/css">
        body {
            border: 3px dashed red;
        }
    </style>
</head>
<body>

<h1>Recipes for Cheese</h1>

<p class="intro">Cheese is a remarkably versatile food, available in literally
hundreds of varieties with different flavors and textures.</p>

</body>
</html>
```

code snippet /chapter8/figure_8-12.html

This CSS and markup results in the output you see in Figure 8-12.

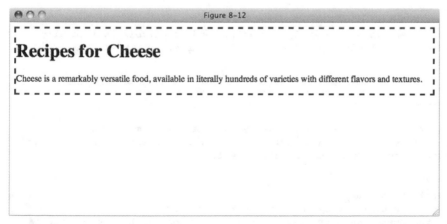

FIGURE 8-12

In Figure 8-12, you see the use of the `border` shorthand property, which specifies the border for all four sides of the box at once.

Unlike the `margin` shorthand property, the `border` property may only be used to specify all four sides of the box at once. If you want a different style, or width, or color for the different sides, you'll need to use the individual shorthand properties.

In the following Try It Out, you recap what is possible with CSS border properties.

TRY IT OUT | **Adding a Border around Content**

Example 8-2

To see the `border` property in action, follow these steps.

1. Enter the following markup:

```
<!DOCTYPE html PUBLIC "-//W3C//DTD HTML 4.01//EN"
    "http://www.w3.org/TR/html4/strict.dtd">
<html lang="en">
<head>
    <meta http-equiv="Content-Type" content="text/html; charset=utf-8">
    <title>Example 8-2</title>
    <style type="text/css">
        body {
            width: 600px;
            margin: 1em auto;
            border: 1px solid #666;
        }
    </style>
</head>
<body>

<h1>Recipes for Cheese</h1>

<p class="intro">Cheese is a remarkably versatile food, available in literally
hundreds of varieties with different flavors and textures.</p>

<div class="recipe">

    <h2>Welsh Rarebit</h2>

    <p class="intro">Welsh Rarebit is a savory dish made from melted cheese, often
    cheddar, on toasted bread, and a variety of other ingredients such as mustard,
    egg, or bacon. Here is one take on this classic.</p>

    <ol>
        <li>Lightly toast the bread</li>
        <li>Place on a baking tray, and spread with butter.</li>
        <li>Add the grated cheddar cheese and 2 tablespoons of beer to a saucepan.
        Place the saucepan over a medium heat, and stir the cheese continuously
        until it has melted. Add a teaspoon of wholegrain mustard and grind in
```

```
a little pepper. Keep stirring.</li>
<li>When thick and smooth, pour over each piece of toast spreading it to
the edges to stop the toast from burning.</li>
<li>Place under the grill for a couple of minutes or until golden
brown.</li>
</ol>

</div>

</body>
</html>
```

2. Save the preceding CSS and markup as `example 8-2.html`. This example results in the output in Figure 8-13.

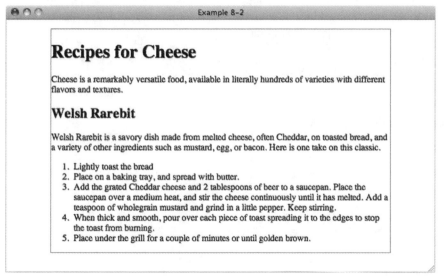

FIGURE 8-13

How It Works

In Example 8-2, you built on example 8-1 by adding a `border` property on the body element.

In the next section, you examine box padding.

PADDING

Padding is the space between the content of an element and its borders, as has been mentioned briefly in previous examples. Refer to the diagram in Figure 8-1 to see where padding appears in the box model. The following table shows the various padding properties.

PROPERTY	VALUE
padding	[<length> | <percentage>] {1,4}
padding-top	<length> | <percentage>
padding-right	
padding-bottom	
padding-left	

Like `margin`, `border-width`, `border-style`, and `border-color`, the `padding` property is a shorthand property, meaning that it is a simplified representation of the other `padding` properties, `padding-top`, `padding-right`, `padding-bottom`, and `padding-left`. In the preceding table, the square brackets are used to group the values. In this context, the `padding` property can accept either a length or a percentage value, and can have one to four space-separated values. We've seen this same effect with margins and borders, so let's Try It Out.

TRY IT OUT   Adding Padding to a Layout

Example 8-3

To see the `padding` property in action, follow these steps.

1.   Enter the following markup:

```
<!DOCTYPE html PUBLIC "-//W3C//DTD HTML 4.01//EN"
    "http://www.w3.org/TR/html4/strict.dtd">
<html lang="en">
<head>
    <meta http-equiv="Content-Type" content="text/html; charset=utf-8">
    <title>Example 8-3</title>
    <style type="text/css">
        body {
            width: 600px;
            margin: 1em auto;
            border: 1px solid #666;
            padding: 10px;
        }
    </style>
</head>
<body>

<h1>Recipes for Cheese</h1>

<p class="intro">Cheese is a remarkably versatile food, available in literally
hundreds of varieties with different flavors and textures.</p>

<div class="recipe">

    <h2>Welsh Rarebit</h2>

    <p class="intro">Welsh Rarebit is a savory dish made from melted cheese, often
```

```
cheddar, on toasted bread, and a variety of other ingredients such as mustard,
egg, or bacon. Here is one take on this classic.</p>

<ol>
    <li>Lightly toast the bread</li>
    <li>Place on a baking tray, and spread with butter.</li>
    <li>Add the grated cheddar cheese and 2 tablespoons of beer to a saucepan.
    Place the saucepan over a medium heat, and stir the cheese continuously
    until it has melted. Add a teaspoon of wholegrain mustard and grind in
    a little pepper. Keep stirring.</li>
    <li>When thick and smooth, pour over each piece of toast spreading it to
    the edges to stop the toast from burning.</li>
    <li>Place under the grill for a couple of minutes or until golden
    brown.</li>
</ol>

</div>

</body>
</html>
```

2. Save the preceding CSS and markup as `example_8-3.html`. This example results in the output in Figure 8-14.

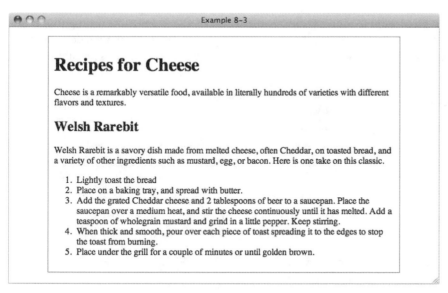

FIGURE 8-14

How It Works

In Example 8-3, you added a `padding` property on the body element, adding space between the content and the border in your new layout.

In Figure 8-14, you see that the `padding` property is similar to the `margin` property. The main differences with the `padding` property are as follows:

➤ The padding area is the area between the inside edge of the border and the outer edge of the content.

➤ The `auto` keyword has no effect with the `padding` property.

➤ The `padding` property cannot accept a negative value (the `margin` property can).

➤ There is no collapsing padding; only margins can collapse.

In the next section, I examine the different length properties supported by CSS.

SETTING DIMENSIONS

CSS 1 introduced the `width` and `height` properties as part of the CSS box model. CSS 2 expands on those properties, providing minimum and maximum dimensions when variable lengths are involved, as is the case with percentage width and height values.

The following sections examine each of CSS's dimension properties individually.

width

The `width` property is a pretty simple property; it sets the width of an element. According to the CSS box model diagram presented in Figure 8-1, `width` is the space measured from inside padding edge to inside padding edge. The following table outlines the `width` property and its possible values.

PROPERTY	VALUE
width	`<length>` | `<percentage>` | `auto` initial value: `auto`

The `width` property accepts a length unit, which is indicated in the preceding table with the `<length>` notation. You've already seen the `width` property in use in your examples so far. In the following code, you see a simple example of the `width` property using a length unit.

Available for download on Wrox.com

```html
<!DOCTYPE html PUBLIC "-//W3C//DTD HTML 4.01//EN"
    "http://www.w3.org/TR/html4/strict.dtd">
<html lang="en">
<head>
    <meta http-equiv="Content-Type" content="text/html; charset=utf-8">
    <title>Figure 8-15</title>
    <style type="text/css">
        body {
            width: 600px;
        }
    </style>
```

```
</head>
<body>

<h1>Recipes for Cheese</h1>

<p class="intro">Cheese is a remarkably versatile food, available in literally
hundreds of varieties with different flavors and textures.</p>

</body>
</html>
```

code snippet /chapter8/figure_8-15.html

This CSS and markup results in the output you see in Figure 8-15.

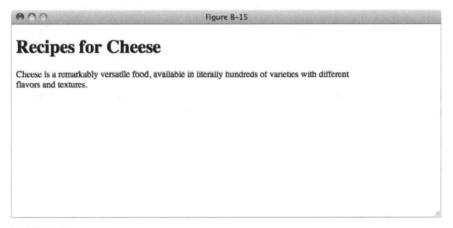

FIGURE 8-15

When you apply a width to an element, you must also take into account the borders and padding as part of the overall horizontal area that the element will occupy, as well as the space between elements determined by their margins.

In the next section, I talk about the height property.

height

Like the width property, the height property sets the amount of space between the top-inside padding edge and the bottom-inside padding edge. The following table outlines the height property and its possible values.

PROPERTY	VALUE
height	<length> | <percentage> | auto
	initial value: auto

The `height` property works in the same way as the `width` property, but is less commonly used as most web pages are designed to scroll vertically, and setting a fixed height causes some strange effects, as you will see in the following snippet.

Available for download on Wrox.com

```
<!DOCTYPE html PUBLIC "-//W3C//DTD HTML 4.01//EN"
    "http://www.w3.org/TR/html4/strict.dtd">
<html lang="en">
<head>
    <meta http-equiv="Content-Type" content="text/html; charset=utf-8">
    <title>Figure 8-16</title>
    <style type="text/css">
        body {
            width: 600px;
            height: 75px;
            border: 1px solid #666;
        }
    </style>
</head>
<body>

<h1>Recipes for Cheese</h1>

<p class="intro">Cheese is a remarkably versatile food, available in literally
hundreds of varieties with different flavors and textures.</p>

</body>
</html>
```

code snippet /chapter8/figure_8-16.html

This CSS and markup results in the output you see in Figure 8-16.

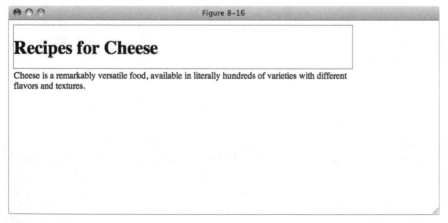

FIGURE 8-16

As you can see, specifying a fixed height causes content larger than that height to overflow outside of the container, in this case the body element. You will most commonly see this when a height has been specified, but the same applies to width if a container contains an element, such as an image, that is wider than it; part of the image would appear outside of the container.

The exception to this rule is IE 6, which will expand a container to fit the size of its content.

I'll cover overflowing content and the quirks of IE 6 in more detail later in this chapter.

The next section continues the discussion of dimensions with auto values for width and height.

auto Values for width and height

By default, width and height properties have an auto value. So, when you do not specify a width or height, the value is the auto keyword. The meaning of the auto keyword changes depending on the type of element that it is applied to. When used on a <div> element, the element spans all the horizontal space available to it and expands vertically to accommodate any content inside of it, including text, images, or other boxes. Elements with this behavior are called *block* elements. Some examples of block elements are <div>, <p>, <h1> through <h6>, <form> and <ul> elements.

The <table> element is an example of an element where the auto value has a different meaning than as, for example, that applied to a block element. Unlike block-level elements, <table> elements don't take up all the horizontal space available to them. Instead, they only take up as much room as needed based on the content they contain. In other words, they take the vertical expanding behavior of block-level elements and apply that to their width too.

Percentage Measurements

When a percentage measurement is used, the size that the percentage is based on is the parent element of the element the percentage width is applied to.

For example, an element with a width value of 50% that has a parent with a width value of 600px will have a computed width of 300px.

In the next section, I describe what happens to the box model when IE is in quirks mode.

Quirks Mode width and height in Internet Explorer

As I mentioned earlier in this chapter, IE is a very different browser in quirks rendering mode.

When discussing width, I said that the horizontal space taken up by an element was equal to width + padding + border + margin. IE in quirks mode behaves a little differently by including padding and border sizes in the width value, so that adding padding and borders actually makes the content area smaller, and the space taken up by the element is equal to width + margin. While there are ways to normalize this across browsers, it requires that you make all browsers behave like IE in quirks mode rather than fixing this problem and so is beyond the scope of this book. I provide a link to documentation on this problem in Appendix B.

Minimum and Maximum Dimensions

The min-width, max-width, min-height, and max-height properties define minimum and maximum boundaries when it is necessary to constrain a width or height from expanding or contracting past a certain point. In a variable width design, where you design content to adapt to multiple screen resolutions, it is sometimes helpful to define where you want the document to stop stretching or stop contracting. For instance, if you have designed primarily with an 800 × 600 or 1024 × 768 screen resolution in mind, a user viewing your website at 1600 × 1200 pixels may see the content stretched pretty thin if an auto keyword or percentage values are used to define the width. This is where the CSS properties min-width, max-width, min-height, and max-height come into play.

min-width and min-height

The min-width property defines a lower-size constraint on an element. The available values for the min-width property are outlined in the following table.

PROPERTY	VALUE
min-width min-height	<length> | <percentage> initial value: 0

 NOTE *IE 6 and less do not support the* min-width *or* min-height *properties.*

The min-width and min-height properties define when an element should stop shrinking to fit the user's window or its content. Consider the example in the following code.

Available for download on Wrox.com

```
<!DOCTYPE html PUBLIC "-//W3C//DTD HTML 4.01//EN"
    "http://www.w3.org/TR/html4/strict.dtd">
<html lang="en">
<head>
    <meta http-equiv="Content-Type" content="text/html; charset=utf-8">
    <title>Figure 8-17</title>
    <style type="text/css">
        body {
            min-width: 1000px;
            min-height: 250px;
            border: 1px solid #666;
        }
    </style>
</head>
```

```
<body>

<h1>Recipes for Cheese</h1>

<p class="intro">Cheese is a remarkably versatile food, available in literally
hundreds of varieties with different flavors and textures.</p>

</body>
</html>
```

code snippet /chapter8/figure_8-17.html

This CSS and markup results in the output you see in Figure 8-17.

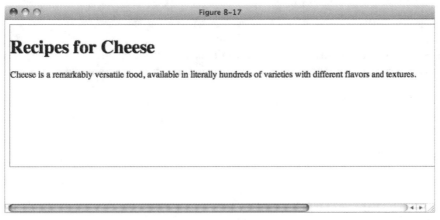

FIGURE 8-17

Figure 8-17 demonstrates that when the browser window or containing element becomes narrower than 1000 pixels, the `<body>` stops shrinking and a scroll bar appears across the bottom of the browser window, and if the content is less than 500px in height, the `<body>` will expand to the `min-height` value.

min-width and min-height in IE 6

IE 6 does not support the `min-width` or `min-height` properties, but support for these properties was introduced in IE 7.0.

Instead `width` and `height` behave just like the `min-width` and `min-height` properties in other browsers. Elements with a `width` or `height` value applied will always expand to the size of their content, even if the content is bigger than the `width` or `height` value. Using conditional comments as explained in Chapter 2 (and see Appendix B for links to more techniques to target IE 6) you can exploit this by providing a `min-width` or `min-height` to more modern browsers and a `width` or `height` property to IE 6.

max-width and max-height

In contrast to the `min-width` property, the `max-width` and `max-height` properties are used to set an upper constraint for width and height for elements.

PROPERTY	VALUE
max-width	`<length>` | `<percentage>` | none
max-height	initial value: none

NOTE As is the case for `min-width` and `min-height`, IE 6.0 does not support the `max-width` or `max-height` properties.

The `max-width` and `max-height` properties allow you to define a maximum length if the area available to the element becomes larger. Consider the example in the following snippet.

Available for download on Wrox.com

```
<!DOCTYPE html PUBLIC "-//W3C//DTD HTML 4.01//EN"
    "http://www.w3.org/TR/html4/strict.dtd">
<html lang="en">
<head>
    <meta http-equiv="Content-Type" content="text/html; charset=utf-8">
    <title>Figure 8-18</title>
    <style type="text/css">
        body {
            width: 600px;
            max-height: 100px;
            border: 1px solid #666;
        }

        .intro {
            max-width: 200px;
        }
    </style>
</head>
<body>

<h1>Recipes for Cheese</h1>

<p class="intro">Cheese is a remarkably versatile food, available in literally
hundreds of varieties with different flavors and textures.</p>

</body>
</html>
```

code snippet /chapter8/figure_8-18.html

This CSS and markup results in the output you see in Figure 8-18.

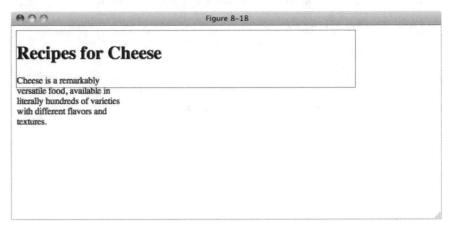

FIGURE 8-18

Figure 8-18 demonstrates that when the browser window or containing element becomes taller than 100 pixels, the <body> element will remain at 100 pixels in height and remaining content will overflow, and if the content of an element with the class of intro is wider than 200px it will wrap or overflow its container.

In the next section, I discuss the overflow property.

OVERFLOWING CONTENT

The CSS overflow property exists to manage content that is susceptible to dimensional constraints, where the content could possibly overflow the boundaries of those dimensional constraints. The following table outlines the overflow property and its possible values.

PROPERTY	VALUE
overflow	visible | hidden | scroll | auto initial value: visible

The two most common uses of the overflow property are to hide content when more content than space is available, or to apply scroll bars so that the extra content can be accessed. By default, the value of the overflow property is the visible keyword, the effects of which you have seen in previous examples. These figures show that when the width and height specified are smaller than the content allows, the content overflows the edges of the box containing it. It is possible to control that overflow by causing scroll bars to appear, or the overflowing content to be invisible.

The following code demonstrates two of the possible values for the `overflow` property.

Available for download on Wrox.com

```
<!DOCTYPE html PUBLIC "-//W3C//DTD HTML 4.01//EN"
    "http://www.w3.org/TR/html4/strict.dtd">
<html lang="en">
<head>
    <meta http-equiv="Content-Type" content="text/html; charset=utf-8">
    <title>Figure 8-19</title>
    <style type="text/css">
        body {
            width: 600px;
        }

        h1 {
            width: 50px;
            overflow: hidden;
        }

        .recipe {
            height: 200px;
            overflow: auto;
        }
    </style>
</head>
<body>

<h1>Recipes for Cheese</h1>

<p class="intro">Cheese is a remarkably versatile food, available in literally
hundreds of varieties with different flavors and textures.</p>

<div class="recipe">

    <h2>Welsh Rarebit</h2>

    <p class="intro">Welsh Rarebit is a savory dish made from melted cheese, often
    Cheddar, on toasted bread, and a variety of other ingredients such as mustard,
    egg, or bacon. Here is one take on this classic.</p>

    <ol>
        <li>Lightly toast the bread</li>
        <li>Place on a baking tray, and spread with butter.</li>
        <li>Add the grated Cheddar cheese and 2 tablespoons of beer to a saucepan.
        Place the saucepan over a medium heat, and stir the cheese continuously
        until it has melted. Add a teaspoon of wholegrain mustard and grind in
        a little pepper. Keep stirring.</li>
```

```
        <li>When thick and smooth, pour over each piece of toast spreading it to
        the edges to stop the toast from burning.</li>
        <li>Place under the grill for a couple of minutes or until golden
        brown.</li>
     </ol>

</div>

</body>
</html>
```

code snippet /chapter8/figure_8-19.html

This CSS and markup results in the output you see in Figure 8-19.

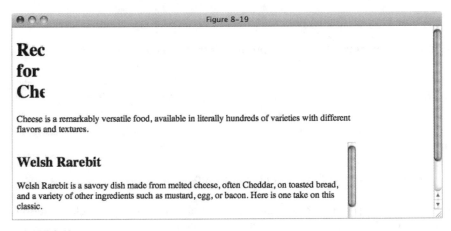

FIGURE 8-19

In Figure 8-19, you can see that even though the h1 text wraps when it is wider than 50 pixels, words that are longer than this width are cropped; the content is hidden. Also the element with the class of recipe scrolls when it's height is more than 200 pixels. The difference between the auto and the scroll keywords is that scroll will always display scroll bars, even if the content is smaller than the specified width or height. auto will only show scroll bars when they are necessary.

Overflowing Just the X or Y axis

Like the overflow property, overflow-x and overflow-y control overflow content, but they also allow users to control the overflowing content with a scroll bar: only a vertical scroll bar for the overflow-y property, and only a horizontal scroll bar for the overflow-x property. Each property accepts the same values as the overflow property, as in the following table.

PROPERTY	VALUE
overflow-x	visible | hidden | scroll | auto initial value: visible
overflow-y	visible | hidden | scroll | auto initial value: visible

 NOTE *IE 6 and IE 7 only support the* overflow-x *and* overflow-y *properties when in standards compliant mode.*

EXERCISES

1. From left to right, what are the seven box model properties that make up the left, center, and right sides of a box?

2. How do you left-, center-, and right-align a block-level box (using the standard method)?

3. When the margin shorthand property has four values, what side of the target element does each value apply margin to, in order?

4. What are the three keyword values of the border-width property?

5. If the border-color shorthand property has three values, what side of the target element does each value apply to, in order?

6. Name the shorthand properties that encompass the border-width, border-style, and border-color properties.

7. Describe briefly the two situations in which margin collapsing occurs?

8. What are the four keywords of the overflow property?

▶ **WHAT YOU LEARNED IN THIS CHAPTER**

In this chapter, I discussed how the box model works in CSS. To recap, in this chapter you learned the following:

TOPIC	KEY CONCEPTS
`margin, border, padding`	How to apply the box model to page elements with margins, borders, and padding properties
`Width, height`	How to specify the width and height of elements, and how content is displayed by default if it is larger than its container
`overflow`	How to control how content is displayed when it is larger than its container

Floating and Vertical Alignment

WHAT YOU WILL LEARN IN THIS CHAPTER:

➤ The `float` property and how it is used to change the flow of elements in a document — for instance, to place text beside an image

➤ The `clear` property and how this property is used to cancel the effects of the float property

➤ The `vertical-align` property and how this property is used to control the vertical alignment of text to create subscript or superscript text or control vertical alignment in table cells

In Chapter 8, I presented a subset of properties that combine to define a concept known as the CSS box model. In this chapter, I continue introducing new properties, this time focusing on two properties most often misunderstood by users new to CSS design: `float` and `clear`. These properties are often misunderstood because of their unique effect on the elements in a document.

I'll begin with a discussion of the `float` property.

FLOATING CONTENT

A simple explanation of the `float` property is that it is used to put content side-by-side. In the coming sections, you look in depth at the `float` property, its idiosyncrasies, and how you can use it to lay out a web page. The following table outlines the `float` property and its values.

PROPERTY	VALUE
float	left | right | none Initial value: none

At this point, the `float` property appears fairly simple. It accepts keyword values of `left`, `right`, and `none`. The effects of the `float` property are intrinsically tied to the CSS box model that you read about in Chapter 8, and specifically as described in the next section. After the `float` property is applied to an element, regardless of the type of element, that element takes on the behavior of a block element, where its dimensions are defined by width, height, padding, borders, and margins. Before you see some examples of this, the following code shows you how the `float` property affects a document's layout.

Available for download on Wrox.com

```html
<!DOCTYPE html PUBLIC "-//W3C//DTD HTML 4.01//EN"
    "http://www.w3.org/TR/html4/strict.dtd">
<html lang="en">
<head>
    <meta http-equiv="Content-Type" content="text/html; charset=utf-8">
    <title>Figure 9-1</title>
    <style type="text/css">
        h1 {
            float: left;
        }
    </style>
</head>
<body>

<h1>Recipes for Cheese</h1>

<p class="intro">Cheese is a remarkably versatile food, available in literally
hundreds of varieties with different flavors and textures.</p>

</body>
</html>
```

code snippet /chapter9/figure_9-1.html

This CSS and markup results in the output in Figure 9-1.

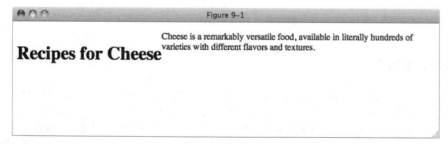

FIGURE 9-1

As you can see, the heading has been floated and so the following paragraph wraps around it. The following code shows a more useful example, creating columns out of content.

Available for download on Wrox.com

```html
<!DOCTYPE html PUBLIC "-//W3C//DTD HTML 4.01//EN"
    "http://www.w3.org/TR/html4/strict.dtd">
<html lang="en">
<head>
    <meta http-equiv="Content-Type" content="text/html; charset=utf-8">
    <title>Figure 9-2</title>
    <style type="text/css">
        .recipe h2 {
            float: left;
        }

        .recipe .intro,
        .recipe ol {
            float: right;
            width: 500px;
        }
    </style>
</head>
<body>

<h1>Recipes for Cheese</h1>

<p class="intro">Cheese is a remarkably versatile food, available in literally
hundreds of varieties with different flavors and textures.</p>

<div class="recipe">

    <h2>Welsh Rarebit</h2>

    <p class="intro">Welsh Rarebit is a savory dish made from melted cheese, often
    Cheddar, on toasted bread, and a variety of other ingredients such as mustard,
    egg, or bacon. Here is one take on this classic.</p>

    <ol>
        <li>Lightly toast the bread</li>
        <li>Place on a baking tray, and spread with butter.</li>
        <li>Add the grated Cheddar cheese and 2 tablespoons of beer to a saucepan.
        Place the saucepan over a medium heat, and stir the cheese continuously
        until it has melted. Add a teaspoon of wholegrain mustard and grind in
        a little pepper. Keep stirring.</li>
        <li>When thick and smooth, pour over each piece of toast spreading it to
        the edges to stop the toast from burning.</li>
        <li>Place under the grill for a couple of minutes or until golden
        brown.</li>
    </ol>

</div>

</body>
</html>
```

code snippet /chapter9/figure_9-2.html

This CSS and markup results in the output in Figure 9-2.

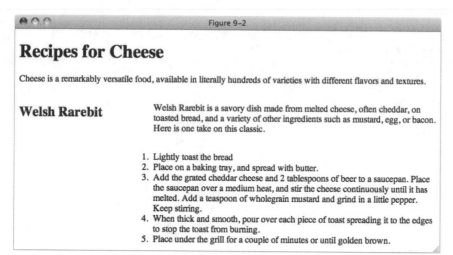

FIGURE 9-2

In Figure 9-2, you can see what happens when there is both a left and right float; the left floated heading is positioned alongside the right floated recipe intro and instructions.

On the surface, the concept of floating is pretty simple, and for most things that you set out to accomplish, this is about as complicated as it will get, but there is quite a complex set of rules under the surface of the `float` property. To understand what happens when an element is floated, you need to know about how the box model is affected and what happens when certain types of elements are floated. These concepts are explored in the coming sections.

Floating Box Model

Because floated elements are repositioned to allow other content to flow around them, they exhibit unique behavior. This behavior is outlined here:

➤ The margins of floated elements do not collapse, no matter what they are next to.

➤ Only the contents of elements following a floated element are affected by the floated element. That is, the backgrounds, margins, borders, padding, and width (the box model and dimensions) of elements following a floated element are not affected.

➤ A floated element is always treated like a block element.

Each rule is important in determining how floated elements are positioned and rendered.

Consider the diagram in Figure 9-3, which shows how the box model is incorporated when an element has been floated.

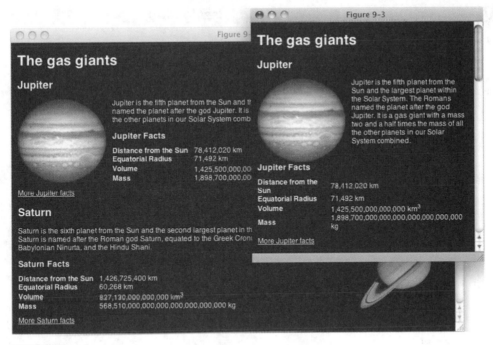

FIGURE 9-3

When an element is floated, it takes on the behavior of a block element, with one major difference: Its sizing becomes shrink-to-fit horizontally and vertically unless you specify width and height properties. That means that if you float a <div> element, its dimensions change such that it only expands enough to accommodate the content within it. In Chapter 8, you learned that the default dimensions of a <div> element are expand-to-fit horizontally, meaning the <div> takes up the whole line, but not so when a <div> element is floated.

Elements within a floated container that are not themselves floated retain their original width unless a width is applied to them, e.g., a paragraph will still take up 100% of the space available to it. If no width had been set on the floated elements in Figure 9-2, the layout would have remained unchanged as the text in the paragraph and the list elements would have retained a width of 100% of the available space.

Now that you've had an overview of the float property, the following Try It Out is a recap of what is possible with the float property.

TRY IT OUT | Create a Page Header with Floated Navigation

Example 9-1

To see the float property in action, follow these steps.

1. Enter the following markup:

```
<!DOCTYPE html PUBLIC "-//W3C//DTD HTML 4.01//EN"
    "http://www.w3.org/TR/html4/strict.dtd">
<html lang="en">
<head>
    <meta http-equiv="Content-Type" content="text/html; charset=utf-8">
    <title>Example 9-1</title>
    <style type="text/css">
        body {
            width: 600px;
            margin: 1em auto;
        }

        h1 {
            float: left;
            margin-top: 0;
        }

        .navigation {
            float: right;
            margin: 0;
            list-style: none;
        }

        .navigation li {
            float: left;
        }

        .navigation a {
            display: block;
            margin-left: 0.5em;
            padding: 0.5em;
            border: 1px solid #CCC;
            color: #233;
            text-decoration: none;
        }

        .navigation a:focus,
        .navigation a:hover {
            background: #233;
            color: #FFF;
        }
    </style>
</head>
<body>

<h1>Recipes for Cheese</h1>

<ul class="navigation">
```

```
      <li><a href="#">Home</a></li>
      <li><a href="#">Recipes</a></li>
      <li><a href="#">Suggestions</a></li>
   </ul>

   </body>
   </html>
```

2. Save the preceding CSS and markup as `example_9-1.html`. This example results in the output in Figure 9-4.

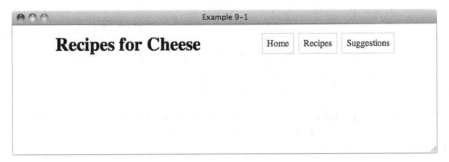

FIGURE 9-4

How It Works

In Example 9-1, you floated the `h1` element left and the element with the class of `navigation` right. This positioned the navigation list alongside the heading, aligned to the right of the body.

In the next section, I present a property that allows you to control floated elements, the `clear` property.

CANCELING FLOATED CONTENT

In this section, I discuss a property intrinsically related to the `float` property: the `clear` property. The `clear` property is used to control floating content. The following table outlines the `clear` property and its possible values.

PROPERTY	VALUE
clear	none | left | right | both Initial value: none

The simplest explanation for the `clear` property is that it is used to cancel the effects of one or more floated elements. Figure 9-5 shows what will happen to the example shown in Figure 9-4 when the heading and navigation are followed by further content.

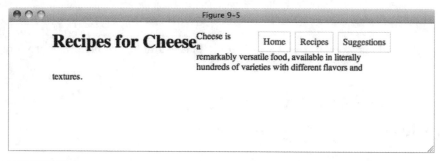

FIGURE 9-5

As you can see, the text in the paragraph falls through the gap between the floated elements instead of appearing after it, as you would want. The following code shows how we `clear` floated elements to ensure that subsequent content follows them.

Available for download on Wrox.com

```
<!DOCTYPE html PUBLIC "-//W3C//DTD HTML 4.01//EN"
    "http://www.w3.org/TR/html4/strict.dtd">
<html lang="en">
<head>
    <meta http-equiv="Content-Type" content="text/html; charset=utf-8">
    <title>Figure 9-6</title>
    <style type="text/css">
        body {
            width: 600px;
            margin: 1em auto;
        }

        h1 {
            float: left;
            margin-top: 0;
        }

        .navigation {
            float: right;
            margin: 0;
            list-style: none;
        }

        .navigation li {
            float: left;
        }

        .navigation a {
            display: block;
            margin-left: 0.5em;
            padding: 0.5em;
            border: 1px solid #CCC;
```

```
            color: #233;
            text-decoration: none;
        }

        .navigation a:focus,
        .navigation a:hover {
            background: #233;
            color: #FFF;
        }

        .intro {
            clear: both;
        }
    </style>
</head>
<body>

<h1>Recipes for Cheese</h1>

<ul class="navigation">
    <li><a href="#">Home</a></li>
    <li><a href="#">Recipes</a></li>
    <li><a href="#">Suggestions</a></li>
</ul>

<p class="intro">Cheese is a remarkably versatile food, available in literally
hundreds of varieties with different flavors and textures.</p>

</body>
</html>
```

code snippet /chapter9/figure_9-6.html

This CSS and markup results in the output you see in Figure 9-6.

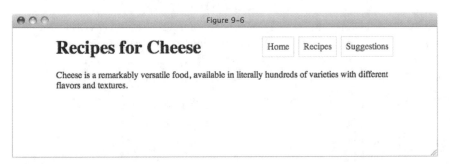

FIGURE 9-6

In Figure 9-6, you see the results of the application of the `clear: both;` declaration on the element with the class name `intro`. The effects of the `float` applied to the heading elements have been canceled, and the text is dropped down below the drawing of the heading.

So the `clear` property is used to control what happens when elements are floated. When you use the `clear` property, you can cancel a `float` on a particular element. Here, I have used `clear: both;` but `clear: left;` and `clear: right;` can be used to clear only left and right floated elements respectively.

In the next section I look at some float bugs in IE 6.

FLOAT BUGS IN IE 6

The following section takes a look at float bugs that arise in IE 6 and a few of the techniques you can use to work around these bugs. The bugs that I discuss here are as follows:

➤ **Peek-a-boo bug:** As the name implies, this bug involves the use of floats where certain content on a page disappears and occasionally reappears.

➤ **Guillotine bug:** This is another bug that comes up in IE when using floats, where content is cut in half.

➤ **Three-pixel jog:** This bug causes 3 pixels of space to mysteriously appear when using floats in IE.

➤ **Double-margin bug:** This bug causes the left or right margins of a floated box to double when using floats in IE.

Even though the following bugs are a problem in IE 6, all of them have been fixed in IE 7.

TARGETING INTERNET EXPLORER

While in most circumstances you will want to write CSS that works in all browsers, in some cases this may not be possible. The most common possibility is that you will experience bugs that only exist in Internet Explorer, like the ones I will show you here.

These bugs often have solutions that cause no harm when applied to all browsers, but this is not always the case, and you may feel that it makes your CSS less readable. In these cases, being able to target CSS or individual declarations at Internet Explorer can be advantageous.

There are two main techniques that I will cover here: conditional comments and hacks.

Conditional Comments

Conditional comments are just like ordinary HTML comments, but with an extra piece of information:

```
<!--[if lte IE 6]>
<![endif]-->
```

The `if` part of the comment is followed by an equation, which in this case it reads "`if less than or equal to IE 6`". This means that if the browser this code is viewed in is Internet Explorer, and the version is 6 or less, then whatever is inside the comment block will be output instead of being a normal comment. Any other browser will treat this as a comment and ignore it. In our example, whatever we put inside the comment (which could be a `link` or `style` element for IE only CSS) will only be output for Internet Explorer versions 6 or less.

You can read more about conditional comments at `www.quirksmode.org/css/condcom.html`.

Hacks

Hacks are tricks you can use to take advantage of bugs in CSS parsers to include CSS that only works in certain browsers. I will show you two hacks here that you may find useful.

First is the *underscore hack*, which allows you to write CSS that only works in IE 6. This works as follows:

```
p {
    _height: 1px;
}
```

As you can see, the normal `height` property has been prefixed with an underscore. Because this is not a valid CSS property, most browsers will ignore it altogehter, but IE 6 does something different. It ignores just the underscore, so to IE 6 this rule looks like:

```
p {
    height: 1px;
}
```

Because IE 6 has ignored the underscore, it will interpret the declaration.

The second hack is the *star hack*. This works in exactly the same way, but targets both IE 6 and IE 7. It works as follows:

```
p {
    *width: 100px;
}
```

The same thing happens here as with the underscore hack. Most browsers will ignore the invalid property, but IE6 and IE7 will ignore the star instead.

With these two hacks you can also target IE7 on its own by using the star hack to apply declarations that apply to both IE6 and IE7, and then using the underscore hack to reset the declaration for IE6:

```
p {
    *width: 100px;
    _width: auto;
}
```

continues

(continued)

Notice that the order is important here, and that each declaration is hacked independently. You can include non-prefixed declarations alongside hacks within a rule, and the non-hacked declarations will apply to all browsers, as follows:

```
p {
      width: 100px;
      _width: 97px;
}
```

This rule will apply a width of 100px to the paragraph in all browsers except for IE6, which would receive a width of 97px. Again, order is important as IE6 will accept either property declaration. The hacked version must be last for it to be applied.

Hacks can be a powerful tool in your arsenal, but use them with care and as little as possible. Overuse will make your CSS hard to read and difficult to maintain. If you find that you need to write a lot of CSS specific to Internet Explorer or a version of IE then consider using conditional comments to include a separate style sheet.

You can read more about hacks at `http://webstandardstips.com/2008/11/18/css-hacks-for-ie-only-style-rules/`.

The Peek-A-Boo Bug

The peek-a-boo bug can come up in several different contexts — in fact, in far too many to list here. It involves content that disappears and reappears seemingly at random (hence, its aptly applied name).

Three properties present in the style sheet trigger this bug:

➤ Floating an element by applying a `float: left;` or `float: right;`.

➤ Including a background on the containing element

➤ Including a `clear` on an element following the float, where the margins of the clearing element come into contact with the floating element.

The following code demonstrates the problem.

Available for download on Wrox.com

```
<!DOCTYPE html PUBLIC "-//W3C//DTD HTML 4.01//EN"
    "http://www.w3.org/TR/html4/strict.dtd">
<html lang="en">
<head>
    <meta http-equiv="Content-Type" content="text/html; charset=utf-8">
    <title>Figure 9-7</title>
    <style type="text/css">
        #container {
            background: #EEE;
```

```
        }

        .float {
            float: left;
            width: 150px;
            height: 150px;
            border: 1px solid #000;
        }

        .clear {
            clear: left;
        }
    </style>
</head>
<body>

<h1>Peek-A-Boo</h1>

<div id="container">
    <p class="float">Floated text</p>
    <p>Content text 1</p>
    <p>Content text 2</p>
    <p>Content text 3</p>
    <p class="clear">Cleared text</p>
</div>

</body>
</html>
```

code snippet /chapter9/figure_9-7.html

This CSS and markup results in the output you see in Figure 9-7. As you can see, the elements between the first and last line of text are missing. Switch to a different window and back and the missing text may reappear!

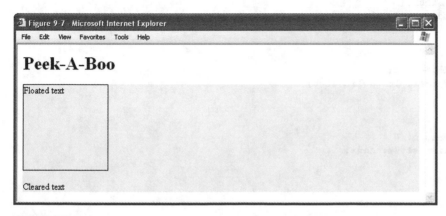

FIGURE 9-7

So, with an overview of what causes the peek-a-boo bug and what it is, what do you do to work around the bug? You have more than one option:

➤ Apply a `position: relative;` declaration to the containing element and floating element.

➤ Prevent the margins of the clearing element from coming into contact with the floating element.

➤ Avoid applying a background to the containing element.

➤ Apply the declaration `zoom: 1;` to the containing element.

➤ Apply the declaration `display: inline-block;` to the containing element.

➤ Apply a fixed width to the containing element.

The Guillotine Bug

Guillotine is another aptly named bug where only part of the content disappears.

The guillotine bug occurs when the following conditions are present:

➤ IE is in standards-compliant rendering mode.

➤ An element is floated inside of a container element.

➤ Links exist inside the container element in non-floated content that appears after the float.

➤ `a:hover` pseudo-class is applied to `<a>` elements that change certain properties.

The following code demonstrates the problem.

Available for download on Wrox.com

```
<!DOCTYPE html PUBLIC "-//W3C//DTD HTML 4.01//EN"
    "http://www.w3.org/TR/html4/strict.dtd">
<html lang="en">
<head>
    <meta http-equiv="Content-Type" content="text/html; charset=utf-8">
    <title>Figure 9-8</title>
    <style type="text/css">
        #container {
          border: 1px solid #000;
        }

        .float {
            float: left;
            border: 1px solid #000;
        }

        ul {
            margin: 0;
            list-style: none;
        }

        a:hover {
            background: #EEE;
        }
    </style>
```

```html
</head>
<body>

<h1>Guillotine</h1>

<div id="container">
    <div class="float">
        <p>Content text 1</p>
        <p>Content text 2</p>
        <p>Content text 3</p>
        <p>Content text 4</p>
        <p>Content text 5</p>
    </div>
    <ul>
        <li><a href="#">Link</a></li>
        <li><a href="#">Link</a></li>
        <li><a href="#">Link</a></li>
        <li><a href="#">Link</a></li>
    </ul>
</div>

</body>
</html>
```

code snippet /chapter9/figure_9-8.html

This CSS and markup results in the output you see in Figure 9-8. As you can see, the elements after the first two lines of text are missing, chopped off at the edge of the container element.

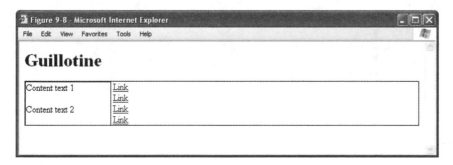

FIGURE 9-8

The guillotine bug is yet another bizarre IE rendering bug. The fix is not nearly as elegant as that for the peek-a-boo bug. To fix the guillotine bug, a clearing element must appear after the containing element. The best method to apply this clearing element without affecting the original design is to apply the following rule to the clearing element:

```css
.clear {
    clear: both;
    visibility: hidden;
}
```

Then in the markup, add the clearing element:

```
<div class="float">Floated Content</div>
<div class="clear"></div>
```

The Three-Pixel Jog

The next Internet Explorer rendering bug, which also involves floated elements, is called the three-pixel jog. As the name implies, this bug causes 3 pixels of space to appear between text inside an element that follows a floated element and the inner border of that element.

The following code demonstrates the problem.

Available for download on Wrox.com

```
<!DOCTYPE html PUBLIC "-//W3C//DTD HTML 4.01//EN"
    "http://www.w3.org/TR/html4/strict.dtd">
<html lang="en">
<head>
    <meta http-equiv="Content-Type" content="text/html; charset=utf-8">
    <title>Figure 9-9</title>
    <style type="text/css">
        .float {
            float: left;
            border: 1px solid #000;
        }
    </style>
</head>
<body>

<h1>Three-Pixel Jog</h1>

<div id="container">
    <div class="float">
        <p>Content text 1</p>
        <p>Content text 2</p>
        <p>Content text 3</p>
        <p>Content text 4</p>
        <p>Content text 5</p>
    </div>
    <div>
        <p>Content text 6</p>
        <p>Content text 7</p>
        <p>Content text 8</p>
        <p>Content text 9</p>
        <p>Content text 10</p>
    </div>
</div>

</body>
</html>
```

code snippet /chapter9/figure_9-9.html

This CSS and markup results in the output you see in Figure 9-9. As you can see, there is a space of 3 pixels between the text in the second column and the border of the first column.

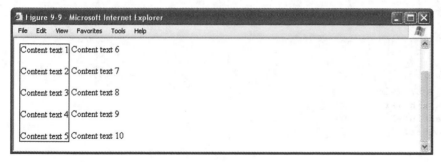

FIGURE 9-9

The three-pixel jog can be corrected by applying either a width or height (other than auto) to the element that follows the float.

```
<!--[if lte IE 6]>
<style type="text/css">
    p {
        height: 1px;
    }
</style>
<![endif]-->
```

You must use conditional comments or the hacks I showed you earlier to target IE 6 only. Because IE 6 and earlier versions have incorrect support for the height property, the content isn't adversely affected by including this declaration. Other browsers won't be so forgiving, however, so this solution must be applied only to Internet Explorer to avoid complications.

In most cases, it is best to not worry about this bug, though, other than you, no one is looking at your site in more than one browser side-by-side, so it is unlikely that such a minor issue will be noticed.

The Double-Margin Bug

Here's yet another Internet Explorer rendering bug involving floated elements. Under certain circumstances left margins on floated elements are doubled.

Three ingredients are required to reproduce this bug:

➤ A containing element

➤ A floated element inside the containing element

➤ A left margin specified on the floated element

The following code demonstrates the problem.

Available for download on Wrox.com

```
<!DOCTYPE html PUBLIC "-//W3C//DTD HTML 4.01//EN"
    "http://www.w3.org/TR/html4/strict.dtd">
<html lang="en">
<head>
    <meta http-equiv="Content-Type" content="text/html; charset=utf-8">
    <title>Figure 9-10</title>
```

```
    <style type="text/css">
        #container {
            border: 1px solid #000;
            float: left;
        }
        .float {
            float: left;
            margin-left: 50px;
            padding-left: 50px;
            border: 1px solid #000;
        }
    </style>
</head>
<body>

<h1>Double-Margin</h1>

<div id="container">
    <div class="float">
        <p>Content text 1</p>
        <p>Content text 2</p>
        <p>Content text 3</p>
        <p>Content text 4</p>
        <p>Content text 5</p>
    </div>
</div>

</body>
</html>
```

code snippet /chapter9/figure_9-10.html

This CSS and markup results in the output you see in Figure 9-10. As you can see, even though the padding between the inner element and its border should be the same as between it and the border of the outer element, the margin is actually double that of the padding.

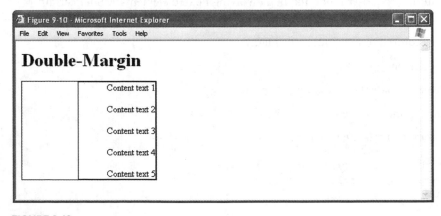

FIGURE 9-10

When these ingredients are present, the left margin of the floated element doubles. The fix for this bug is very simple. All you need to do is apply a `display: inline;` declaration to the floated element. If you recall from earlier in this chapter, all floated elements are always block elements. Using the `display: inline;` declaration tricks IE 6 into correct behavior. As is the case with the three-pixel jog, you can target IE 6 specifically by including this declaration within a rule inside of a style sheet that resides in conditional comments.

VERTICALLY ALIGNING CONTENT

The `vertical-align` property is used primarily in two contexts. In one context, it is used to vertically align text appearing within the lines of a paragraph. One example of this creates subscript or superscript text. The `vertical-align` property may also be used to align the content appearing inside a table cell. The following table outlines the `vertical-align` property and its possible values.

PROPERTY	VALUE
vertical-align	baseline | sub | super | top | text-top | middle | bottom | text-bottom | \<percentage> | \<length> Initial value: baseline

The `vertical-align` property applies exclusively to inline elements, such as `<img/>` and `<span>`. It has different meaning when applied to table cells. I discuss its use in cells in an upcoming section. In the next section, however, I look at how to format subscript text with the `vertical-align` property.

Subscript and Superscript Text

Within a paragraph, you may need several different types of styles that are only applied to snippets of the text, such as bold or italic fonts. Subscript text is an example of styles that often apply only to a selection of text, rather than to a whole paragraph. *Subscript text* is text that appears slightly smaller than the text surrounding it and slightly lower than the baseline of the surrounding text. The *baseline* is the invisible line created for each line of text against which the bottom of each letter is aligned. In other words, the baseline is the line that letters "sit" on. *Superscript text*, on the other hand, is text raised above the baseline and that appears slightly smaller than the surrounding text. The following code demonstrates subscript and superscript text.

Available for download on Wrox.com

```
<!DOCTYPE html PUBLIC "-//W3C//DTD HTML 4.01//EN"
    "http://www.w3.org/TR/html4/strict.dtd">
<html lang="en">
<head>
    <meta http-equiv="Content-Type" content="text/html; charset=utf-8">
    <title>Figure 9-11</title>
    <style type="text/css">
        h1 span {
            font-size: 0.5em;
        }

        .superscript {
```

```
            vertical-align: super;
        }

        .subscript {
            vertical-align: sub;
        }
    </style>
</head>
<body>

<h1><span class="superscript">Tasty</span> Recipes for <span class="subscript">
Tasty</span> Cheese</h1>

</body>
</html>
```

code snippet /chapter9/figure_9-11.html

This CSS and markup results in the output in Figure 9-11.

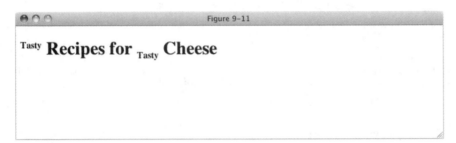

FIGURE 9-11

Figure 9-11 shows that the content of the <span> element with the class of superscript appears slightly higher, which is a result of applying the vertical-align: super; declaration. The figure also shows that the content of the <span> element with the class of subscript appears slightly lower, which is a result of applying the vertical-align: sub; declaration.

The next section continues the discussion of the vertical-align property with top, middle, and bottom vertical alignment text.

The top, middle, and bottom Keywords

The top, middle, and bottom keywords are used to control vertical alignment of selections of text that are slightly smaller than the surrounding text. The top keyword is demonstrated in the following snippet.

Available for
download on
Wrox.com

```
<!DOCTYPE html PUBLIC "-//W3C//DTD HTML 4.01//EN"
    "http://www.w3.org/TR/html4/strict.dtd">
<html lang="en">
<head>
    <meta http-equiv="Content-Type" content="text/html; charset=utf-8">
    <title>Figure 9-12</title>
```

```
<style type="text/css">
    h1 span {
        font-size: 0.5em;
    }

    .top {
        vertical-align: top;
    }

    .middle {
        vertical-align: middle;
    }

    .bottom {
        vertical-align: bottom;
    }
</style>
</head>
<body>

<h1><span class="top">Super</span> <span class="middle">Tasty</span> Recipes for
<span class="bottom">Tasty</span> Cheese</h1>

</body>
</html>
```

code snippet /chapter9/figure_9-12.html

This CSS and markup results in the output in Figure 9-12.

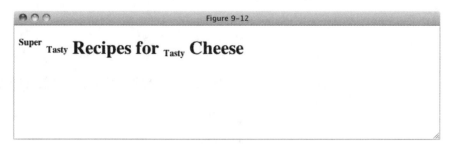

FIGURE 9-12

In Figure 9-12, you see that each <span> element is aligned to the top, middle, and bottom of the line box.

The text-top and text-bottom Keywords

Like the top, middle, and bottom values, the text-top and text-bottom keywords raise or lower a subset of text. The difference in the text-top keyword as opposed to the top keyword is that the text-top keyword causes alignment to happen with respect to the tallest character of the font of the surrounding text. Likewise, the text-bottom keyword aligns with respect to the lowest character, for instance the letters *p, y,* or *g,* which drop below the baseline. The `text-top` and `text-bottom` keyword values produce output similar to that produced by the `top` and `bottom` keywords. The most important difference between `top` and `text-top` is that `top` causes the top of the text to align with the top of the line containing that inline box, determined by the `line-height` (see chapter 6 for a recap), whereas `text-top` aligns with respect to the tallest character in the font. You can see this in the following code.

Available for download on Wrox.com

```
<!DOCTYPE html PUBLIC "-//W3C//DTD HTML 4.01//EN"
    "http://www.w3.org/TR/html4/strict.dtd">
<html lang="en">
<head>
    <meta http-equiv="Content-Type" content="text/html; charset=utf-8">
    <title>Figure 9-13</title>
    <style type="text/css">
        h1 span {
            font-size: 0.5em;
        }

        .text-top {
            vertical-align: top;
        }

        .text-bottom {
            vertical-align: bottom;
        }
    </style>
</head>
<body>

<h1><span class="text-top">Tasty</span> Recipes for <span class="text-bottom">
Tasty</span> Cheese</h1>

</body>
</html>
```

code snippet /chapter9/figure_9-13.html

This CSS and markup results in the output you see in Figure 9-13.

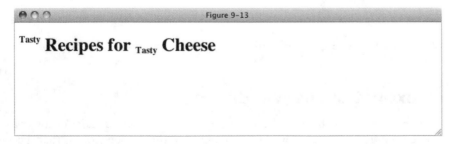

FIGURE 9-13

The next section discusses percentage and length values as applied to the `vertical-align` property.

Percentage and Length Value

If the selection of keywords I presented in the previous sections weren't enough for you, the `vertical-align` property also allows percentage and length values to be applied. The following code demonstrates this:

Available for download on Wrox.com

```html
<!DOCTYPE html PUBLIC "-//W3C//DTD HTML 4.01//EN"
    "http://www.w3.org/TR/html4/strict.dtd">
<html lang="en">
<head>
    <meta http-equiv="Content-Type" content="text/html; charset=utf-8">
    <title>Figure 9-14</title>
    <style type="text/css">
        h1 span {
            font-size: 0.5em;
            line-height: 10px;
        }

        .align-pixel {
            vertical-align: 5px;
        }

        .align-percent {
            vertical-align: 50%;
        }
    </style>
</head>
<body>

<h1><span class="align-pixel">Tasty</span> Recipes for <span class="align-percent">
Tasty</span> Cheese</h1>

</body>
</html>
```

code snippet /chapter9/figure_9-14.html

This CSS and markup results in the output in Figure 9-14.

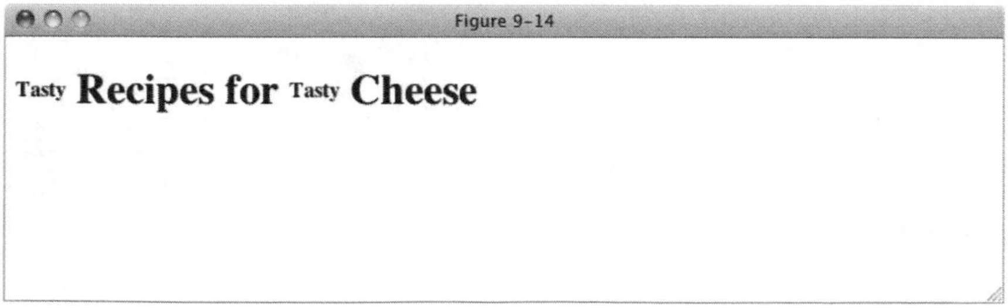

Figure 9-14

Tasty **Recipes for** Tasty **Cheese**

FIGURE 9-14

Giving the `vertical-align` property percentage or length values positioned text above the text base line by the value given. In the case of percentage values, the distance is based on the `line-height` of the positioned element. In Figure 9-14, the `line-height` of each element has been set to 10px, and the `vertical-align` value of the second span to 50%. 50% of 10px is 5px, so it will have the same offset as the first span.

Vertically Aligning the Contents of Table Cells

The `vertical-align` property has a completely different meaning when it is applied to table cells. When applied to table cells, only the `baseline`, `top`, `middle`, and `bottom` keywords are applicable, and the `vertical-align` property is used to align the entire contents of the cell. As these keywords behave in the same way as we have seen before, but with the context of the table cell rather than the bounding box determined by line-height, let's Try It Out!

TRY IT OUT   **Vertically Aligning Text in a Table**

Example 9-2

To see the `vertical-align` property in action, follow these steps.

1.   Enter the following markup:

```
<!DOCTYPE html PUBLIC "-//W3C//DTD HTML 4.01//EN"
    "http://www.w3.org/TR/html4/strict.dtd">
<html lang="en">
<head>
    <meta http-equiv="Content-Type" content="text/html; charset=utf-8">
    <title>Example 9-2</title>
    <style type="text/css">
        table {
            width: 200px;
            text-align: left;
        }

        th {
            vertical-align: bottom;
            border-bottom: 2px solid #666;
        }

        td {
            vertical-align: top;
            border-bottom: 1px solid #666;
        }
    </style>
</head>
<body>

<table>
    <caption>Ingredients</caption>
    <thead>
```

```
            <tr>
                <th>Ingredient</th>
                <th>Quantity of Ingredient</th>
            </tr>
        </thead>
        <tbody>
            <tr>
                <td>Bread</th>
                <td>2 medium thickness slices</td>
            </tr>
            <tr>
                <td>Butter</td>
                <td>Enough for 2 slices of bread</td>
            </tr>
            <tr>
                <td>Grated Cheddar</td>
                <td>1.5 handfuls</td>
            </tr>
            <tr>
                <td>Beer</td>
                <td>One splash</td>
            </tr>
            <tr>
                <td>Wholegrain mustard</td>
                <td>One dollop</td>
            </tr>
            <tr>
                <td>Pepper</td>
                <td>To taste</td>
            </tr>
        </tbody>
    </table>

    </body>
    </html>
```

2. Save the preceding CSS and markup as example_9-2.html. This example results in the output in Figure 9-15

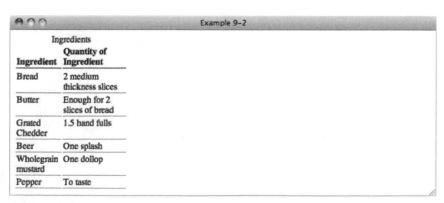

FIGURE 9-15

How It Works

In Example 9-2, you set the text in <th> elements to align to the bottom of the cell and the text in <td> elements to align to the top of the cell.

EXERCISES

1. When an element is floated, what rule governs its dimensions?

2. What happens when an inline element, such as a <span> element, is floated?

3. What are the three keywords of the float property?

4. If an element is floated to the right, and you don't want the following element to wrap around it, what declaration would you apply to that element?

5. What declarations would you use to create subscript and superscript text?

6. When vertically aligning an inline element to the middle, how is the element positioned on the line?

7. What is the difference between the text-top and top keywords of the vertical-align property?

8. If you are aligning table cells to the baseline, what determines the baseline?

▶ WHAT YOU LEARNED IN THIS CHAPTER

This chapter focused on three key areas of CSS design. In this chapter, you learned the following:

TOPIC	KEY CONCEPTS
float	The `float` property is a seemingly complex property that has a unique place in CSS design. The `float` property is used for layout — for instance, to include content in the flow of paragraph text in such a way that text wraps around the floated element.
clear	The `clear` property is used to control the effects of the `float` property in situations where you don't want all the content following a floated element to float beside it.
vertical-align	The `vertical-align` property is used to vertically align inline elements such as the `<span>` element or the `<img>` element relative to the line containing those inline elements; this property can be used, for instance, to create subscript or superscript text.
	The `vertical-align` property may also be applied to table cells to control vertical alignment of the content within table cells. If the `vertical-align` property is applied to table cells, only a subset of properties are applicable. These include the `baseline`, `top`, `middle`, and `bottom` properties. The behavior of these properties is completely different when applied to table cells as opposed to normal inline content.

10

Styling Lists

WHAT YOU WILL LEARN IN THIS CHAPTER:

➤   The markup for basic ordered and unordered lists

➤   The `list-style-type` property and how it's used to present different types of lists through a variety of marker styles for bulleted lists and numbered lists

➤   The `list-style-image` property and how it's used to provide a custom marker for each list item

➤   The `list-style-position` property and how it's used to control the positioning of list item markers

Lists are a very versatile group of elements in HTML, used for all sort of things, such as site and page navigation, tab controls, and simple lists of items such as for tasks or shopping basket contents.

LIST MARKUP

Lists consist of two parts. The first is the list container element, which is either `<ul>` for lists without any particular order or `<ol>` for lists that have a specific order to the items within it, and in which the order matters.

The second part of a list is one or more `<li>` elements, which contains each item. There must be at least one `<li>` in every list. There is no maximum number of items, but very long lists can be hard to read and are best broken up into sections.

The most common example of an unordered list in modern websites is site navigation. Navigation is a list of links, but while they will have a visual order, they don't usually have a fixed order that is integral to the content — they make sense in any order.

Available for
download on
Wrox.com

```
<ul>
    <li>Home</li>
    <li>About Us</li>
    <li>Products</li>
    <li>Contact Us</li>
</ul>
```

code snippet /chapter10/figure10-1.html

As Figure 10-1 shows, by default each item is preceded by a bullet.

FIGURE 10-1

An example of an ordered list is a recipe, in which each step must be followed in order.

Available for
download on
Wrox.com

```
<ol>
    <li>Lightly toast the bread. Place on a baking tray, and spread with
    butter.</li>
    <li>Add the grated Cheddar cheese and 2 tablespoons of beer to a saucepan.
    Place the saucepan over a medium heat, and stir the cheese continuously
    until it has melted. Add a teaspoon of wholegrain mustard and grind in
    a little pepper. Keep stirring.</li>
    <li>When thick and smooth, pour over each piece of toast spreading it to the
    edges to stop the toast from burning.</li>
    <li>Place under the grill for a couple of minutes or until golden brown.</li>
</ol>
```

code snippet /chapter10/figure10-2.html

As Figure 10.2 shows, by default each item is preceded by a number.

FIGURE 10-2

THE LIST-STYLE-TYPE PROPERTY

The `list-style-type` property changes the style of the bullet or format of the number that precedes each list item. You can change an ordered list to a list using Roman numerals for markers, or you can change a bulleted list to one using squares instead of circles for markers. The following table outlines the `list-style-type` property and its possible values (as of CSS 2.1).

PROPERTY	VALUE
list-style-type	disc | circle | square | decimal | decimal-leading-zero | lower-roman | upper-roman | lower-greek | lower-latin | upper-latin | armenian | georgian | none
	Initial value for unordered list: disc
	Initial value for unordered list: decimal

> **NOTE** It is possible to style an unordered list with styles that suggest an order (for example `list-style-type: decimal`); but I strongly advise against this, as the styling of an element should follow the semantics implied in the markup. If it looks like an ordered list, it should be an ordered list.

Styling Unordered Lists

There are four styles for unordered list bullets: `disc`, `circle`, `square`, and `none`. The default value is `disc`. All major browsers support these values.

The syntax for these unordered list types is shown in the following code, and the result of running this code is shown in Figure 10-3.

Available for download on Wrox.com

```
<!DOCTYPE html PUBLIC "-//W3C//DTD HTML 4.01//EN"
    "http://www.w3.org/TR/html4/strict.dtd">
<html lang="en">
<head>
    <meta http-equiv="Content-Type" content="text/html; charset=utf-8">
    <title>Figure 10-3</title>
    <style type="text/css">
        .demo-disc {
            list-style-type: disc;
        }

        .demo-circle {
            list-style-type: circle;
        }

        .demo-square {
```

```
            list-style-type: square;
        }

        .demo-none {
            list-style-type: none;
        }
    </style>
</head>
<body>

<h1>Unordered list bullet styles</h1>

<h2>Disc</h2>

<ul class="demo-disc">
    <li>Home</li>
    <li>About Us</li>
    <li>Products</li>
    <li>Contact Us</li>
</ul>

<h2>Circle</h2>

<ul class="demo-circle">
    <li>Home</li>
    <li>About Us</li>
    <li>Products</li>
    <li>Contact Us</li>
</ul>

<h2>Square</h2>

<ul class="demo-square">
    <li>Home</li>
    <li>About Us</li>
    <li>Products</li>
    <li>Contact Us</li>
</ul>

<h2>None</h2>

<ul class="demo-none">
    <li>Home</li>
    <li>About Us</li>
    <li>Products</li>
    <li>Contact Us</li>
</ul>

</body>
</html>
```

code snippet /chapter10/figure10-3.html

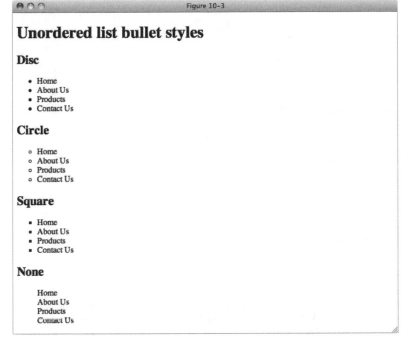

FIGURE 10-3

Styling Ordered Lists

The number that precedes list items in an ordered list can be formatted with the following keywords: decimal, decimal-leading-zero, lower-roman, upper-roman, lower-greek, lower-latin, upper-latin, Armenian, georgian, none. The default value is decimal.

Support for the full range of ordered list styles is not as complete as the styles for ordered lists:

➤ armenian is not supported by Safari, Firefox, or Opera for Mac OS X.

➤ decimal-leading-zero, lower-greek, lower-latin, upper-latin, armenian, and Georgian are not supported by IE6 or IE7.

This means that just like unordered lists, there are ultimately four keywords that can be reliably used across all major browsers: decimal, lower-roman, upper-roman, none.

The syntax for these ordered list types is shown in the following code, and the result of running this code is shown in Figure 10-4.

Available for download on Wrox.com

```
<!DOCTYPE html PUBLIC "-//W3C//DTD HTML 4.01//EN"
    "http://www.w3.org/TR/html4/strict.dtd">
<html lang="en">
<head>
    <meta http-equiv="Content-Type" content="text/html; charset=utf-8">
    <title>Figure 10-4</title>
    <style type="text/css">
        .demo-decimal {
```

```
            list-style-type: decimal;
        }

        .demo-lower-roman {
            list-style-type: lower-roman;
        }

        .demo-upper-roman {
            list-style-type: upper-roman;
        }

        .demo-none {
            list-style-type: none;
        }
    </style>
</head>
<body>

<h1>Ordered list number styles</h1>

<h2>Decimal</h2>

<ol class="demo-decimal">
    <li>Lightly toast the bread. Place on a baking tray, and spread with butter.</li>
    <li>Add the grated Cheddar cheese and 2 tablespoons of beer to a saucepan.
Place the saucepan over a medium heat, and stir the cheese continuously until it
has melted. Add a teaspoon of wholegrain mustard and grind in a little pepper. Keep
stirring.</li>
    <li>When thick and smooth, pour over each piece of toast spreading it to the
edges to stop the toast from burning.</li>
    <li>Place under the grill for a couple of minutes or until golden brown.</li>
</ol>

<h2>Lower Roman</h2>

<ol class="demo-lower-roman">
    <li>Lightly toast the bread. Place on a baking tray, and spread with butter.</li>
    <li>Add the grated Cheddar cheese and 2 tablespoons of beer to a saucepan.
Place the saucepan over a medium heat, and stir the cheese continuously until it
has melted. Add a teaspoon of wholegrain mustard and grind in a little pepper. Keep
stirring.</li>
    <li>When thick and smooth, pour over each piece of toast spreading it to the
edges to stop the toast from burning.</li>
    <li>Place under the grill for a couple of minutes or until golden brown.</li>
</ol>

<h2>Upper Roman</h2>

<ol class="demo-upper-roman">
    <li>Lightly toast the bread. Place on a baking tray, and spread with butter.</li>
    <li>Add the grated Cheddar cheese and 2 tablespoons of beer to a saucepan.
Place the saucepan over a medium heat, and stir the cheese continuously until it
has melted. Add a teaspoon of wholegrain mustard and grind in a little pepper. Keep
stirring.</li>
```

```
    <li>When thick and smooth, pour over each piece of toast spreading it to the
edges to stop the toast from burning.</li>
    <li>Place under the grill for a couple of minutes or until golden brown.</li>
</ol>

<h2>None</h2>

<ol class="demo-none">
    <li>Lightly toast the bread. Place on a baking tray, and spread with butter.</li>
    <li>Add the grated Cheddar cheese and 2 tablespoons of beer to a saucepan.
Place the saucepan over a medium heat, and stir the cheese continuously until it
has melted. Add a teaspoon of wholegrain mustard and grind in a little pepper. Keep
stirring.</li>
    <li>When thick and smooth, pour over each piece of toast spreading it to the
edges to stop the toast from burning.</li>
    <li>Place under the grill for a couple of minutes or until golden brown.</li>
</ol>

</body>
</html>
```

code snippet /chapter10/figure10-4.html

Ordered list number styles

Decimal

1. Lightly toast the bread. Place on a baking tray, and spread with butter.
2. Add the grated Cheddar cheese and 2 tablespoons of beer to a saucepan. Place the saucepan over a medium heat, and stir the cheese continuously until it has melted. Add a teaspoon of wholegrain mustard and grind in a little pepper. Keep stirring.
3. When thick and smooth, pour over each piece of toast spreading it to the edges to stop the toast from burning.
4. Place under the grill for a couple of minutes or until golden brown.

Lower Roman

i. Lightly toast the bread. Place on a baking tray, and spread with butter.
ii. Add the grated Cheddar cheese and 2 tablespoons of beer to a saucepan. Place the saucepan over a medium heat, and stir the cheese continuously until it has melted. Add a teaspoon of wholegrain mustard and grind in a little pepper. Keep stirring.
iii. When thick and smooth, pour over each piece of toast spreading it to the edges to stop the toast from burning.
iv. Place under the grill for a couple of minutes or until golden brown.

Upper Roman

I. Lightly toast the bread. Place on a baking tray, and spread with butter.
II. Add the grated Cheddar cheese and 2 tablespoons of beer to a saucepan. Place the saucepan over a medium heat, and stir the cheese continuously until it has melted. Add a teaspoon of wholegrain mustard and grind in a little pepper. Keep stirring.
III. When thick and smooth, pour over each piece of toast spreading it to the edges to stop the toast from burning.
IV. Place under the grill for a couple of minutes or until golden brown.

None

Lightly toast the bread. Place on a baking tray, and spread with butter.
Add the grated Cheddar cheese and 2 tablespoons of beer to a saucepan. Place the saucepan over a medium heat, and stir the cheese continuously until it has melted. Add a teaspoon of wholegrain mustard and grind in a little pepper. Keep stirring.
When thick and smooth, pour over each piece of toast spreading it to the edges to stop the toast from burning.
Place under the grill for a couple of minutes or until golden brown.

FIGURE 10-4

Now we'll put this together in a more practical Try It Out example, changing the `list-style-type` property to create a site navigation.

TRY IT OUT **Change the Marker Style of a List**

Example 10-1

To apply the `list-style-type` property, follow these steps.

1. Enter the following markup into your text editor:

```
<!DOCTYPE html PUBLIC "-//W3C//DTD HTML 4.01//EN"
    "http://www.w3.org/TR/html4/strict.dtd">
<html lang="en">
<head>
    <meta http-equiv="Content-Type" content="text/html; charset=utf-8">
    <title>Example 10-1</title>
    <style type="text/css">
        body {
            width: 600px;
            margin: 1em auto;
            padding-top: 3em;
        }

        #header-wrapper {
            position: fixed;
            top: 0;
            left: 0;
            width: 100%;
            padding-bottom: 0.5em;
            background: #FFF;
        }

        #header {
            width: 600px;
            margin: 0 auto;
        }

        h1 {
            float: left;
            margin-top: 0.2em;
        }

        .navigation {
            float: right;
        }

        .navigation li {
            display: inline;
        }

        .navigation a {
            margin-left: 0.5em;
```

```
            padding: 0.5em;
            border: 1px solid #CCC;
        }

        .recipe ol {
            list-style-type: upper-roman;
        }

        .recipe ol ol {
            list-style-type: lower-roman;
        }
    </style>
</head>
<body>

<div id="header-wrapper">

    <div id="header">

        <h1>Recipes for Cheese</h1>

        <ul class="navigation">
            <li><a href="#">Home</a></li>
            <li><a href="#">Recipes</a></li>
            <li><a href="#">Suggestions</a></li>
        </ul>

    </div>

</div>

<p class="intro">Cheese is a remarkably versatile food, available in literally
hundreds of varieties with different flavors and textures.</p>

<div class="recipe">

    <h2>Welsh Rarebit</h2>

    <p class="intro">Welsh Rarebit is a savory dish made from melted cheese, often
Cheddar, on toasted bread, and a variety of other ingredients such as mustard, egg, or
bacon. Here is one take on this classic.</p>

    <ol>
       <li>
            Lightly toast the bread:
            <ol>
                <li>Turn grill to medium heat.</li>
                <li>Place bread under the grill.</li>
                <li>When golden brown, remove the toasted bread from the grill.</li>
            </ol>
       </li>
       <li>Place on a baking tray, and spread with butter.</li>
       <li>Add the grated Cheddar cheese and 2 tablespoons of beer to a saucepan.
Place the saucepan over a medium heat, and stir the cheese continuously until it
```

```
has melted. Add a teaspoon of wholegrain mustard and grind in a little pepper. Keep
stirring.</li>
        <li>When thick and smooth, pour over each piece of toast spreading it to the
edges to stop the toast from burning.</li>
        <li>Place under the grill for a couple of minutes or until golden brown.</li>
    </ol>

</div>

</body>
</html>
```

2. Save the preceding CSS and markup as `example_10-1.html`. This example results in the rendered output in Figure 10-5.

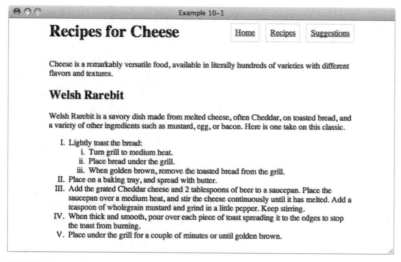

FIGURE 10-5

How It Works

Example 10-1 shows two uses of the `list-style-type` property: The first shows that you can suppress the default bullet display so you can use unordered lists for site navigation, and the second shows that you can set a different format of the number that precedes the ordered list and that a child list can have a format different from that of its parent.

THE LIST-STYLE-IMAGE PROPERTY

As with the `list-style-type` property, you can use the `list-style-image` property to change the marker used for list items. The following table outlines the `list-style-image` property and its possible values.

PROPERTY	VALUE
list-style-image	\<uri\> | none
	Initial value: none

The `list-style-image` property is quite straightforward; it accepts the URLof the image, which is denoted in the preceding table by the `<uri>` notation.

The syntax for using images as list markers is shown in the following code, and the result of running this code is shown in Figure 10-6.

Available for download on Wrox.com

```
<!DOCTYPE html PUBLIC "-//W3C//DTD HTML 4.01//EN"
    "http://www.w3.org/TR/html4/strict.dtd">
<html lang="en">
<head>
    <meta http-equiv="Content-Type" content="text/html; charset=utf-8">
    <title>Figure 10-6</title>
    <style type="text/css">
        li {
                list-style-image: url(arrow.png);
        }

        .alternate {
                list-style-image: url(arrow2.png);
        }
    </style>
</head>
<body>

<h1>List Style Image</h1>

<ul>
    <li>List markers can be customized!</li>
    <li>You can use any image you like.</li>
    <li class="alternate">Size and position, however, cannot be controlled.</li>
</ul>

</body>
</html>
```

code snippet /chapter10/figure10-6.html

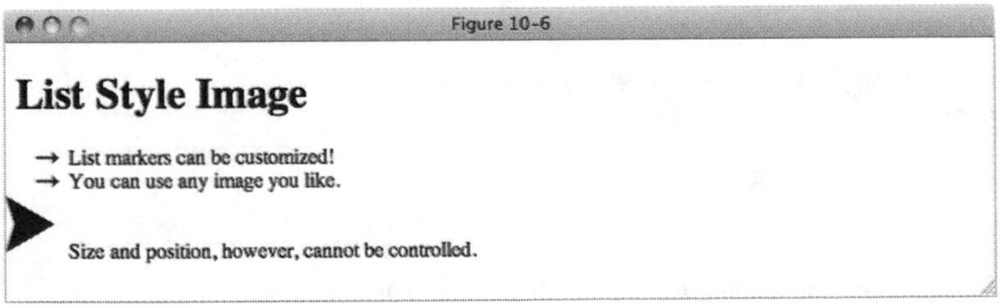

List Style Image

→ List markers can be customized!
→ You can use any image you like.

▶ Size and position, however, cannot be controlled.

FIGURE 10-6

As you can see in Figure 10-6, the `arrow.png` and `arrow2.png` icons have replaced the list bullets.

THE LIST-STYLE-POSITION PROPERTY

You can use the `list-style-position` property to control the placement of list item markers and whether the list item marker appears on the inside of the list item element or outside of it. Where the list marker is placed is only obvious when the `<li>` element has a border. The following table outlines the `list-style-position` property and its possible values.

PROPERTY	VALUE
list-style-position	inside	outside Initial value: outside

You can highlight the effects of the `list-style-position` property.

The syntax for positioning list markers is shown in the following code, and the result of running this code is shown in Figure 10-7.

Available for download on Wrox.com

```
<!DOCTYPE html PUBLIC "-//W3C//DTD HTML 4.01//EN"
    "http://www.w3.org/TR/html4/strict.dtd">
<html lang="en">
<head>
    <meta http-equiv="Content-Type" content="text/html; charset=utf-8">
    <title>Figure 10-7</title>
    <style type="text/css">
        li li {
            background: #CCF;
        }

        .inside {
            list-style-position: inside;
        }

        .outside {
            list-style-position: outside;
        }
    </style>
</head>
<body>

<h1>List Style Position</h1>

<ul>
    <li>The markers for these list items are on the inside.
        <ul class="inside">
            <li>One</li>
            <li>Two</li>
        </ul>
    </li>
    <li>The markers for these list items are on the outside.
        <ul class="outside">
```

```
                <li>One</li>
                <li>Two</li>
            </ul>
        </li>
    </ul>

    </body>
    </html>
```

code snippet /chapter10/figure10-7.html

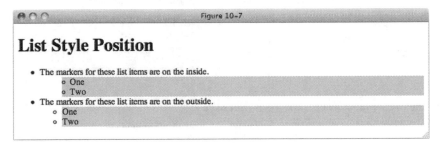

FIGURE 10-7

In Figure 10-7, you can see that the list-style-position property is used to control whether the list marker appears on the inside of the <li> element's borders or on the outside.

The next section wraps up the discussion of CSS list properties with the list-style shorthand property. Using this property, you can combine several properties into one.

THE LIST-STYLE SHORTHAND PROPERTY

Like the shorthand properties I presented in previous chapters, the list-style shorthand property allows multiple properties to be combined into one property. The following table outlines the list-style shorthand property and the values it allows.

PROPERTY	VALUE
list-style	<'list-style-type'> || <'list-style-position'> || <'list-style-image'> Initial value: n/a

The list-style property enables you to specify from one to three values, with each value corresponding to the list style properties I have discussed throughout this chapter: list-style-type, list-style-image, and list-style-position.

The following Try It Out shows you how the list-style property works.

Example 10-2.

To try out the list-style property, follow these steps.

1. Enter the following markup into your text editor:

```
<!DOCTYPE html PUBLIC "-//W3C//DTD HTML 4.01//EN"
    "http://www.w3.org/TR/html4/strict.dtd">
<html lang="en">
<head>
    <meta http-equiv="Content-Type" content="text/html; charset=utf-8">
    <title>Example 10-2</title>
    <style type="text/css">
        li {
            background: #CCF;
        }

        .arrow {
            list-style: square url(arrow.png) outside;
        }

        .arrow-inside {
            list-style: url(arrow.png) inside;
        }

        .marker-inside {
            list-style: square inside;
        }

        .marker-image {
            list-style: square url(arrow.png);
        }

        .arrow-only {
            list-style: url(arrow.png);
        }

        .marker {
            list-style: circle;
        }

        .position {
            list-style: inside;
        }
    </style>
</head>
<body>

<ul>
    <li class="arrow">All three styles can be provided.</li>
    <li class="arrow-inside">The image and the position.</li>
    <li class="marker-inside">The marker and the position.</li>
```

```
        <li class="marker-image">The marker and the image.</li>
        <li class="arrow-only">Just the image.</li>
        <li class="marker">Just the marker.</li>
        <li class="position">Just the position.</li>
    </ul>

    </body>
    </html>
```

2. Save the preceding CSS and markup as `example_10-2.html`. This example results in the rendered output in Figure 10-8.

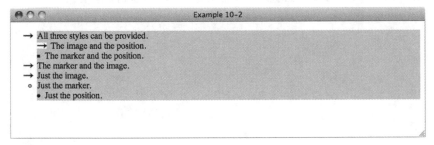

FIGURE 10-8

How It Works

The `list-style` property exists as a shortcut for specifying list styles. It can still be useful to use `list-style-type`, `list-style-image`, and `list-style-position` properties, as sometimes you just want to change one property at a time. In other cases, however, you will want to change all three and can use the list-style short hand.

In Example 10-2, you recapped what's possible with the `list-style` property by writing out an example that implements every possible combination of the `list-style-type`, `list-style-image`, and `list-style-position` properties.

EXERCISES

1. Name the keywords of the `list-style-type` property supported by all major browsers.

2. What properties does the `list-style` property allow you to specify in a single declaration?

3. Can size and position be controlled with the `list-style-image` property? If so, how?

► **WHAT YOU LEARNED IN THIS CHAPTER**

The CSS list properties provide complete control over how list elements are presented. To recap, in this chapter you learned the following:

TOPIC	KEY CONCEPTS
List types	There are two types of lists: ordered and unordered.
`list-style-type`	This property is used the most; it is for changing the marker displayed before each item.
`list-style`	This property can be used as a short hand for all three of the list properties.

11

Positioning

WHAT YOU WILL LEARN IN THIS CHAPTER:

➤ The `position` property and the four types of positioning that CSS has to offer: static, relative, absolute, and fixed

➤ The offset properties `top`, `right`, `bottom`, and `left`, and how these are used to deliver an element to a specific position in a web document

➤ The `z-index` property and how this property is used to layer the elements of a document

This chapter examines the various properties that CSS provides to position elements in a document. *Positioning* can be thought of as layering, in that the various elements of a page can be layered on top of others and given specific places to appear in the browser's window.

Like floating elements, positioning offers some unique characteristics that allow behavior you might not always expect. This chapter begins the discussion of positioning with none other than the `position` property.

INTRODUCTION TO POSITIONING

The `position` property is used to give elements different types of positioning. Positioning gives you the ability to dictate with precision where in a document you want an element to appear. You can choose whether an element appears relative to a container element, or relative to the browser window. You can layer elements one on top of another.

The following table outlines the `position` property and its values, and the four offset properties, `top`, `right`, `bottom`, and `left`, and their possible values.

PROPERTY	VALUE
position	static | relative | absolute | fixed Initial value: static
top	\<length> | \<percentage> | auto Initial value: auto
right	\<length> | \<percentage> | auto Initial value: auto
bottom	\<length> | \<percentage> | auto Initial value: auto
left	\<length> | \<percentage> | auto Initial value: auto

In the next section, I begin the discussion of positioning with absolute positioning.

Absolute Positioning

Absolute positioning allows you to render an element to a particular place in a document. The best way to grasp this concept is to see a demonstration of it in action, as shown in the following code:

Available for
download on
Wrox.com

```
<!DOCTYPE html PUBLIC "-//W3C//DTD HTML 4.01//EN"
    "http://www.w3.org/TR/html4/strict.dtd">
<html lang="en">
<head>
    <meta http-equiv="Content-Type" content="text/html; charset=utf-8">
    <title>Figure 11-1</title>
    <style type="text/css">
        body {
            width: 600px;
            margin: 1em auto;
        }

        h1 {
            float: left;
            margin-top: 0.2em;
        }

        .navigation {
            float: right;
        }

        .navigation li {
            display: inline;
```

```
        }

        .navigation a {
            margin-left: 0.5em;
            padding: 0.5em;
            border: 1px solid #CCC;
        }

        .navigation ul a {
            display: block;
        }
    </style>
</head>
<body>

<h1>Recipes for Cheese</h1>

<ul class="navigation">
    <li><a href="#">Home</a></li>
    <li>
        <a href="#">Recipes</a>
        <ul>
            <li><a href="#">Snacks</a></li>
            <li><a href="#">Meals</a></li>
            <li><a href="#">Desserts</a></li>
        </ul>
    </li>
    <li><a href="#">Suggestions</a></li>
</ul>

</body>
</html>
```

code snippet /chapter11/figure_11-1.html

The result is shown in Figure 11-1.

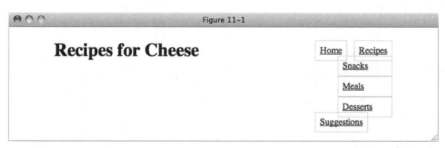

FIGURE 11-1

In the code for Figure 11-1, you can see that I have added a sub-list to the navigation that you first saw in Chapter 9. The rule with selector `.navigation ul a` applies `display: block;` to the links inside the sub-list, so that they appear vertically. The sub-list has the default static position and has broken our layout, but this is a great example of where absolute positioning is useful. Let's add a little more CSS:

Available for download on Wrox.com

```html
<!DOCTYPE html PUBLIC "-//W3C//DTD HTML 4.01//EN"
    "http://www.w3.org/TR/html4/strict.dtd">
<html lang="en">
<head>
    <meta http-equiv="Content-Type" content="text/html; charset=utf-8">
    <title>Figure 11-2</title>
    <style type="text/css">
        body {
            width: 600px;
            margin: 1em auto;
        }

        h1 {
            float: left;
            margin-top: 0.2em;
        }

        .navigation {
            float: right;
        }

        .navigation li {
            display: inline;
        }

        .navigation a {
            margin-left: 0.5em;
            padding: 0.5em;
            border: 1px solid #CCC;
        }

        .navigation ul {
            position: absolute;
            top: 20px;
            left: 40px;
        }

        .navigation ul a {
            display: block;
        }
    </style>
</head>
<body>

<h1>Recipes for Cheese</h1>

<ul class="navigation">
    <li><a href="#">Home</a></li>
    <li>
        <a href="#">Recipes</a>
        <ul>
```

```
            <li><a href="#">Snacks</a></li>
            <li><a href="#">Meals</a></li>
            <li><a href="#">Desserts</a></li>
        </ul>
    </li>
    <li><a href="#">Suggestions</a></li>
</ul>

</body>
</html>
```

code snippet /chapter11/figure_11-2.html

In Figure 11-2, you see what the document looks like when I add `position: absolute;`, `top: 20px;`, and `left: 40px;` to the sub-list.

FIGURE 11-2

A number of things have happened here.

1. The list has been taken out of the document flow (that is, it no longer takes up space in the document or influences the positioning of other elements).

2. It has been positioned 20px from the top and 40px from the left of the top left-hand corner of the viewport. By default, all absolutely positioned elements are positioned relative to the viewport.

3. It has been given a position on the z-axis; in other words, it appears above other elements, in this case the `h1`. I'll cover this in more detail later in the chapter.

`bottom` and `right` work in the same way; however in their case, the bottom edge of the positioned element is positioned relative to the bottom of the viewport and the right-hand edge to the right of the viewport, as you can see in Figure 11-3.

FIGURE 11-3

It is important to note that the list is positioned relative to the viewport as it appears when you first load the page — it will scroll with the rest of the content, as you can see in Figure 11-4, in which more content has been added.

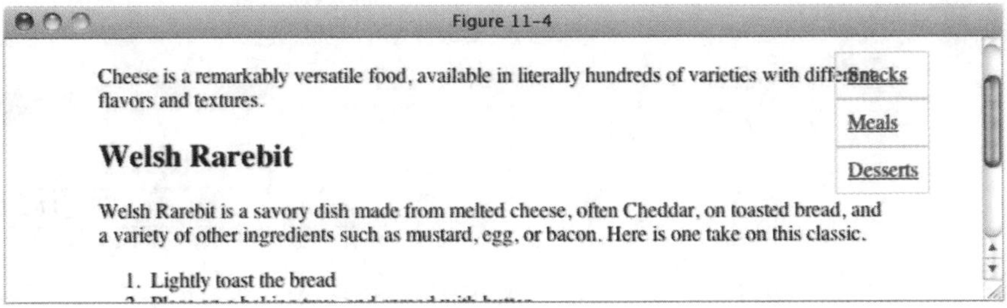

FIGURE 11-4

In Figure 11-4, you can see that when you scroll down, the boxes stay where they were initially positioned when the page was loaded up.

You can modify what element is used as the point of reference for absolutely positioned elements. The rules are pretty simple: If an absolutely positioned element is contained within another element that has a position other than static, then that element is used as the point of reference for positioned elements. One common way to change the point of reference for positioned elements is to give the containing element a "relative" position, and that is the topic of the next section.

Relative Positioning

Relative positioning is very similar to the default static positioning; elements to which relative positioning is applied do not leave the document flow. There are three differences between relative positioning and static positioning:

1. Elements with a relative position can be used as a point of reference for elements nested within them that are absolutely positioned.

2. The position of a relatively positioned element can be adjusted using the offset properties.

3. A relatively positioned element can have a position on the z-axis.

To observe how a relatively positioned element can be used as a point of reference for absolutely positioned descendant elements, I'll continue in the following Try It Out with the navigation example. In the navigation example, you don't want the sub-list positioned relative to the viewport, but instead relative to the list element that it is a child of. I'll demonstrate how a relatively positioned element can be used as a point of reference for absolutely positioned descendant elements in the following Try It Out.

TRY IT OUT   **Positioning Sub-Navigation**

Example 11-1

To position the sub-navigation list using `position: absolute;` and `position: relative;`, follow these steps.

1.   Enter the following markup:

```
<!DOCTYPE html PUBLIC "-//W3C//DTD HTML 4.01//EN"
    "http://www.w3.org/TR/html4/strict.dtd">
<html lang="en">
<head>
    <meta http-equiv="Content-Type" content="text/html; charset=utf-8">
    <title>Example 11-1</title>
    <style type="text/css">
        body {
            width: 600px;
            margin: 1em auto;
        }

        h1 {
            float: left;
            margin-top: 0.2em;
        }

        .navigation {
            float: right;
        }

        .navigation li {
            position: relative;
            display: inline;
        }

        .navigation a {
            margin-left: 0.5em;
            padding: 0.5em;
            border: 1px solid #CCC;
        }

        .navigation ul {
            position: absolute;
            top: 2em;
            left: 0;
            width: 8em;
            padding: 0;
        }

        .navigation ul a {
            display: block;
        }
    </style>
</head>
<body>

<h1>Recipes for Cheese</h1>

<ul class="navigation">
```

```
      <li><a href="#">Home</a></li>
      <li>
          <a href="#">Recipes</a>
          <ul>
              <li><a href="#">Snacks</a></li>
              <li><a href="#">Meals</a></li>
              <li><a href="#">Desserts</a></li>
          </ul>
      </li>
      <li><a href="#">Suggestions</a></li>
  </ul>

  </body>
  </html>
```

2. Save the preceding CSS and markup as `example_11-1.html`. This example results in the output in Figure 11-5.

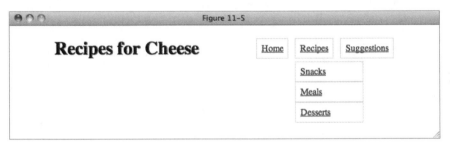

FIGURE 11-5

How It Works

In Figure 11-5, you can see that with the addition of a `position: relative;` declaration to the `li` elements in the navigation list, the sub-navigation list is now positioned relative to its container `li` instead of the viewport. `top: 2em;` shifts it from the top of the container `li` to just below it and `left: 0;` positions it to the left hand edge. You will note that other than providing a point of reference for the absolutely positioned element that `position: relative;` has had no effect on any of the `li` elements.

> **NOTE** When no position is defined for any of an element's ancestors, all elements are positioned relative to the browser's viewport by default. If an element does have a relative, absolute, or fixed position and is the ancestor of an element with absolute positioning, that element is used as the point of reference for the absolutely positioned element.

Applying Offset Positioning to Relatively Positioned Elements

The position of elements with relative positioning can be adjusted using combinations of the four offset properties, top, right, bottom, and left. For example, the top and left properties can be used to adjust the position of a relatively positioned element. This works similarly to the margin property that you saw in Chapter 8 with one important difference — the space reserved by the element is not changed or moved within the document. This will be made clearer with the following example:

Available for
download on
Wrox.com

```html
<!DOCTYPE html PUBLIC "-//W3C//DTD HTML 4.01//EN"
    "http://www.w3.org/TR/html4/strict.dtd">
<html lang="en">
<head>
    <meta http-equiv="Content-Type" content="text/html; charset=utf-8">
    <title>Figure 11-6</title>
    <style type="text/css">
        body {
            width: 600px;
            margin: 1em auto;
        }

        h1 {
            float: left;
            margin-top: 0.2em;
        }

        .navigation {
            float: right;
        }

        .navigation li {
            display: inline;
        }

        .navigation a {
            margin-left: 0.5em;
            padding: 0.5em;
            border: 1px solid #CCC;
        }

        .intro {
            clear: both;
        }

        .recipe {
            border: 1px solid #CCC;
        }

        .recipe h2 {
            position: relative;
            top: 75px;
            left: -50px;
        }
```

```
        </style>
</head>
<body>

<h1>Recipes for Cheese</h1>

<ul class="navigation">
    <li><a href="#">Home</a></li>
    <li><a href="#">Recipes</a></li>
    <li><a href="#">Suggestions</a></li>
</ul>

<p class="intro">Cheese is a remarkably versatile food, available in literally
hundreds of varieties with different flavors and textures.</p>

<div class="recipe">

    <h2>Welsh Rarebit</h2>

    <p class="intro">Welsh Rarebit is a savory dish made from melted cheese, often
    Cheddar, on toasted bread, and a variety of other ingredients such as mustard,
    egg, or bacon. Here is one take on this classic.</p>

    <ol>
        <li>Lightly toast the bread</li>
        <li>Place on a baking tray, and spread with butter.</li>
        <li>Add the grated Cheddar cheese and 2 tablespoons of beer to a saucepan.
        Place the saucepan over a medium heat, and stir the cheese continuously
        until it has melted. Add a teaspoon of wholegrain mustard and grind in
        a little pepper. Keep stirring.</li>
        <li>When thick and smooth, pour over each piece of toast spreading it to
        the edges to stop the toast from burning.</li>
        <li>Place under the grill for a couple of minutes or until golden
        brown.</li>
    </ol>

</div>

</body>
</html>
```

code snippet /chapter11/figure_11-6.html

In Figure 11-6, you see what happens when the offset properties top and left are applied to a relatively positioned h2 element. Just as with absolute positioning the relatively positioned element appears above statically positioned content, but the top: 75px; and left: -50px; declarations move the h2 relative to its original starting position, and the space that it would normally take up in the document still remains.

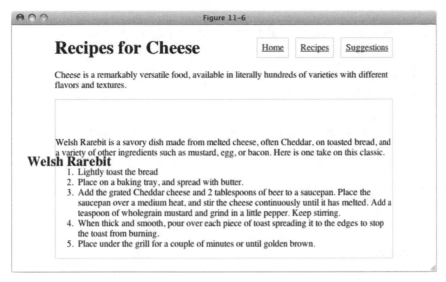

FIGURE 11-6

A recap of relative positioning:

➤ Relative positioning is just like static positioning, in that the elements remain in the normal document flow, but that's where the similarities end.

➤ Relatively positioned elements can be used as a point of reference for absolutely positioned elements.

➤ Relatively positioned elements can accept combinations of the four offset properties, `top` and `left`, `top` and `right`, `bottom` and `left`, and `bottom` and `right`. The browser will ignore combinations of the offset properties beyond those mentioned here. For example, you can't combine the `top` and `bottom` offset properties on the same relatively positioned element.

➤ Relatively positioned content can be stacked and layered along the z-axis (more on this later in this chapter).

In the next section, I continue the concept of positioning with fixed positioning, which is similar to absolute positioning, in that the element leaves the normal flow of the document, but unlike absolute positioning, the context of a fixed positioned element cannot be altered by nesting the element in a relatively positioned element or another absolutely positioned element. Fixed position elements are always positioned relative to the browser's viewport, and remain in that position, even if the document is scrolled.

Fixed Positioning

Fixed positioning is used to make an element remain in the same fixed position, even if the document is being scrolled. Alas, IE 6 does not support fixed positioning, so the examples that follow will not work in IE 6. My advice is to accept this limitation and not utilize fixed position content in IE 6; however, Appendix B has links to resources that will allow you to emulate its affect.

Elements with a fixed position are always positioned relative to the viewport, regardless of whether they are contained in an element with relative or absolute positioning applied. Here is an example of fixed positioning:

Available for download on Wrox.com

```
<!DOCTYPE html PUBLIC "-//W3C//DTD HTML 4.01//EN"
    "http://www.w3.org/TR/html4/strict.dtd">
<html lang="en">
<head>
    <meta http-equiv="Content-Type" content="text/html; charset=utf-8">
    <title>Figure 11-7</title>
    <style type="text/css">
        body {
            width: 600px;
            margin: 1em auto;
        }

        #header {
            position: fixed;
            width: 600px;
            margin: 0 auto;
        }

        h1 {
            float: left;
            margin-top: 0.2em;
        }

        .navigation {
            float: right;
        }

        .navigation li {
            display: inline;
        }

        .navigation a {
            margin-left: 0.5em;
            padding: 0.5em;
            border: 1px solid #CCC;
        }
    </style>
</head>
<body>

<div id="header">

    <h1>Recipes for Cheese</h1>

    <ul class="navigation">
        <li><a href="#">Home</a></li>
        <li><a href="#">Recipes</a></li>
        <li><a href="#">Suggestions</a></li>
```

```
    </ul>

</div>

<p class="intro">Cheese is a remarkably versatile food, available in literally
hundreds of varieties with different flavors and textures.</p>

<div class="recipe">

    <h2>Welsh Rarebit</h2>

    <p class="intro">Welsh Rarebit is a savory dish made from melted cheese, often
    Cheddar, on toasted bread, and a variety of other ingredients such as mustard,
    egg, or bacon. Here is one take on this classic.</p>

    <ol>
        <li>Lightly toast the bread</li>
        <li>Place on a baking tray, and spread with butter.</li>
        <li>Add the grated Cheddar cheese and 2 tablespoons of beer to a saucepan.
        Place the saucepan over a medium heat, and stir the cheese continuously
        until it has melted. Add a teaspoon of wholegrain mustard and grind in
        a little pepper. Keep stirring.</li>
        <li>When thick and smooth, pour over each piece of toast spreading it to
        the edges to stop the toast from burning.</li>
        <li>Place under the grill for a couple of minutes or until golden
        brown.</li>
    </ol>

</div>

</body>
</html>
```

code snippet/chapter11/figure_11-7.html

In Figure 11-7, you can see how fixed position is similar to absolute positioning — both remove the positioned element from the normal document.

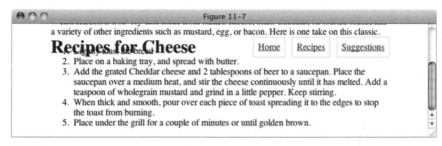

FIGURE 11-7

For this to be a useful technique, you will have to reserve space for the positioned content, which you'll do in the following exercise.

TRY IT OUT Using Fixed Positioning

Example 11-2

To position the page header so it remains in place even when the page scrolls, follow these steps.

1. Enter the following markup:

```
<!DOCTYPE html PUBLIC "-//W3C//DTD HTML 4.01//EN"
    "http://www.w3.org/TR/html4/strict.dtd">
<html lang="en">
<head>
    <meta http-equiv="Content-Type" content="text/html; charset=utf-8">
    <title>Example 11-2</title>
    <style type="text/css">
        body {
            width: 600px;
            margin: 1em auto;
            padding-top: 3em;
        }

        #header-wrapper {
            position: fixed;
            top: 0;
            left: 0;
            width: 100%;
            padding-bottom: 0.5em;
            background: #FFF;
        }

        #header {
            width: 600px;
            margin: 0 auto;
        }

        h1 {
            float: left;
            margin-top: 0.2em;
        }

        .navigation {
            float: right;
        }

        .navigation li {
            display: inline;
        }

        .navigation a {
            margin-left: 0.5em;
            padding: 0.5em;
            border: 1px solid #CCC;
        }
    </style>
```

```
</head>
<body>

<div id="header-wrapper">

    <div id="header">

        <h1>Recipes for Cheese</h1>

        <ul class="navigation">
            <li><a href="#">Home</a></li>
            <li><a href="#">Recipes</a></li>
            <li><a href="#">Suggestions</a></li>
        </ul>

    </div>

</div>

<p class="intro">Cheese is a remarkably versatile food, available in literally
hundreds of varieties with different flavors and textures.</p>

<div class="recipe">

    <h2>Welsh Rarebit</h2>

    <p class="intro">Welsh Rarebit is a savory dish made from melted cheese, often
    Cheddar, on toasted bread, and a variety of other ingredients such as mustard,
    egg, or bacon. Here is one take on this classic.</p>

    <ol>
        <li>Lightly toast the bread</li>
        <li>Place on a baking tray, and spread with butter.</li>
        <li>Add the grated Cheddar cheese and 2 tablespoons of beer to a saucepan.
        Place the saucepan over a medium heat, and stir the cheese continuously
        until it has melted. Add a teaspoon of wholegrain mustard and grind in
        a little pepper. Keep stirring.</li>
        <li>When thick and smooth, pour over each piece of toast spreading it to
        the edges to stop the toast from burning.</li>
        <li>Place under the grill for a couple of minutes or until golden
        brown.</li>
    </ol>

</div>

</body>
</html>
```

2. Save the preceding CSS and markup as `example_11-2.html`. This example results in the output in Figures 11-8 and 11-9.

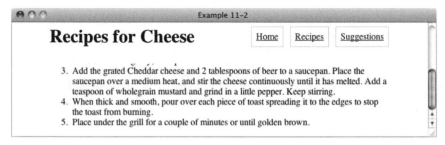

FIGURE 11-8

FIGURE 11-9

How It Works

In Figure 11-8 and Figure 11-9, you can see that with the addition of a `position: fixed;` declaration to the element with id `header-wrapper`, the page heading and navigation become fixed to the viewport.

`top: 0;` and `left: 0;` are applied to fix `header-wrapper` to the top left of the viewport, while `width: 100%;` and `background: #FFF;` ensure that it takes up the full width of the screen and has a solid white background to prevent other content showing through.

To reserve space in the document for the fixed content, padding is applied to the top of the `body` element with `padding-top: 3em;`. The amount of padding required is determined by the height of the content being positioned. It is best to be conservative and allow for a little more than you think. By using em units, you can be confident that if the text is resized that there will still be enough space reserved, and your fixed position element will not cover any content before the page is scrolled.

Finally, the element with the id of `header` is centered using `width: 600px;` and `margin: 0 auto;`.

As you can see in Figure 11-9, even when you scroll down the page, the content remains in place.

In the next section, I discuss how you can control layering of positioned elements with the `z-index` property.

THE Z-AXIS AND THE Z-INDEX PROPERTY

The z-index property is used to control layering of positioned elements along an invisible z-axis, which you might imagine as an invisible line coming out of the computer screen. The following table outlines the z-index property and its possible values.

PROPERTY	VALUE
z-index	auto | <integer>
	Initial value: auto

The z-index property controls elements' positions along the invisible z-axis, if those elements are positioned relative, absolute, or fixed. To explain how this works, I'll use the following markup with a few basic styles to make things clear:

Available for download on Wrox.com

```
<!DOCTYPE html PUBLIC "-//W3C//DTD HTML 4.01//EN"
    "http://www.w3.org/TR/html4/strict.dtd">
<html lang="en">
<head>
    <meta http-equiv="Content-Type" content="text/html; charset=utf-8">
    <title>Figure 11-10</title>
    <style type="text/css">
        div {
            width: 100px;
            height: 100px;
            border: 1px solid #000;
            font-size: 25px;
            text-align: center;
        }

        .z1 {
            background: #CC5;
        }

        .z2 {
            background: #CCF;
        }

        .z3 {
            width: 50px;
            height: 50px;
            background: #FCC;
        }

        .z4 {
            background: #5CC;
        }
    </style>
</head>
<body>
```

```
<div class="z1">1</div>

<div class="z2">
    2
    <div class="z3">
        3
    </div>
</div>

<div class="z4">4</div>

</body>
</html>
```

code snippet /chapter11/figure_11-10.html

This will look like Figure 11-10.

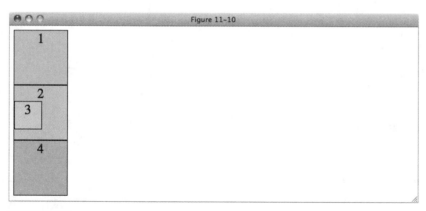

FIGURE 11-10

In Figure 11-10, the content is positioned much as you might expect. Each of the div elements is one after each other in order, with the nested div with class z3 inside the div with class z2. Now I'll add absolute positioning with the default z-index value of auto:

Available for download on Wrox.com

```
<!DOCTYPE html PUBLIC "-//W3C//DTD HTML 4.01//EN"
    "http://www.w3.org/TR/html4/strict.dtd">
<html lang="en">
<head>
    <meta http-equiv="Content-Type" content="text/html; charset=utf-8">
    <title>Figure 11-11</title>
    <style type="text/css">
        div {
            position: absolute;
            z-index: auto;
            width: 100px;
            height: 100px;
```

```
        border: 1px solid #000;
        font-size: 25px;
        text-align: center;
    }

    .z1 {
        top: 10px;
        left: 50px;
        background: #CC5;
    }

    .z2 {
        top: 70px;
        left: 120px;
        background: #CCF;
    }

    .z3 {
        top: -10px;
        left: -30px;
        width: 50px;
        height: 50px;
        background: #FCC;
    }

    .z4 {
        top: 90px;
        left: 30px;
        background: #5CC;
    }
    </style>
</head>
<body>

<div class="z1">1</div>

<div class="z2">
    2
    <div class="z3">
        3
    </div>
</div>

<div class="z4">4</div>

</body>
</html>
```

code snippet /chapter11/figure_11-11.html

In Figure 11-11, you can see that positioned elements with the default z-index value of auto are layered over each other in order, with the first element in the source order on the bottom and each subsequent positioned element, including nested positioned elements, appearing above the previous positioned element.

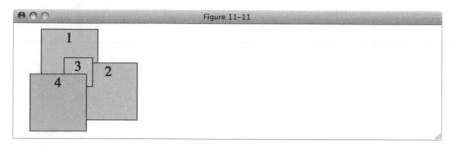

FIGURE 11-11

You can change this stacking order using an integer value for the z-index property:

Available for
download on
Wrox.com

```
<!DOCTYPE html PUBLIC "-//W3C//DTD HTML 4.01//EN"
    "http://www.w3.org/TR/html4/strict.dtd">
<html lang="en">
<head>
    <meta http-equiv="Content-Type" content="text/html; charset=utf-8">
    <title>Figure 11-12</title>
    <style type="text/css">
        div {
            position: absolute;
            z-index: auto;
            width: 100px;
            height: 100px;
            border: 1px solid #000;
            font-size: 25px;
            text-align: center;
        }

        .z1 {
            top: 10px;
            left: 50px;
            background: #CC5;
        }

        .z2 {
            top: 70px;
            left: 120px;
            background: #CCF;
        }

        .z3 {
            z-index: 1;
            top: -10px;
            left: -30px;
            width: 50px;
            height: 50px;
            background: #FCC;
        }

        .z4 {
```

```
            top: 90px;
            left: 30px;
            background: #5CC;
        }
    </style>
</head>
<body>

<div class="z1">1</div>

<div class="z2">
    2
    <div class="z3">
        3
    </div>
</div>

<div class="z4">4</div>

</body>
</html>
```

code snippet /chapter11/figure_11-12.html

The result is shown in Figure 11-12.

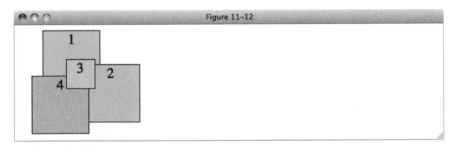

FIGURE 11-12

In Figure 11-12 I have added a z-index value of 1 to the div with class z3. This has had the effect of creating what is known as a stacking context, and positions the div above the other div elements with a value of auto. Only elements with an integer value z-index create stacking contexts, and to explain what that means in the next example, first I will apply an integer z-index to the fourth div:

Available for download on Wrox.com

```
<!DOCTYPE html PUBLIC "-//W3C//DTD HTML 4.01//EN"
    "http://www.w3.org/TR/html4/strict.dtd">
<html lang="en">
<head>
    <meta http-equiv="Content-Type" content="text/html; charset=utf-8">
    <title>Figure 11-13</title>
    <style type="text/css">
```

```
        div {
            position: absolute;
            z-index: auto;
            width: 100px;
            height: 100px;
            border: 1px solid #000;
            font-size: 25px;
            text-align: center;
        }

        .z1 {
            top: 10px;
            left: 50px;
            background: #CC5;
        }

        .z2 {
            top: 70px;
            left: 120px;
            background: #CCF;
        }

        .z3 {
            z-index: 1;
            top: -10px;
            left: -30px;
            width: 50px;
            height: 50px;
            background: #FCC;
        }

        .z4 {
            z-index: 3;
            top: 90px;
            left: 30px;
            background: #5CC;
        }
    </style>
</head>
<body>

<div class="z1">1</div>

<div class="z2">
    2
    <div class="z3">
        3
    </div>
</div>

<div class="z4">4</div>

</body>
</html>
```

As you might expect, the fourth div in Figure 11-13 is now above the second and third div elements, as it has a z-index value of 3 compared to their values of auto and 1, respectively.

FIGURE 11-13

Now I'm going to add z-index values to the remaining div elements: 1 to z1, and 2 to z2. I'll also increase the z-index of z3 to 4, one higher than the z-index of z4.

Available for
download on
Wrox.com

```
<!DOCTYPE html PUBLIC "-//W3C//DTD HTML 4.01//EN"
    "http://www.w3.org/TR/html4/strict.dtd">
<html lang="en">
<head>
    <meta http-equiv="Content-Type" content="text/html; charset=utf-8">
    <title>Figure 11-14</title>
    <style type="text/css">
        div {
            position: absolute;
            z-index: auto;
            width: 100px;
            height: 100px;
            border: 1px solid #000;
            font-size: 25px;
            text-align: center;
        }

        .z1 {
            z-index: 1;
            top: 10px;
            left: 50px;
            background: #CC5;
        }

        .z2 {
            z-index: 2;
            top: 70px;
            left: 120px;
            background: #CCF;
        }

        .z3 {
            z-index: 4;
            top: -10px;
            left: -30px;
```

```
                    width: 50px;
                    height: 50px;
                    background: #FCC;
            }

            .z4 {
                    z-index: 3;
                    top: 90px;
                    left: 30px;
                    background: #5CC;
            }
        </style>
    </head>
    <body>

    <div class="z1">1</div>

    <div class="z2">
        2
        <div class="z3">
            3
        </div>
    </div>

    <div class="z4">4</div>

    </body>
    </html>
```

code snippet /chapter11/figure_11-14.html

Figure 11-14 might not be what you expected! Although z1 and z2 are layered in the order specified by their z1 values, the fourth div is still positioned above the third div, even though it has a lower value.

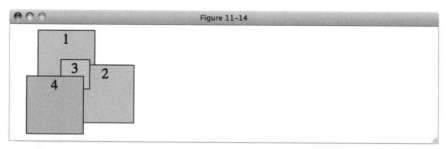

FIGURE 11-14

This is the stacking context in action. Because the div with class z2 is an absolutely positioned element with an integer z-index value, it creates a new stacking context. All elements within a stacking context are first layered according to the context, and then by their z-index value within the context. No elements within a stacking context will appear above the z-index of the element that created the context.

Within a static context, positioned elements behave as if elements outside of the context don't exist for stacking purposes, that is we can add another div element to the element with the class of z2 and specify the order of stacking with respect to the element with the class of z3, but not with any of the elements outside of z2:

Available for download on Wrox.com

```html
<!DOCTYPE html PUBLIC "-//W3C//DTD HTML 4.01//EN"
    "http://www.w3.org/TR/html4/strict.dtd">
<html lang="en">
<head>
    <meta http-equiv="Content-Type" content="text/html; charset=utf-8">
    <title>Figure 11-15</title>
    <style type="text/css">
        div {
            position: absolute;
            z-index: auto;
            width: 100px;
            height: 100px;
            border: 1px solid #000;
            font-size: 25px;
            text-align: center;
        }

        .z1 {
            z-index: 1;
            top: 10px;
            left: 50px;
            background: #CC5;
        }

        .z2 {
            z-index: 2;
            top: 70px;
            left: 120px;
            background: #CCF;
        }

        .z3 {
            z-index: 99;
            top: -10px;
            left: -30px;
            width: 50px;
            height: 50px;
            background: #FCC;
        }

        .z3b {
            z-index: 1;
            top: -30px;
```

```
            left: -65px;
            width: 50px;
            height: 50px;
            background: #FCC;
        }

        .z4 {
            z-index: 3;
            top: 90px;
            left: 30px;
            background: #5CC;
        }
    </style>
</head>
<body>

<div class="z1">1</div>

<div class="z2">
    2
    <div class="z3">
        3
    </div>
    <div class="z3b">
        3b
    </div>
</div>

<div class="z4">4</div>

</body>
</html>
```

code snippet /chapter11/figure_11-15.html

In Figure 11-15, you can see this in action. The new div element is positioned behind its sibling as it has a lower z-index value. The third div is still not positioned above the div with the class of z3, despite having a much higher z-index value of 99.

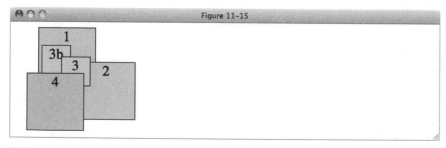

FIGURE 11-15

> **NOTE** *It is easy to get to the point where you have to specify very large z-index values if you don't carefully keep control — as each new element must be placed above another, values go from 10 or less, to hundreds and then thousands! It is best to rely on management of z-index values than just having a free-for-all over which content appears on top. If you are working with other people to develop a site, decide from the start what content needs to appear on top and determine values accordingly. Remember that elements inside a stacking context are isolated from the z-index values outside the context, so you can start back at 1.*
>
> *There is a good reason to keep z-index values below 100. Assistive technologies such as the speech recognition software Dragon NaturallySpeaking insert elements into the page which show the user the text that the software has recognized. These elements have a z-index of 100, so positioning content above this could interfere with your users' ability to browse your site.*

The IE 6/IE 7 z-index Bug

IE 6 and IE 7 support the z-index property but with a bug that was fixed for IE 8. Positioned elements with a z-index value of auto are given a z-index value anyway, starting at 0 and increasing by 1 for each positioned element in order. This means that every positioned element generates a stacking context, as you can see in Figure 11-16 when you look at the code I showed you for Figure 11-12 in IE 6:

Available for download on Wrox.com

```
<!DOCTYPE html PUBLIC "-//W3C//DTD HTML 4.01//EN"
    "http://www.w3.org/TR/html4/strict.dtd">
<html lang="en">
<head>
    <meta http-equiv="Content-Type" content="text/html; charset=utf-8">
    <title>Figure 11-16</title>
    <style type="text/css">
        div {
            position: absolute;
            z-index: auto;
            width: 100px;
            height: 100px;
            border: 1px solid #000;
            font-size: 25px;
            text-align: center;
        }

        .z1 {
            top: 10px;
            left: 50px;
            background: #CC5;
        }

        .z2 {
            top: 70px;
```

```
            left: 120px;
            background: #CCF;
        }

        .z3 {
            z-index: 1;
            top: -10px;
            left: -30px;
            width: 50px;
            height: 50px;
            background: #FCC;
        }

        .z4 {
            top: 90px;
            left: 30px;
            background: #5CC;
        }
    </style>
</head>
<body>

<div class="z1">1</div>

<div class="z2">
    2
    <div class="z3">
        3
    </div>
</div>

<div class="z4">4</div>

</body>
</html>
```

code snippet /chapter11/figure_11-16.html

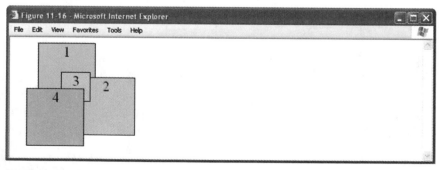

FIGURE 11-16

Even though only the div with the class of z3 has an integer z-index value, all of the positioned div elements have a stacking context in IE 6 and IE 7, so the third div is not stacked above the fourth as it would be in all other browsers, but within the stacking context of the second div.

Unfortunately, there is no solution to this problem, other than to be aware of the limitations that positioning has in these browsers. Most of the time when you nest positioned elements you will also want to take advantage of a new stacking context as well, so fortunately this is not as big an issue as it may seem.

EXERCISES

1. What is the default value of the top, right, bottom, and left properties?

2. What are offset properties used for?

3. If the <body> element has a sole child that is positioned absolutely, what point of reference is used for its positioning?

4. If the <body> element has a sole child that is positioned relatively, with an id name of *relative-element*, and that relatively positioned element has a child that is absolutely positioned, what point of reference is used for the absolutely positioned element?

5. If the element from Exercise 4, *relative-element,* has a fixed position child, what point of reference is used for its positioning?

6. You have five elements that are all absolutely positioned siblings, but no z-index is specified for any of them. In what order will they be stacked?

► WHAT YOU LEARNED IN THIS CHAPTER

In this chapter, you saw the power of positioning in web design. Positioning offers web designers solutions to challenges both simple and complex. In this chapter, you learned the following:

TOPIC	KEY CONCEPTS
Absolute positioning	Absolute positioned elements are positioned relative to the viewport, by default.
Relative positioning	Relative positioning allows you to change the point of reference used for absolute positioning. In addition, the four offset properties can be used on relatively positioned content to adjust its position with respect to its static origin.
Fixed positioning	Fixed position elements remain in the same place when a document is scrolled, and fixed position elements are always positioned relative to the viewport.
`z-index`	By default, elements are stacked in ascending order, but this layering can be controlled with the `z-index` property.

12

Styling Tables

WHAT YOU WILL LEARN IN THIS CHAPTER:

➤ The optional table elements that can make it easier to style a table and that make the structure more intuitive

➤ Controlling placement of the table caption

➤ Controlling the layout of the table

➤ Controlling the spacing between table cells

Tables are primarily a method to show the relationship between data, much as a spreadsheet application does. Tables can be complex creatures in HTML, but if used properly, they allow information to be presented in a neat, organized, and consistent manner.

OPTIONAL TABLE ELEMENTS

The `<table>` element has several optional elements that can be used to enhance the presentation and semantic value of a table, including captions, columns, headings, and footers. Take a look at a `<table>` element that makes use of all these optional elements. When I get into the discussion of styling tables, beginning with the section "Table Captions," you'll need to understand what is possible in a table. The following markup shows a table complete with all the required and optional elements.

Available for download on Wrox.com

```
<!DOCTYPE html PUBLIC "-//W3C//DTD HTML 4.01//EN"
    "http://www.w3.org/TR/html4/strict.dtd">
<html lang="en">
<head>
    <meta http-equiv="Content-Type" content="text/html; charset=utf-8">
    <title>Figure 12-1</title>
</head>
```

```html
<body>

<table>
    <caption>Ingredients</caption>
    <colgroup>
        <col class="ingredient">
        <col class="quantity">
    </colgroup>
    <thead>
        <tr>
            <th>Ingredient</th>
            <th>Quantity of Ingredient</th>
        </tr>
    </thead>
    <tfoot>
        <tr>
            <th>Ingredient</th>
            <th>Quantity of Ingredient</th>
        </tr>
    </tfoot>
    <tbody>
        <tr>
            <td>Bread</td>
            <td>2 medium thickness slices</td>
        </tr>
        <tr>
            <td>Butter</td>
            <td>Enough for 2 slices of bread</td>
        </tr>
        <tr>
            <td>Grated Cheddar</td>
            <td>1.5 handfuls</td>
        </tr>
        <tr>
            <td>Beer</td>
            <td>One splash</td>
        </tr>
        <tr>
            <td>Wholegrain mustard</td>
            <td>One dollop</td>
        </tr>
        <tr>
            <td>Pepper</td>
            <td>To taste</td>
        </tr>
    </tbody>
</table>

</body>
</html>
```

code snippet /chapter12/figure_12-1.html

Figure 12-1 shows what this table looks like with no additional styling.

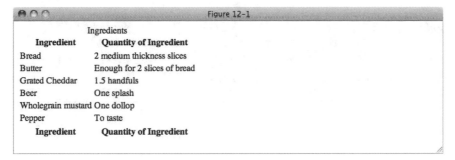

FIGURE 12-1

In the preceding markup, you can see that HTML tables support many additional, optional elements.

➤   The <caption> element is used to provide the table with a caption or the name of the table.

➤   The <colgroup> element is used to enclose each of the table <col> elements. <colgroup> elements are not displayed.

➤   <col> elements are used to control certain properties of each table column, the most common being the column width. <col> elements are not displayed and contain no content.

➤   The <thead> element encloses information about column headers. If you print a table that spans more than one page, the information in the <thead> element is repeated at the top of each page.

➤   The <tbody> element contains the main table data.

➤   The <tfoot> element is similar to the <thead> element, and is sometimes used to repeat column headers in long tables but may contain summary or footnote content. When you print a table that spans more than one page, the information in the <tfoot> element is repeated at the bottom of each page.

In the coming sections, you learn more about what properties CSS offers for tweaking the visual presentation of HTML tables.

TABLE CAPTIONS

Captions are presented in the <caption> element. By default, they are rendered above the table in the document. You use the caption-side property to control the placement of the table caption.

The following table shows the caption-side property and its values.

PROPERTY	VALUE
caption-side	top | bottom Initial value: top

> **NOTE** *Although IE 6 and IE 7 support the* <caption> *element for tables, neither IE 6 nor IE 7 supports the CSS* caption-side *property. The* <caption> *element is displayed but is always positioned above the table.*
>
> *All other browsers (including IE 8 and 9) have full support.*

Using the caption-side property, you can control whether the caption appears above or below the table. The following is a demonstration of the caption-side property positioning the caption at the bottom of the table.

Available for download on Wrox.com

```
<!DOCTYPE html PUBLIC "-//W3C//DTD HTML 4.01//EN"
    "http://www.w3.org/TR/html4/strict.dtd">
<html lang="en">
<head>
    <meta http-equiv="Content-Type" content="text/html; charset=utf-8">
    <title>Figure 12-2</title>
    <style type="text/css">
        table {
            caption-side: bottom;
        }
    </style>
</head>
<body>

<table>
    <caption>Ingredients</caption>
    <colgroup>
        <col class="ingredient">
        <col class="quantity">
    </colgroup>
    <thead>
        <tr>
            <th>Ingredient</th>
            <th>Quantity of Ingredient</th>
        </tr>
    </thead>
    <tfoot>
        <tr>
            <th>Ingredient</th>
            <th>Quantity of Ingredient</th>
        </tr>
    </tfoot>
    <tbody>
        <tr>
            <td>Bread</td>
            <td>2 medium thickness slices</td>
        </tr>
        <tr>
            <td>Butter</td>
            <td>Enough for 2 slices of bread</td>
```

```
        </tr>
        <tr>
            <td>Grated Cheddar</td>
            <td>1.5 handfuls</td>
        </tr>
        <tr>
            <td>Beer</td>
            <td>One splash</td>
        </tr>
        <tr>
            <td>Wholegrain mustard</td>
            <td>One dollop</td>
        </tr>
        <tr>
            <td>Pepper</td>
            <td>To taste</td>
        </tr>
    </tbody>
</table>

</body>
</html>
```

code snippet /chapter12/figure_12-2.html

In Figure 12-2, you see how the `caption-side` property works; the table caption appears beneath the table.

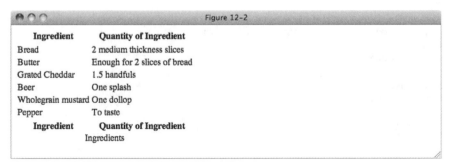

FIGURE 12-2

In the next section, I continue the discussion of tables with the styles allowed in table columns.

TABLE COLUMNS

In HTML, the `<colgroup>` and `<col>` elements allow the vertical columns of a table to be controlled. This is useful for controlling the width of a column of data, background color, or text color.

NOTE *IE is the only browser that supports the setting of text color on* <col> *elements. This is non-standard behavior, so don't expect to see it in other browsers in the future.*

All browsers have support for width and background color properties.

I have already shown how to use the width and background-color properties in previous chapters, and they work in exactly the same way on <col> elements. Even though the <col> elements themselves are not visible, the styles applied to them carry over to the cells that appear in those columns in the table. In the following Try It Out, I show how width and background-color can be applied to <col> elements.

TRY IT OUT   **Styling Columns**

Example 12-1

To apply styles to <col> elements, follow these steps.

1.   Enter the following markup:

```
<!DOCTYPE html PUBLIC "-//W3C//DTD HTML 4.01//EN"
    "http://www.w3.org/TR/html4/strict.dtd">
<html lang="en">
<head>
    <meta http-equiv="Content-Type" content="text/html; charset=utf-8">
    <title>Example 12-1</title>
    <style type="text/css">
        .ingredient {
            width: 200px;
            background-color: #CC5;
            color: red;
        }


        .quantity {
            width: 400px;
            background-color: #CCF;
        }
    </style>
</head>
<body>

<table>
    <caption>Ingredients</caption>
    <colgroup>
        <col class="ingredient">
        <col class="quantity">
    </colgroup>
    <thead>
        <tr>
```

```
                <th>Ingredient</th>
                <th>Quantity of Ingredient</th>
            </tr>
        </thead>
        <tfoot>
            <tr>
                <th>Ingredient</th>
                <th>Quantity of Ingredient</th>
            </tr>
        </tfoot>
        <tbody>
            <tr>
                <td>Bread</td>
                <td>2 medium thickness slices</td>
            </tr>
            <tr>
                <td>Butter</td>
                <td>Enough for 2 slices of bread</td>
            </tr>
            <tr>
                <td>Grated Cheddar</td>
                <td>1.5 handfuls</td>
            </tr>
            <tr>
                <td>Beer</td>
                <td>One splash</td>
            </tr>
            <tr>
                <td>Wholegrain mustard</td>
                <td>One dollop</td>
            </tr>
            <tr>
                <td>Pepper</td>
                <td>To taste</td>
            </tr>
        </tbody>
    </table>

</body>
</html>
```

2. Save the preceding CSS and markup as example_12-1.html. This example results in the output in Figure 12-3.

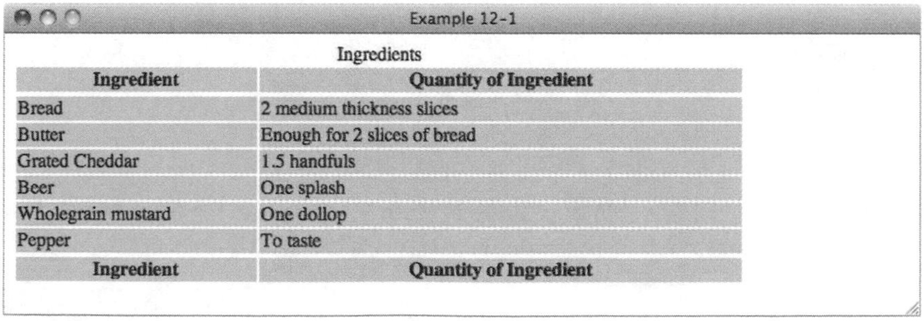

Example 12-1	
Ingredients	
Ingredient	**Quantity of Ingredient**
Bread	2 medium thickness slices
Butter	Enough for 2 slices of bread
Grated Cheddar	1.5 handfuls
Beer	One splash
Wholegrain mustard	One dollop
Pepper	To taste
Ingredient	**Quantity of Ingredient**

FIGURE 12-3

How It Works

In Example 12-1, we gave each <col> element a class and used this class to apply styles that affected the column they were associated with. The <col> element with class `ingredient` is given a `width` of 200px and a light green `background-color`. The <col> element with class `quantity` is given a `width` of 400px and a light blue `background-color`.

These styles are applied to each cell within the <thead>, <tbody>, and <tfoot> elements.

Now that you have seen the various elements available for use in a <table> element, the following section explores how you control table width with the `table-layout` property.

CONTROLLING TABLE LAYOUT

The following table outlines the `table-layout` property and its values.

PROPERTY	VALUE
table-layout	auto | fixed Initial value: auto

As you learned in Chapter 8, by default, a table expands and contracts to accommodate the data contained inside. As data fills the table, it continues to expand as long as there is space. When you look at them this way, tables are inherently fluid.

By adding borders, you can see in Figure 12-4 that, by default, table cells and the table itself expands to the width of the content. 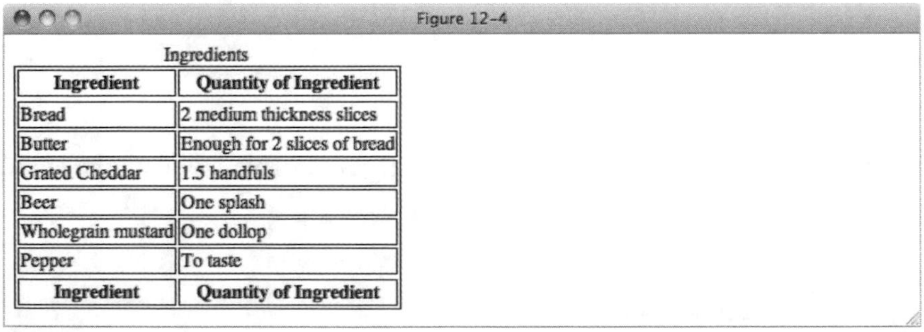

FIGURE 12-4

Sometimes, however, it is necessary to force a table into a fixed width for both the table and the cells. The following is a demonstration of what happens when you specify a fixed width for the table.

Available for
download on
Wrox.com

```
<!DOCTYPE html PUBLIC "-//W3C//DTD HTML 4.01//EN"
    "http://www.w3.org/TR/html4/strict.dtd">
<html lang="en">
<head>
    <meta http-equiv="Content-Type" content="text/html; charset=utf-8">
    <title>Figure 12-5</title>
    <style type="text/css">
        table,
        .control {
            width: 100px;
        }

        table,
        th,
        td,
        .control {
            border: 1px solid #000;
        }
    </style>
</head>
<body>

<div class="control">
    <p>100px wide</p>
</div>

<table>
    <caption>Ingredients</caption>
    <colgroup>
        <col class="ingredient">
        <col class="quantity">
    </colgroup>
    <thead>
        <tr>
            <th>Ingredient</th>
            <th>Quantity of Ingredient</th>
        </tr>
    </thead>
    <tfoot>
        <tr>
            <th>Ingredient</th>
            <th>Quantity of Ingredient</th>
        </tr>
    </tfoot>
    <tbody>
        <tr>
            <td>Bread</td>
            <td>2 medium thickness slices</td>
        </tr>
        <tr>
            <td>Butter</td>
            <td>Enough for 2 slices of bread</td>
        </tr>
        <tr>
```

```
                <td>Grated Cheddar</td>
                <td>1.5 handfuls</td>
            </tr>
            <tr>
                <td>Beer</td>
                <td>One splash</td>
            </tr>
            <tr>
                <td>Wholegrain mustard</td>
                <td>One dollop</td>
            </tr>
            <tr>
                <td>Pepper</td>
                <td>To taste</td>
            </tr>
        </tbody>
    </table>

</body>
</html>
```

code snippet /chapter12/figure_12-5.html

I've given the table a width of 100px and added a snippet of markup to show what a 100px width should look like, as you can see in Figure 12-5

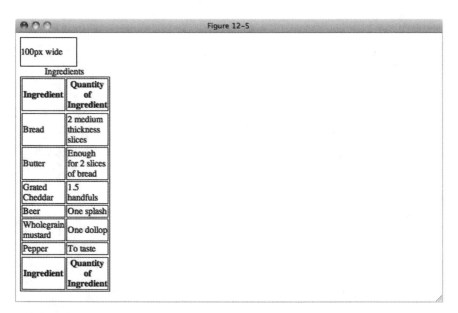

FIGURE 12-5

As you can see in Figure 12-5, the table is wider than 100px because the text contained in the cells is too wide.

Should it be a requirement that a table does not expand to fit its contents, you can use the `table-layout: fixed;` declaration to force the width as follows:

Available for
download on
Wrox.com

```
<!DOCTYPE html PUBLIC "-//W3C//DTD HTML 4.01//EN"
    "http://www.w3.org/TR/html4/strict.dtd">
<html lang="en">
<head>
    <meta http-equiv="Content-Type" content="text/html; charset=utf-8">
    <title>Figure 12-6</title>
    <style type="text/css">
        table {
            table-layout: fixed;
        }

        table,
        .control {
            width: 100px;
        }

        table,
        th,
        td,
        .control {
            border: 1px solid #000;
        }
    </style>
</head>
<body>

<div class="control">
    <p>100px wide</p>
</div>

<table>
    <caption>Ingredients</caption>
    <colgroup>
        <col class="ingredient">
        <col class="quantity">
    </colgroup>
    <thead>
        <tr>
            <th>Ingredient</th>
            <th>Quantity of Ingredient</th>
        </tr>
    </thead>
    <tfoot>
        <tr>
            <th>Ingredient</th>
            <th>Quantity of Ingredient</th>
        </tr>
    </tfoot>
    <tbody>
        <tr>
            <td>Bread</td>
```

```
            <td>2 medium thickness slices</td>
        </tr>
        <tr>
            <td>Butter</td>
            <td>Enough for 2 slices of bread</td>
        </tr>
        <tr>
            <td>Grated Cheddar</td>
            <td>1.5 handfuls</td>
        </tr>
        <tr>
            <td>Beer</td>
            <td>One splash</td>
        </tr>
        <tr>
            <td>Wholegrain mustard</td>
            <td>One dollop</td>
        </tr>
        <tr>
            <td>Pepper</td>
            <td>To taste</td>
        </tr>
    </tbody>
</table>

</body>
</html>
```

code snippet /chapter12/figure_12-6.html

This results in the output in Figure 12-6.

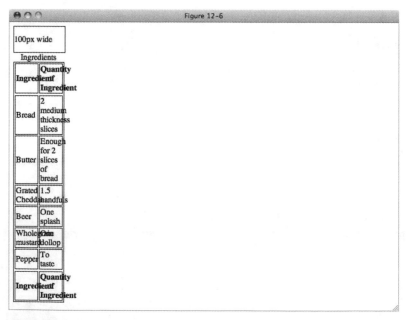

FIGURE 12-6

The table is forced to maintain its width of 100 pixels, regardless of how much data is contained in its table cells. If the content inside the cells results in a width larger than 100 pixels, the content overflows.

> **NOTE** *When content overflows in all versions of IE the content is clipped, as if a* `overflow: hidden;` *declaration has been applied to each* `th` *and* `td`.
>
> *All other browsers display the content as per Figure 12-6. By applying the* `overflow` *property, which I covered in Chapter 8, whenever you use* `table-layout: fixed;` *you can avoid inconsistencies across browsers.*

Now that I've explored the `table-layout` property, in the following sections I examine the other CSS properties that exist for controlling table layout.

COLLAPSING BORDERS

Tables, by default, include some spacing between each of the cells appearing in the table. As you have seen in the previous examples, each cell has its own border with a space between the borders of its neighboring cells. The `border-collapse` property allows you to remove this space completely, and for finer control, the `border-spacing` property allows you to specify the spacing.

The following table outlines the `border-collapse` property and its values.

PROPERTY	VALUE
border-collapse	collapse | separate Initial value: separate

By default, the `border-collapse` property has a value of `separate`. If you set the value to `collapse`, you remove the spacing between each cell. The following demonstrates the `border-collapse` property in action:

Available for download on Wrox.com

```
<!DOCTYPE html PUBLIC "-//W3C//DTD HTML 4.01//EN"
    "http://www.w3.org/TR/html4/strict.dtd">
<html lang="en">
<head>
    <meta http-equiv="Content-Type" content="text/html; charset=utf-8">
    <title>Figure 12-7</title>
    <style type="text/css">
        table {
            border-collapse: collapse;
        }

        table,
        th,
        td {
```

```
                    border: 1px solid #000;
            }
        </style>
</head>
<body>

<table>
    <caption>Ingredients</caption>
    <colgroup>
        <col class="ingredient">
        <col class="quantity">
    </colgroup>
    <thead>
        <tr>
            <th>Ingredient</th>
            <th>Quantity of Ingredient</th>
        </tr>
    </thead>
    <tfoot>
        <tr>
            <th>Ingredient</th>
            <th>Quantity of Ingredient</th>
        </tr>
    </tfoot>
    <tbody>
        <tr>
            <td>Bread</td>
            <td>2 medium thickness slices</td>
        </tr>
        <tr>
            <td>Butter</td>
            <td>Enough for 2 slices of bread</td>
        </tr>
        <tr>
            <td>Grated Cheddar</td>
            <td>1.5 handfuls</td>
        </tr>
        <tr>
            <td>Beer</td>
            <td>One splash</td>
        </tr>
        <tr>
            <td>Wholegrain mustard</td>
            <td>One dollop</td>
        </tr>
        <tr>
            <td>Pepper</td>
            <td>To taste</td>
        </tr>
    </tbody>
</table>

</body>
</html>
```

code snippet /chapter12/figure_12-7.html

If you apply the `collapse` value, all the cells are squeezed together, and the borders between cells are combined. Figure 12-7 shows what happens.

FIGURE 12-7

Notice that the border on the `<table>` element is also collapsed.

The next section talks about how you can control spacing between table cells with greater precision with the `border-spacing` property.

CONTROLLING BORDER SPACING

The following table outlines the `border-spacing` property and its values.

PROPERTY	VALUE
border-spacing	`<length> <length>?` Initial value: 0

> **NOTE** *IE 6 and IE 7 do not support the* `border-spacing` *property. Instead, if you must support these browsers, a common workaround is to remove borders from the table cells completely, and instead wrap the contents of each cell in a* `<div>` *element, to which you apply the borders and padding you need.*

The `border-spacing` property allows more control over cell spacing than `border-collapse` because it allows the length to be specified.

If, as in the following example, you provide a single length value of 15px, 15 pixels of space are added between each cell, both vertically and horizontally:

Available for download on Wrox.com

```
<!DOCTYPE html PUBLIC "-//W3C//DTD HTML 4.01//EN"
    "http://www.w3.org/TR/html4/strict.dtd">
<html lang="en">
<head>
    <meta http-equiv="Content-Type" content="text/html; charset=utf-8">
    <title>Figure 12-8</title>
    <style type="text/css">
        table {
            border-spacing: 15px;
        }

        table,
        th,
        td {
            border: 1px solid #000;
        }
    </style>
</head>
<body>

<table>
    <caption>Ingredients</caption>
    <colgroup>
        <col class="ingredient">
        <col class="quantity">
    </colgroup>
    <thead>
        <tr>
            <th>Ingredient</th>
            <th>Quantity of Ingredient</th>
        </tr>
    </thead>
    <tfoot>
        <tr>
            <th>Ingredient</th>
            <th>Quantity of Ingredient</th>
        </tr>
    </tfoot>
    <tbody>
        <tr>
            <td>Bread</td>
            <td>2 medium thickness slices</td>
        </tr>
        <tr>
            <td>Butter</td>
            <td>Enough for 2 slices of bread</td>
        </tr>
        <tr>
            <td>Grated Cheddar</td>
            <td>1.5 handfuls</td>
        </tr>
```

```
        <tr>
            <td>Beer</td>
            <td>One splash</td>
        </tr>
        <tr>
            <td>Wholegrain mustard</td>
            <td>One dollop</td>
        </tr>
        <tr>
            <td>Pepper</td>
            <td>To taste</td>
        </tr>
    </tbody>
</table>

</body>
</html>
```

code snippet /chapter12/figure_12-8.html

The result is shown in Figure 12-8.

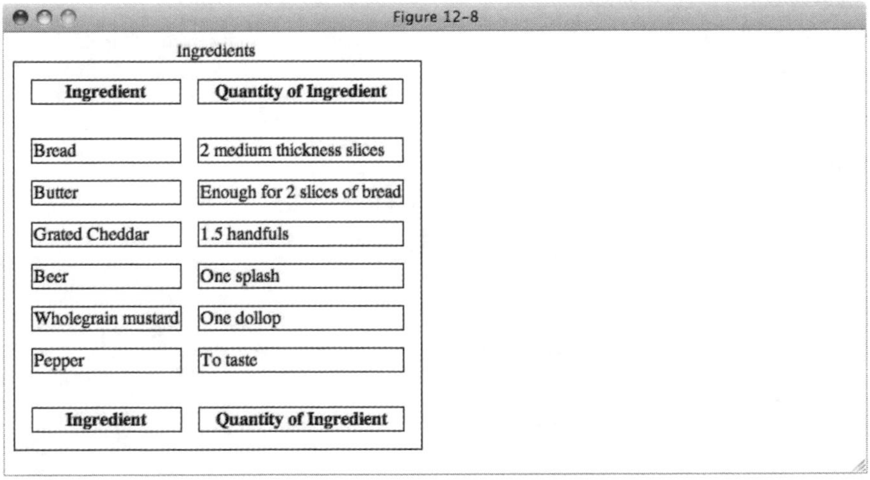

FIGURE 12-8

You can see that the space between cells in <thead> and <tbody>, and between cells in <tfoot> and <tbody>, is doubled as their containing element (<thead>, <tfoot> or <tbody>) sets a new context for cell boundaries.

The border-spacing property has the following syntax:

```
border-spacing: <horizontal spacing length> <vertical spacing length>;
```

If the optional second value is present, this property allows the vertical and horizontal spacing to be specified. For our final example of this chapter, let's Try It Out.

TRY IT OUT Style Borders for Separating Rows and Columns

Example 12-2

To see the `border-spacing` property in action, follow these steps.

1. Enter the following markup:

```
<!DOCTYPE html PUBLIC "-//W3C//DTD HTML 4.01//EN"
    "http://www.w3.org/TR/html4/strict.dtd">
<html lang="en">
<head>
    <meta http-equiv="Content-Type" content="text/html; charset=utf-8">
    <title>Example 12-2</title>
    <style type="text/css">
        table {
            border-spacing: 15px 5px;
        }

        table,
        th,
        td {
            border: 1px solid #000;
        }
    </style>
</head>
<body>

<table>
    <caption>Ingredients</caption>
    <colgroup>
        <col class="ingredient">
        <col class="quantity">
    </colgroup>
    <thead>
        <tr>
            <th>Ingredient</th>
            <th>Quantity of Ingredient</th>
        </tr>
    </thead>
    <tfoot>
        <tr>
            <th>Ingredient</th>
            <th>Quantity of Ingredient</th>
        </tr>
    </tfoot>
    <tbody>
        <tr>
            <td>Bread</td>
```

```
                <td>2 medium thickness slices</td>
            </tr>
            <tr>
                <td>Butter</td>
                <td>Enough for 2 slices of bread</td>
            </tr>
            <tr>
                <td>Grated Cheddar</td>
                <td>1.5 handfuls</td>
            </tr>
            <tr>
                <td>Beer</td>
                <td>One splash</td>
            </tr>
            <tr>
                <td>Wholegrain mustard</td>
                <td>One dollop</td>
            </tr>
            <tr>
                <td>Pepper</td>
                <td>To taste</td>
            </tr>
        </tbody>
    </table>

    </body>
    </html>
```

2. Save the preceding CSS and markup as `example_12-2.html`. This example results in the output in Figure 12-9.

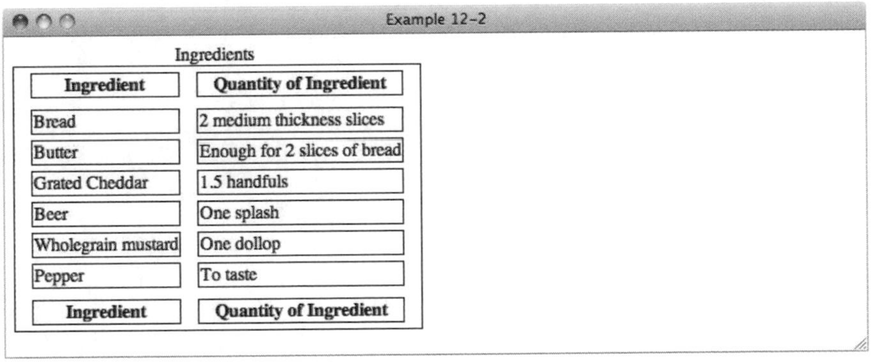

FIGURE 12-9

How It Works

In Example 12-2, we applied a `border-spacing: 15px 5px;` declaration to the `<table>` element, which added 15px of horizontal spacing and 5px vertical spacing between each cell.

EXERCISES

1. Describe what the `table-layout: fixed;` declaration does.

2. When sizing using the `table-layout: fixed;` declaration, how does the browser determine the width of table columns?

3. What purpose does the optional `<thead>` element serve?

4. In what containing element does the main table data appear?

► **WHAT YOU LEARNED IN THIS CHAPTER**

In this chapter, I showed you what is possible with HTML tables and CSS. You learned the following:

TOPIC	KEY CONCEPTS
Table structure and optional elements	Tables have a lot of optional elements that make the structure easier to style. These include columns, heading groupings, body groupings, and footer groupings.
Positioning of table caption elements	You control the placement of a table's caption by using the `caption-side` property.
Table layout	You control a table's layout by using the `table-layout` property. With this property, it is possible to force a table into a certain width.
Controlling border spacing	You can remove the spacing between table cells by using the `border-collapse` property. You can also adjust the spacing between table cells by using the `border-spacing` property.

13

Create a Complete Layout

WHAT YOU WILL LEARN IN THIS CHAPTER:

➤   How to create a complete layout from scratch

➤   How to add gradient backgrounds with CSS

➤   How to use custom fonts

Throughout this book, you have learned everything you need to create a complete layout for a website. In this chapter, I go through this process from HTML to CSS, and show you a few new tricks.

CREATING THE PAGE WITH HTML

Throughout this chapter, I show you how to build the page you see in Figure 13-1.

Many parts of this layout should be familiar to you from previous chapters, but you may notice that the page has a gradient background from dark gray to white, and the h1 element uses a non-standard font. I'll show you how this is done later in the chapter, but the first thing you will do in the following example is create the markup.

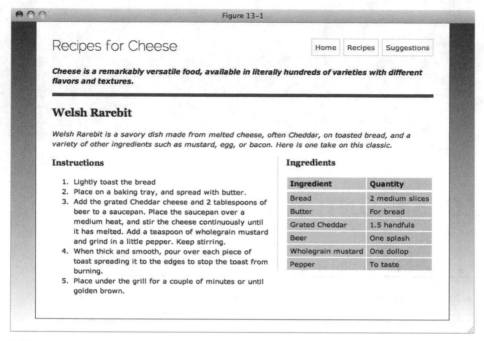

FIGURE 13-1

TRY IT OUT Markup Content before Adding CSS

Example 13-1

To create the markup that the complete layout uses, follow these steps.

1. Enter the following markup:

```
<!DOCTYPE html PUBLIC "-//W3C//DTD HTML 4.01//EN"
    "http://www.w3.org/TR/html4/strict.dtd">
<html lang="en">
<head>
    <meta http-equiv="Content-Type" content="text/html; charset=utf-8">
    <title>Example 13-1</title>
</head>
<body>

<div class="header">

    <h1>Recipes for Cheese</h1>

    <ul class="navigation">
        <li><a href="#">Home</a></li>
        <li><a href="#">Recipes</a></li>
        <li><a href="#">Suggestions</a></li>
```

```
    </ul>

    <p class="intro">Cheese is a remarkably versatile food, available in literally
    hundreds of varieties with different flavors and textures.</p>

</div>

<h2>Welsh Rarebit</h2>

<p class="intro">Welsh Rarebit is a savory dish made from melted cheese, often
Cheddar, on toasted bread, and a variety of other ingredients such as mustard,
 egg, or bacon. Here is one take on this classic.</p>

<div class="ingredients">

    <h3>Ingredients</h3>

    <table>
        <colgroup>
            <col class="ingredient">
            <col class="quantity">
        </colgroup>
        <thead>
            <tr>
                <th>Ingredient</th>
                <th>Quantity</th>
            </tr>
        </thead>
        <tbody>
            <tr>
                <td>Bread</td>
                <td>2 medium slices</td>
            </tr>
            <tr>
                <td>Butter</td>
                <td>For bread</td>
            </tr>
            <tr>
                <td>Grated Cheddar</td>
                <td>1.5 handfuls</td>
            </tr>
            <tr>
                <td>Beer</td>
                <td>One splash</td>
            </tr>
            <tr>
                <td>Wholegrain mustard</td>
                <td>One dollop</td>
            </tr>
            <tr>
                <td>Pepper</td>
                <td>To taste</td>
            </tr>
        </tbody>
```

```
        </table>

    </div>

    <h3>Instructions</h3>

    <ol>
        <li>Lightly toast the bread</li>
        <li>Place on a baking tray, and spread with butter.</li>
        <li>Add the grated Cheddar cheese and 2 tablespoons of beer to a saucepan.
        Place the saucepan over a medium heat, and stir the cheese continuously until
        it has melted. Add a teaspoon of wholegrain mustard and grind in a little
        pepper. Keep stirring.</li>
        <li>When thick and smooth, pour over each piece of toast spreading it to the
        edges to stop the toast from burning.</li>
        <li>Place under the grill for a couple of minutes or until golden brown.</li>
    </ol>

    </body>
    </html>
```

2. Save the preceding CSS and markup as `example_13-1.html`. This example results in the output in Figure 13-2 in Safari and other desktop browsers.

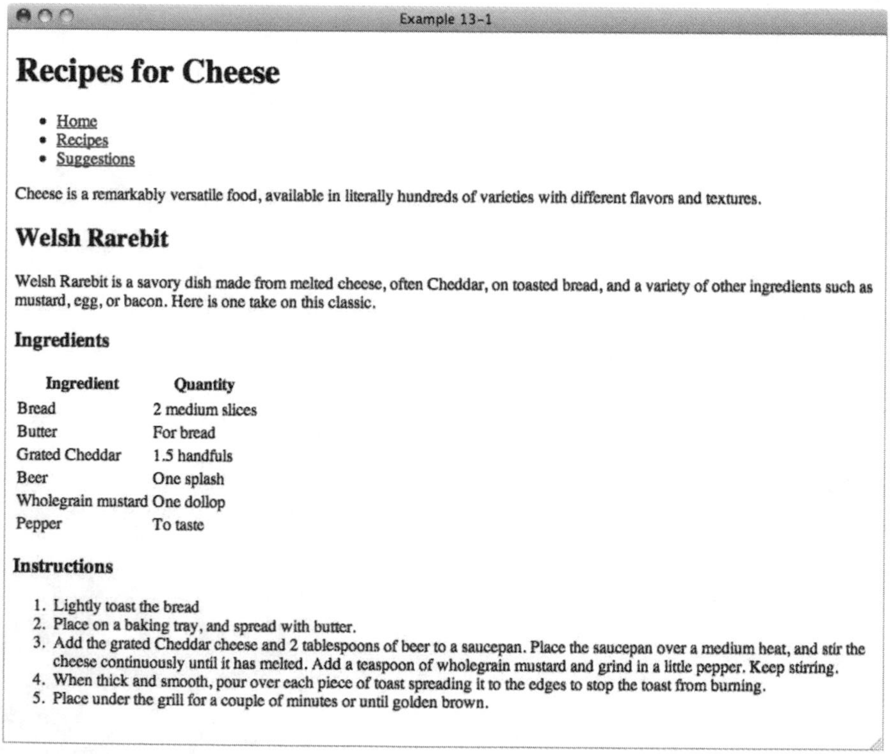

FIGURE 13-2

How It Works

In Example 13-1, you have written the basic HTML for the page. I've kept the markup as simple as possible, but with a few concessions to the design you will have to implement, such as wrapping the page header elements and the ingredients section in `div` elements with classes of `header` and `ingredients`, respectively, as I know that you will need to add specific styles to these elements to achieve the positioning you need.

The most important thing at this stage is that the content in Figure 13-2 works with only the default browser styles, particularly that the meaning of each section is clear and in the correct order.

Next, you're going to start adding CSS, specifically styling the text to match the fonts used in the design.

STYLING TEXT AND CUSTOM FONTS

In Chapter 5, I showed you how to apply font faces to text, so you may want to take a look back if you can't remember how.

There are three fonts used on the page:

➤ Verdana for the main text

➤ Georgia for the headings that are part of the main page content

➤ Raleway for the site title in the `example` element.

The first two fonts are fairly common, and a large number of visitors to a site can be expected to have them, so let's deal with them first.

```
body {
    font: 82%/1.4 Verdana, Arial, Helvetica, sans-serif;
}

h2,
h3 {
    font-family: Georgia, Times, Times New Roman, serif;
}
```

In Figure 13-3, you can see the results of this code.

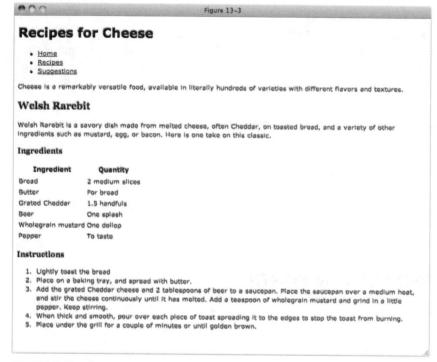

FIGURE 13-3

Figure 13-3 shows the result of applying default fonts; already the page is cleaner and easier to read, because I am using sans-serif fonts for the main content that most people find more readable on screen. Also of note is that on the body element I have also set a font size of 82%, and a line-height of 1.4, which makes the main text 13px in size, and gives each line a little more spacing, again making the page more readable for most visitors. By specifying the font size with a percentage value I have not broken the font resizing facility in Internet Explorer.

The third font, Raleway, is a bit more difficult, as it is not a commonly installed font. Fortunately, you can make fonts available to visitors of your site that they may not have installed with the @font-face rule:

```
@font-face {
    font-family: Raleway;
    src: url(raleway_thin.eot);
    src: local(raleway_thin), url(raleway_thin.ttf) format(opentype);
}
```

This creates a new font-face reference that you can use in your CSS. There are two parts to this rule.

First is the font-family property; in this case, it behaves slightly differently than you are used to. Instead of applying a font to an element in the page, it provides a label you can use to reference the font later. It can be any string that is valid in CSS (see Chapter 2), but you should make sure that it identifies the font so that you don't get confused later. I have given this font the label Raleway.

Next is the src attribute. There are two src attributes in this rule because Internet Explorer requires a different file format for fonts than other browsers do. The first src declaration is for Internet

Explorer, and the value is simply the URI of the font file. The second src declaration is for all other browsers, which support the Open Type format for fonts. This declaration must come second so that it overrides the first src declaration for supporting browsers. There are two extra parts to this declaration: local, which indicates that the font should be looked for in the user's installed fonts first, and so should be given the filename of the font without an extension (in this case, raleway_thin) as the value; and format, which should be given the value opentype. format is optional, but because Internet Explorer doesn't support it, it will ignore the second src declaration.

The following Try It Out puts this into action

TRY IT OUT | **Using Custom Fonts**

Example 13-2

To use a font that is not installed on a user's computer, follow these steps. You should download the files for this example as they include the font files you will need.

1. Enter the following markup:

```
<!DOCTYPE html PUBLIC "-//W3C//DTD HTML 4.01//EN"
    "http://www.w3.org/TR/html4/strict.dtd">
<html lang="en">
<head>
    <meta http-equiv="Content-Type" content="text/html; charset=utf-8">
    <title>Example 13-2</title>
        <style type="text/css">
        @font-face {
            font-family: Raleway;
            src: url(raleway_thin.eot);
            src: local(raleway_thin), url(raleway_thin.ttf) format(opentype);
        }

        body {
            font: 82%/1.4 Verdana, Arial, Helvetica, sans-serif;
        }

        h1 {
            font-family: Raleway, Georgia, Times, Times New Roman, serif;
        }

        h2,
        h3 {
            font-family: Georgia, Times, Times New Roman, serif;
        }
    </style>
</head>
<body>

<div class="header">

    <h1>Recipes for Cheese</h1>

    <ul class="navigation">
```

```
            <li><a href="#">Home</a></li>
            <li><a href="#">Recipes</a></li>
            <li><a href="#">Suggestions</a></li>
        </ul>

        <p class="intro">Cheese is a remarkably versatile food, available in literally
        hundreds of varieties with different flavors and textures.</p>

</div>

<h2>Welsh Rarebit</h2>

<p class="intro">Welsh Rarebit is a savory dish made from melted cheese, often
Cheddar, on toasted bread, and a variety of other ingredients such as mustard,
egg, or bacon. Here is one take on this classic.</p>

<div class="ingredients">

    <h3>Ingredients</h3>

    <table>
        <colgroup>
            <col class="ingredient">
            <col class="quantity">
        </colgroup>
        <thead>
            <tr>
                <th>Ingredient</th>
                <th>Quantity</th>
            </tr>
        </thead>
        <tbody>
            <tr>
                <td>Bread</td>
                <td>2 medium slices</td>
            </tr>
            <tr>
                <td>Butter</td>
                <td>For bread</td>
            </tr>
            <tr>
                <td>Grated Cheddar</td>
                <td>1.5 handfuls</td>
            </tr>
            <tr>
                <td>Beer</td>
                <td>One splash</td>
            </tr>
            <tr>
                <td>Wholegrain mustard</td>
                <td>One dollop</td>
            </tr>
            <tr>
                <td>Pepper</td>
                <td>To taste</td>
            </tr>
```

```
            </tbody>
        </table>

    </div>

    <h3>Instructions</h3>

    <ol>
        <li>Lightly toast the bread</li>
        <li>Place on a baking tray, and spread with butter.</li>
        <li>Add the grated Cheddar cheese and 2 tablespoons of beer to a saucepan.
        Place the saucepan over a medium heat, and stir the cheese continuously until
        it has melted. Add a teaspoon of wholegrain mustard and grind in a little
        pepper. Keep stirring.</li>
        <li>When thick and smooth, pour over each piece of toast spreading it to the
        edges to stop the toast from burning.</li>
        <li>Place under the grill for a couple of minutes or until golden brown.</li>
    </ol>

    </body>
</html>
```

2. Save the preceding CSS and markup as `example_13-2.html`. This example results in the output in Figure 13-4 in Safari and other desktop browsers.

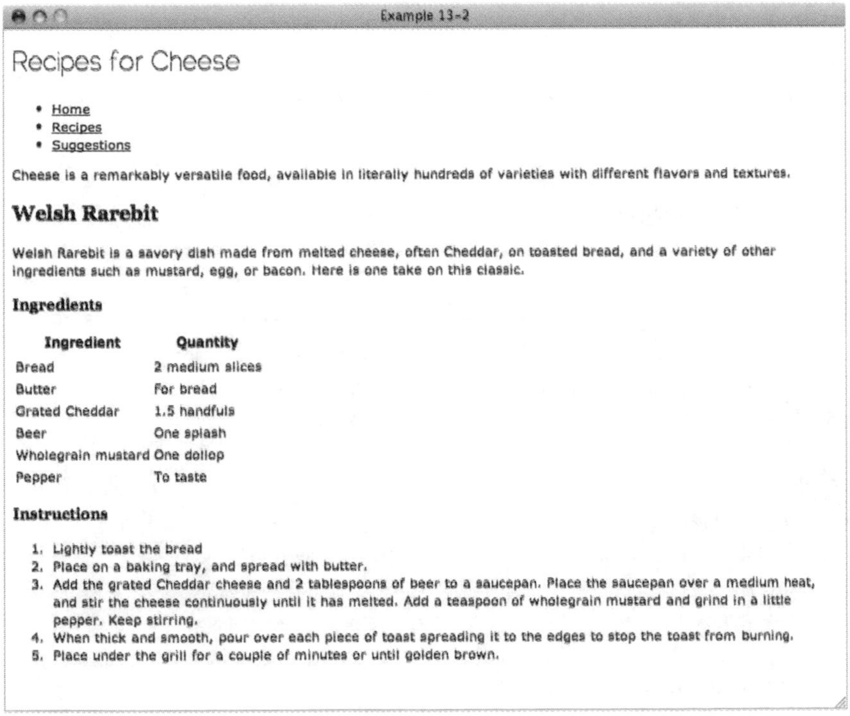

FIGURE 13-4

How It Works

In Example 13-2, you have added font styling to the page.

First you've applied a font size, line height, and font family to the body element, with the following declaration:

```
body {
    font: 82%/1.4 Verdana, Arial, Helvetica, sans-serif;
}
```

Next, you set a font family to all h1 and h3 elements:

```
h2,
h3 {
    font-family: Georgia, Times, Times New Roman, serif;
}
```

Finally, you add an @font-face rule to make the Raleway font available to use in the same way that you normally would:

```
@font-face {
    font-family: Raleway;
    src: url(raleway_thin.eot);
    src: local(raleway_thin), url(raleway_thin.ttf) format(opentype);
}

h1 {
    font-family: Raleway, Georgia, Times, Times New Roman, serif;
}
```

As you can see, you still specify fallback fonts, which in this case would be used by older browsers that don't support the @font-face rule or if the font file has not downloaded.

 NOTE *Use custom fonts with caution. Each file needs to be downloaded from the server hosting your website, and adds to the overall size of a page. The Raleway font files are 74KB, for example, and could account for a significant proportion of the user's download time. Until the file has downloaded, the text using the font will not be displayed.*

There aren't many fonts available that are free for you to use in this way. You will find Raleway by Matt McIneney, and other free-to-use fonts at www.theleagueofmoveabletype.com.

Next I will add the CSS that forms the layout of the page.

BUILDING THE LAYOUT

You will have already learned everything required to create the layout for the site, so instead of going through each part, instead I encourage you to Try It Out straight away. Experiment with the styles to come up with your own variations, and to help you figure out if there are any aspects of CSS that you don't fully understand yet. At the end, I will show you where to look in the book to refresh your memory or if you need to re-read any chapters.

TRY IT OUT Building a Layout

Example 13-3

To complete the layout of the example page, follow these steps. You should download the files for this example, as they include the font files you will need.

1. Enter the following markup:

```
<!DOCTYPE html PUBLIC "-//W3C//DTD HTML 4.01//EN"
    "http://www.w3.org/TR/html4/strict.dtd">
<html lang="en">
<head>
    <meta http-equiv="Content-Type" content="text/html; charset=utf-8">
    <title>Example 13-3</title>
    <style type="text/css">
        @font-face {
            font-family: Raleway;
            src: url(raleway_thin.eot);
            src: local(raleway_thin), url(raleway_thin.ttf) format(opentype);
        }

        body {
            width: 700px;
            margin: 0 auto;
            padding: 29px;
            border: 1px solid #233;
            border-top: none;
            background: #FFF;
            font: 82%/1.4 Verdana, Arial, Helvetica, sans-serif;
        }

        h1 {
            float: left;
            margin-top: 0;
            font-family: Raleway, Georgia, Times, Times New Roman, serif;
        }

        h2,
```

```
h3 {
    font-family: Georgia, Times, Times New Roman, serif;
}

.header {
    border-bottom: 6px solid #233;
}

.navigation {
    float: right;
    margin: 0;
    list-style: none;
}

.navigation li {
    float: left;
}

.navigation a {
    display: block;
    margin-left: 0.5em;
    padding: 0.5em;
    border: 1px solid #CCC;
    color: #233;
    text-decoration: none;
}

.navigation a:focus,
.navigation a:hover {
    background: #233;
    color: #FFF;
}

.header .intro {
    clear: both;
    font-weight: bold;
}

.intro {
    font-style: italic;
}

.ingredients {
    float: right;
    margin: 0 0 15px 15px;
    padding-left: 15px;
    border-left: 1px solid #CCC;
}

.ingredients h3 {
    margin-top: 0;
}

.ingredients th {
```

```
                text-align: left;
            }

            .ingredients th,
            .ingredients td {
                padding: 2px 5px;
            }

            .ingredients .ingredient {
                background-color: #CC5;
            }

            .ingredients .quantity {
                background-color: #CCF;
            }
        </style>
    </head>
    <body>

    <div class="header">

        <h1>Recipes for Cheese</h1>

        <ul class="navigation">
            <li><a href="#">Home</a></li>
            <li><a href="#">Recipes</a></li>
            <li><a href="#">Suggestions</a></li>
        </ul>

        <p class="intro">Cheese is a remarkably versatile food, available in literally
        hundreds of varieties with different flavors and textures.</p>

    </div>

    <h2>Welsh Rarebit</h2>

    <p class="intro">Welsh Rarebit is a savory dish made from melted cheese, often
    Cheddar, on toasted bread, and a variety of other ingredients such as mustard,
    egg, or bacon. Here is one take on this classic.</p>

    <div class="ingredients">

        <h3>Ingredients</h3>

        <table>
            <colgroup>
                <col class="ingredient">
                <col class="quantity">
            </colgroup>
            <thead>
                <tr>
                    <th>Ingredient</th>
                    <th>Quantity</th>
                </tr>
```

```
            </thead>
            <tbody>
                <tr>
                    <td>Bread</td>
                    <td>2 medium slices</td>
                </tr>
                <tr>
                    <td>Butter</td>
                    <td>For bread</td>
                </tr>
                <tr>
                    <td>Grated Cheddar</td>
                    <td>1.5 handfuls</td>
                </tr>
                <tr>
                    <td>Beer</td>
                    <td>One splash</td>
                </tr>
                <tr>
                    <td>Wholegrain mustard</td>
                    <td>One dollop</td>
                </tr>
                <tr>
                    <td>Pepper</td>
                    <td>To taste</td>
                </tr>
            </tbody>
        </table>

</div>

<h3>Instructions</h3>

<ol>
    <li>Lightly toast the bread</li>
    <li>Place on a baking tray, and spread with butter.</li>
    <li>Add the grated Cheddar cheese and 2 tablespoons of beer to a saucepan.
    Place the saucepan over a medium heat, and stir the cheese continuously until
    it has melted. Add a teaspoon of wholegrain mustard and grind in a little
    pepper. Keep stirring.</li>
    <li>When thick and smooth, pour over each piece of toast spreading it to the
    edges to stop the toast from burning.</li>
    <li>Place under the grill for a couple of minutes or until golden brown.</li>
</ol>

</body>
</html>
```

2. Save the preceding CSS and markup as `example_13-3.html`. This example results in the output in Figure 13-5 in Safari and other desktop browsers.

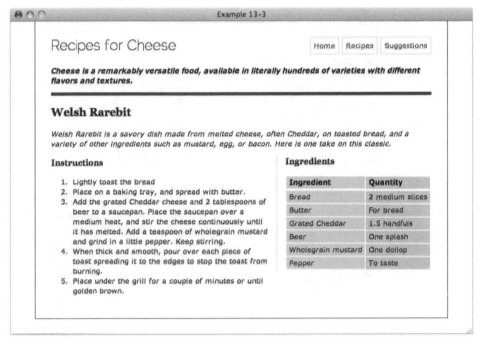

FIGURE 13-5

How It Works

In Example 13-3, you have completed the layout of the example page.

If you don't understand any aspects of the CSS used here, you should review the following chapters:

Chapter 3 for using selectors and pseudo-classes

Chapter 7 for setting background colors

Chapter 8 for understanding widths, margins, and padding

Chapter 10 for styling lists

Chapter 12 for styling tables

Last in this chapter, I will show you how to create gradient backgrounds with CSS.

GRADIENT BACKGROUNDS

In Chapter 7 you learned how to set solid background colors and background images, but you can also create gradient backgrounds with CSS. There are different types of gradient, but here I will cover a linear gradient of two colors from top to bottom. See Appendix B for links to further information about creating gradient backgrounds.

As with the `@font-face` rule you saw earlier in this chapter, you need to write different declarations for different browsers as follows:

```
background-image: -moz-linear-gradient(top, #233, #FFF);
background-image: -webkit-gradient(linear, left top, left bottom, from(#233),
to(#FFF));
-ms-filter: "progid:DXImageTransform.Microsoft.Gradient(StartColorStr=#223333,
EndColorStr=#FFFFFF)";
background-image: linear-gradient(top, #233, #FFF);
```

Three of the four the previous declarations apply to the `background-image` property, and I will cover these first.

The first and second declarations apply the gradient to Mozilla Firefox and to webkit browsers (Apple Safari and Google Chrome). The values for the `background-image` property in both cases are prefixed with `-moz-` and `-webkit-` respectively, which are known as vendor prefixes. Vendor prefixes allow browsers to implement the unfinished CSS3 specification without having to worry if the final recommendation is different. As you can see, the values that follow each vendor prefix are different, which demonstrates that there is still uncertainty about how gradients will be implemented.

The final of the four declarations does not have a vendor prefix, and this is because this is the currently proposed format in the CSS3 recommendation. You will see a similar use of vendor prefixes for other CSS3 properties, and it is common practice for the non-prefixed version of a declaration to be added last so that as browsers finalize support the browser neutral declaration will take precedence.

The other common vendor prefixes are `-o-` for the Opera browser (which doesn't support CSS3 gradients at the time of writing) and `-ms-` for Internet Explorer.

The `-ms-` prefix is used in the third of the four declarations and follows a very different format; instead, you can implement gradient using proprietary Microsoft filters. This filter works in both IE8 and IE9.

Despite the differences, each of these declarations works the same way. They all require two RGB or hexadecimal color values, in this case `#233` and `#FFF` for Firefox, Chrome, and Safari, and `#223333` and `#FFFFFF` for Internet Explorer, which does not correctly support short hexadecimal form.

Let's Try It Out to put this into practice.

TRY IT OUT **Adding a Gradient Background**

Example 13-4

To finish the page by adding a gradient background, follow these steps. You should download the files for this example, as they include the font files you will need.

1. Enter the following markup:

```
<!DOCTYPE html PUBLIC "-//W3C//DTD HTML 4.01//EN"
    "http://www.w3.org/TR/html4/strict.dtd">
<html lang="en">
<head>
    <meta http-equiv="Content-Type" content="text/html; charset=utf-8">
    <title>Example 13-4</title>
```

```css
<style type="text/css">
    @font-face {
        font-family: Raleway;
        src: url(raleway_thin.eot);
        src: local(raleway_thin), url(raleway_thin.ttf) format(opentype);
    }

    html {
        height: 100%;
        background-color: #233;
        background-image: -moz-linear-gradient(top, #233, #FFF);
        background-image: -webkit-gradient(linear, left top, left bottom,
        from(#233), to(#FFF));
        -ms-filter: "progid:DXImageTransform.Microsoft.Gradient
        (StartColorStr=#223333, EndColorStr=#FFFFFF)";
        background-image: linear-gradient(top, #233, #FFF);
    }

    body {
        width: 700px;
        margin: 0 auto;
        padding: 29px;
        border: 1px solid #233;
        border-top: none;
        background: #FFF;
        font: 82%/1.4 Verdana, Arial, Helvetica, sans-serif;
    }

    h1 {
        float: left;
        margin-top: 0;
        font-family: Raleway, Georgia, Times, Times New Roman, serif;
    }

    h2,
    h3 {
        font-family: Georgia, Times, Times New Roman, serif;
    }

    .header {
        border-bottom: 6px solid #233;
    }

    .navigation {
        float: right;
        margin: 0;
        list-style: none;
    }

    .navigation li {
        float: left;
    }

    .navigation a {
        display: block;
        margin-left: 0.5em;
```

```css
        padding: 0.5em;
        border: 1px solid #CCC;
        color: #233;
        text-decoration: none;
    }

    .navigation a:focus,
    .navigation a:hover {
        background: #233;
        color: #FFF;
    }

    .header .intro {
        clear: both;
        font-weight: bold;
    }

    .intro {
        font-style: italic;
    }

    .ingredients {
        float: right;
        margin: 0 0 15px 15px;
        padding-left: 15px;
        border-left: 1px solid #CCC;
    }

    .ingredients h3 {
        margin-top: 0;
    }

    .ingredients th {
        text-align: left;
    }

    .ingredients th,
    .ingredients td {
        padding: 2px 5px;
    }

    .ingredients .ingredient {
        background-color: #CC5;
    }

    .ingredients .quantity {
        background-color: #CCF;
    }
    </style>
</head>
<body>

<div class="header">

    <h1>Recipes for Cheese</h1>

    <ul class="navigation">
```

```
          <li><a href="#">Home</a></li>
          <li><a href="#">Recipes</a></li>
          <li><a href="#">Suggestions</a></li>
     </ul>

     <p class="intro">Cheese is a remarkably versatile food, available in literally
     hundreds of varieties with different flavors and textures.</p>

</div>

<h2>Welsh Rarebit</h2>

<p class="intro">Welsh Rarebit is a savory dish made from melted cheese, often
Cheddar, on toasted bread, and a variety of other ingredients such as mustard,
egg, or bacon. Here is one take on this classic.</p>

<div class="ingredients">

     <h3>Ingredients</h3>

     <table>
          <colgroup>
               <col class="ingredient">
               <col class="quantity">
          </colgroup>
          <thead>
               <tr>
                    <th>Ingredient</th>
                    <th>Quantity</th>
               </tr>
          </thead>
          <tbody>
               <tr>
                    <td>Bread</td>
                    <td>2 medium slices</td>
               </tr>
               <tr>
                    <td>Butter</td>
                    <td>For bread</td>
               </tr>
               <tr>
                    <td>Grated Cheddar</td>
                    <td>1.5 handfuls</td>
               </tr>
               <tr>
                    <td>Beer</td>
                    <td>One splash</td>
               </tr>
               <tr>
                    <td>Wholegrain mustard</td>
                    <td>One dollop</td>
               </tr>
```

```
            <tr>
                <td>Pepper</td>
                <td>To taste</td>
            </tr>
        </tbody>
    </table>

</div>

<h3>Instructions</h3>

<ol>
    <li>Lightly toast the bread</li>
    <li>Place on a baking tray, and spread with butter.</li>
    <li>Add the grated Cheddar cheese and 2 tablespoons of beer to a saucepan.
    Place the saucepan over a medium heat, and stir the cheese continuously until
    it has melted. Add a teaspoon of wholegrain mustard and grind in a little
    pepper. Keep stirring.</li>
    <li>When thick and smooth, pour over each piece of toast spreading it to the
    edges to stop the toast from burning.</li>
    <li>Place under the grill for a couple of minutes or until golden brown.</li>
</ol>

</body>
</html>
```

2. Save the preceding CSS and markup as `example_13-4.html`. This example results in the output in Figure 13-6 in Safari and other desktop browsers.

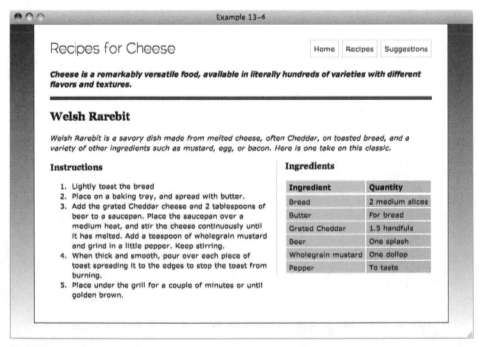

FIGURE 13-6

How It Works

In Example 13-4,you added a gradient background to the html element with the following rule:

```
html {
    height: 100%;
    background-color: #233;
    background-image: -moz-linear-gradient(top, #233, #FFF);
    background-image: -webkit-gradient(linear, left top, left bottom, from(#233),
    to(#FFF));
    -ms-filter: "progid:DXImageTransform.Microsoft.Gradient
    (StartColorStr=#223333, EndColorStr=#FFFFFF)";
    background-image: linear-gradient(top, #233, #FFF);
}
```

In addition to applying the gradient, you've also added a height declaration, making the html element take up the full height of the browser window (if the content is shorter) and a background-color declaration.

The height makes the gradient apply to the full height of the page and doesn't stop at the end of the content. You can see the result in Figure 13-6.

The background-color declaration is important for browsers that don't support gradient backgrounds. In IE6, for example, you will see a solid background instead of a gradient, as in Figure 13-7.

FIGURE 13-7

That is the end of this section on CSS properties. In the next part of this book, you'll look at advanced selectors, styling for print, customizing the mouse cursor, controlling opacity and visibility, and styling content for mobile devices.

EXERCISES

1. What is the first step in implementing a web page from a design?

2. Which rule is used to add support for custom fonts?

3. What are the drawbacks to using custom fonts?

4. What are vendor prefixes?

5. How would you apply a gradient background, and what must you do to support browsers that don't implement gradient backgrounds?

▶ WHAT YOU LEARNED IN THIS CHAPTER

In this chapter, I showed you some of the challenges of writing CSS for mobile devices. You learned the following:

TOPIC	KEY CONCEPTS
Custom fonts	How to use the @font-face rule to specify custom fonts, and the drawbacks to using them in designs.
Vendor prefixes	Vendor prefixes allow browser vendors to implement features of CSS that have yet to be finalized.
Applying gradient backgrounds	How to implement gradient backgrounds in four different ways to support a wide range of browsers.

PART III
Advanced CSS and Alternative Media

14

Advanced Selectors

WHAT YOU WILL LEARN IN THIS CHAPTER:

➤ How to use direct child selectors

➤ How to use next sibling selectors

➤ How to use attribute selectors

➤ How to use pseudo-elements

➤ How to use structural pseudo-classes

In Chapter 3, I covered the basic selectors in CSS. There I discussed the most common and widely supported selectors, class and ID selectors, which target elements based on their class and ID attributes. I also covered the universal selector, which targets everything, and descendant selectors, which target elements that are ancestors of other elements. In addition, I covered a small range of pseudo-classes, :link, :visited, :focus, :hover, and :active, used for styling links and other interactive elements.

In this chapter I show you a range of advanced selectors that can be used to more precisely target elements of a web page, a greater range of pseudo-classes, and I introduce pseudo-elements.

DIRECT CHILD SELECTORS

Direct child selectors operate much like descendant selectors in that they also rely on an ancestral relationship to decide where to apply style. Descendant selectors, however, are more ambiguous because they apply to any descendant of an element; the descendant can be a grandchild or a great-grandchild, or a great-great-grandchild, and so on. Direct child selectors apply only to immediate children of the element. This is achieved by introducing a new syntax for the selector:

```
body > .intro {
    font-weight: bold;
}
```

Like descendant selectors, direct child selectors are chained together, but instead of a space, a greater than, or right angled bracket, is used to separate each element in the selector.

 NOTE *All major browsers except for IE 6 support direct child selectors.*

The following Try It Out shows how to use direct child selectors.

TRY IT OUT **Direct Child Selectors**

Example 14-1

To use a direct child selector, follow these steps.

1. Enter the following markup:

```
<!DOCTYPE html PUBLIC "-//W3C//DTD HTML 4.01//EN"
    "http://www.w3.org/TR/html4/strict.dtd">
<html lang="en">
<head>
    <meta http-equiv="Content-Type" content="text/html; charset=utf-8">
    <title>Example 14-1</title>
    <style type="text/css">
        .intro {
            font-style: italic;
        }

        body > .intro {
            font-weight: bold;
        }
    </style>
</head>
<body>

<h1>Recipes for Cheese</h1>

<p class="intro">Cheese is a remarkably versatile food, available in literally
hundreds of varieties with different flavors and textures.</p>

<div class="content">

    <h2>Submit a recipe</h2>

    <p class="intro">We would love to hear from you about your delicious recipes
    for cheese. Please complete our form (all fields required) or email us at
    <a href="mailto:recipes@example.com">recipes@example.com</a>.</p>

    <form method="post" action="">
        <div>
            <label for="submit-name">Name</label>
            <input type="text" name="name" id="submit-name">
```

```
            </div>
            <div>
                <label for="submit-email">Email</label>
                <input type="text" name="email" id="submit-email">
            </div>
            <div>
                <label for="submit-recipe-name">Recipe Name</label>
                <input type="text" name="recipe-name" id="submit-recipe-name">
            </div>
            <div>
                <label for="submit-ingredients">Ingredients</label>
                <textarea name="ingredients" id="submit-ingredients" rows="5" cols="50">
                </textarea>
            </div>
            <div>
                <label for="submit-recipe">Recipe</label>
                <textarea name="recipe" id="submit-recipe" rows="5" cols="50">
                </textarea>
            </div>
            <div>
                <input type="submit" value="Send recipe">
            </div>
        </form>

    </div>

    </body>
    </html>
```

2. Save the preceding CSS and markup as `example_14-1.html`. This example results in the output in Figure 14-1.

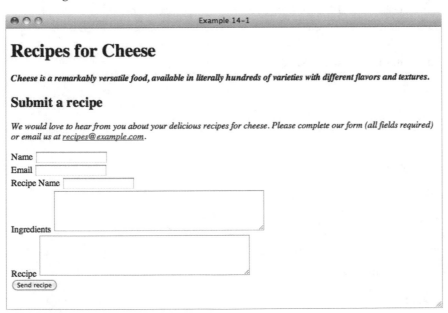

FIGURE 14-1

How It Works

In Example 14-1, you made each element with the class name `intro` italic with `font-style: italic;`, and used a descendent selector `body > .into` to make only the elements with the class name of `intro`, which are also a direct child of the `body` element bold with `font-weight: bold;`.

You can see in the figure that while both paragraphs are italic only the first is bold, because the second paragraph is a child of the element with the class name `content` and not the `body`.

NEXT SIBLING SELECTOR

The official name of the selector I discuss in this section, according to the W3C, is the *adjacent sibling combinator*. I think that's too long and complicated, so I've shortened it to just *next sibling*. The next sibling selector selects an element's next sibling, in other words the element following another element if it matches the second part of the selector.

This syntax for this selector is:

```
h1 + .intro {
    font-weight: bold;
}
```

This will select any elements with the class name `intro` that immediately follow an `h1` element.

Next sibling selectors are chained together with a plus sign.

 NOTE *All major browsers except for IE 6 support next sibling selectors.*

The following Try It Out shows how to use next sibling selectors.

TRY IT OUT Next Sibling Selector

Example 14-2

To use a next sibling selector, follow these steps.

1. Enter the following markup:

```
<!DOCTYPE html PUBLIC "-//W3C//DTD HTML 4.01//EN"
    "http://www.w3.org/TR/html4/strict.dtd">
<html lang="en">
<head>
    <meta http-equiv="Content-Type" content="text/html; charset=utf-8">
    <title>Example 14-2</title>
    <style type="text/css">
        .intro {
```

```
            font-style: italic;
        }

        h1 + .intro {
            font-weight: bold;
        }
    </style>
</head>
<body>

<h1>Recipes for Cheese</h1>

<p class="intro">Cheese is a remarkably versatile food, available in literally
hundreds of varieties with different flavors and textures.</p>

<div class="content">

    <h2>Submit a recipe</h2>

    <p class="intro">We would love to hear from you about your delicious recipes
    for cheese. Please complete our form (all fields required) or email us at
    <a href="mailto:recipes@example.com">recipes@example.com</a>.</p>

    <form method="post" action="">
        <div>
            <label for="submit-name">Name</label>
            <input type="text" name="name" id="submit-name">
        </div>
        <div>
            <label for="submit-email">Email</label>
            <input type="text" name="email" id="submit-email">
        </div>
        <div>
            <label for="submit-recipe-name">Recipe Name</label>
            <input type="text" name="recipe-name" id="submit-recipe-name">
        </div>
        <div>
            <label for="submit-ingredients">Ingredients</label>
            <textarea name="ingredients" id="submit-ingredients" rows="5" cols="50">
            </textarea>
        </div>
        <div>
            <label for="submit-recipe">Recipe</label>
            <textarea name="recipe" id="submit-recipe" rows="5" cols="50">
            </textarea>
        </div>
        <div>
            <input type="submit" value="Send recipe">
        </div>
    </form>

</div>

</body>
</html>
```

2. Save the preceding CSS and markup as `example_14-2.html`. This example results in the output in Figure 14-2.

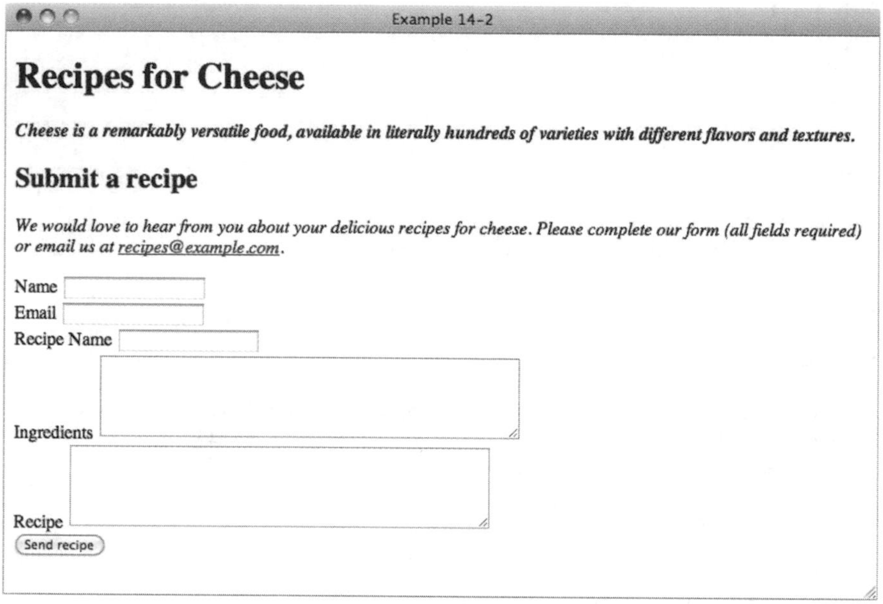

FIGURE 14-2

How It Works

In Example 14-2, you made each element with the class name `intro` italic with `font-style: italic;` and used a next sibling selector `h1 + .intro` to make only the elements with the class name of `intro` that immediately follow an `h1` element bold with `font-weight: bold;`.

You will see that this results in the same output as Example 1, giving you two ways to achieve the same effect under different circumstances.

ATTRIBUTE SELECTORS

Attribute selectors are used to apply style sheet declarations based on the presence of attributes or attribute values of an HTML element.

There are several types of attribute selectors, and CSS is capable of detecting attributes based on the following criteria:

➤ The presence of an attribute

➤ The value of an attribute

➤ Whether the attribute value begins with a specific string

➤ Whether the attribute value ends with a specific string

➤ Whether the attribute value contains a specific string anywhere in the value, be it at the beginning, end, or middle

The following sections examine each type of attribute selector in greater depth and provide examples of the syntax for each.

 NOTE *All major browsers except for IE 6 support attribute selectors.*

Select by Presence of an Attribute

The simplest attribute selector is one that applies a style sheet rule based on the presence of an attribute. It doesn't matter what the value given to the attribute is, just that the element has the specified attribute.

This syntax for attribute selectors is:

```
input[name] {
    border: 2px dashed #000;
}
```

The following Try It Out shows how to select by presence of an attribute.

TRY IT OUT   Attribute Selector: Presence of an Attribute

Example 14-3

To use a select based on the presence of an attribute, follow these steps.

1.   Enter the following markup:

```
<!DOCTYPE html PUBLIC "-//W3C//DTD HTML 4.01//EN"
    "http://www.w3.org/TR/html4/strict.dtd">
<html lang="en">
<head>
    <meta http-equiv="Content-Type" content="text/html; charset=utf-8">
    <title>Example 14-3</title>
    <style type="text/css">
        input {
            background: #CC5;
        }

        input[name] {
            border: 2px dashed #000;
        }
```

```
      </style>
  </head>
  <body>

  <h1>Recipes for Cheese</h1>

  <p class="intro">Cheese is a remarkably versatile food, available in literally
  hundreds of varieties with different flavors and textures.</p>

  <div class="content">

      <h2>Submit a recipe</h2>

      <p class="intro">We would love to hear from you about your delicious recipes
      for cheese. Please complete our form (all fields required) or email us at
      <a href="mailto:recipes@example.com">recipes@example.com</a>.</p>

      <form method="post" action="">
          <div>
              <label for="submit-name">Name</label>
              <input type="text" name="name" id="submit-name">
          </div>
          <div>
              <label for="submit-email">Email</label>
              <input type="text" name="email" id="submit-email">
          </div>
          <div>
              <label for="submit-recipe-name">Recipe Name</label>
              <input type="text" name="recipe-name" id="submit-recipe-name">
          </div>
          <div>
              <label for="submit-ingredients">Ingredients</label>
              <textarea name="ingredients" id="submit-ingredients" rows="5" cols="50">
              </textarea>
          </div>
          <div>
              <label for="submit-recipe">Recipe</label>
              <textarea name="recipe" id="submit-recipe" rows="5" cols="50">
              </textarea>
          </div>
          <div>
              <input type="submit" value="Send recipe">
          </div>
      </form>

  </div>

  </body>
  </html>
```

2. Save the preceding CSS and markup as `example_14-3.html`. This example results in the output in Figure 14-3.

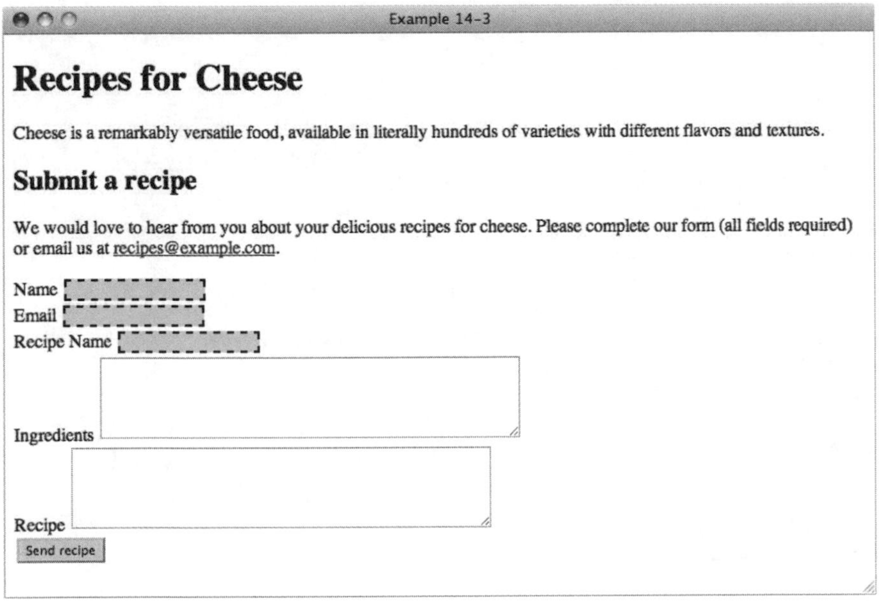

FIGURE 14-3

How It Works

In Example 14-3, you used a simple type selector to give all input elements a green background. Then using a combined type and attribute selector, input[name], you added a dashed border to only those inputs that have a name attribute — the final input, `<input type="submit" value="Send recipe">`, does not have a name attribute and therefore does not have a dotted border.

Select by Attribute Value

You are not limited to detecting the presence of an attribute, attribute value selectors delegate style declarations based on an attribute's presence and value.

The syntax is very similar:

```
input[name="email"] {
    border: 2px dashed #000;
}
```

Here you have specified both an attribute (name) and a value for that attribute (email) to select on — only input elements with name attribute values of email will match this selector.

The following Try It Out shows how to select by attribute value.

TRY IT OUT | Attribute Selector: Attribute Value

Example 14-4

To use a selector based on the presence of an attribute with a specific value, follow these steps.

1. Enter the following markup:

```
<!DOCTYPE html PUBLIC "-//W3C//DTD HTML 4.01//EN"
    "http://www.w3.org/TR/html4/strict.dtd">
<html lang="en">
<head>
    <meta http-equiv="Content-Type" content="text/html; charset=utf-8">
    <title>Example 14-4</title>
    <style type="text/css">
        input {
            background: #CC5;
        }

        input[name="email"] {
            border: 2px dashed #000;
        }
    </style>
</head>
<body>

<h1>Recipes for Cheese</h1>

<p class="intro">Cheese is a remarkably versatile food, available in literally
hundreds of varieties with different flavors and textures.</p>

<div class="content">

    <h2>Submit a recipe</h2>

    <p class="intro">We would love to hear from you about your delicious recipes
    for cheese. Please complete our form (all fields required) or email us at
    <a href="mailto:recipes@example.com">recipes@example.com</a>.</p>

    <form method="post" action="">
        <div>
            <label for="submit-name">Name</label>
            <input type="text" name="name" id="submit-name">
        </div>
        <div>
            <label for="submit-email">Email</label>
            <input type="text" name="email" id="submit-email">
        </div>
        <div>
            <label for="submit-recipe-name">Recipe Name</label>
            <input type="text" name="recipe-name" id="submit-recipe-name">
        </div>
        <div>
            <label for="submit-ingredients">Ingredients</label>
```

```
                    <textarea name="ingredients" id="submit-ingredients" rows="5" cols="50">
                    </textarea>
                </div>
                <div>
                    <label for="submit-recipe">Recipe</label>
                    <textarea name="recipe" id="submit-recipe" rows="5" cols="50">
                    </textarea>
                </div>
                <div>
                    <input type="submit" value="Send recipe">
                </div>
            </form>

    </div>

    </body>
    </html>
```

2. Save the preceding CSS and markup as `example_14-4.html`. This example results in the output in Figure 14-4.

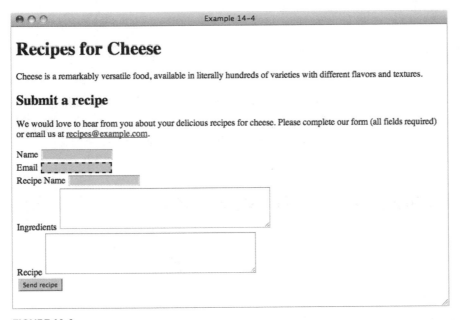

FIGURE 14-4

How It Works

In Example 14-4, you used a simple type selector to give all `input` elements a green background as you did in Example 14-3. Then using a combined type, attribute, and value selector, `input[name="email"]`, you added a dashed border to only those `input` elements that have a `name` attribute value equal to `email`.

Attribute Substring Selectors

Taking the flexibility of attribute selectors even further, the selectors in the following sections choose elements based on whether a particular string appears at the beginning of an attribute's value, at the end of an attribute's value, or anywhere inside an attribute's value. You can select an element based on what appears at the beginning of an attribute's value.

 NOTE *A string that appears inside another string is referred to as a substring.*

Selection Based on Attribute Values That Begin with a String

The first type of substring attribute selector chooses elements with an attribute value that begins with a particular string.

The syntax for this selector is:

```
a[href^="mailto:"] {
    padding-left: 23px;
    background: transparent url(icon-email.png) no-repeat center left;
}
```

The ^ character following the href attribute means to select elements where the value of the preceding attribute begins with the value that follows.

The following Try It Out shows how to use attributes that begin with a string as a selector.

TRY IT OUT | **Attribute Selector: Attribute Begins with a String**

Example 14-5

To use a selector based on the presence of an attribute with a value that starts with a given string, follow these steps.

1. Enter the following markup:

```
<!DOCTYPE html PUBLIC "-//W3C//DTD HTML 4.01//EN"
    "http://www.w3.org/TR/html4/strict.dtd">
<html lang="en">
<head>
    <meta http-equiv="Content-Type" content="text/html; charset=utf-8">
    <title>Example 14-5</title>
    <style type="text/css">
        a[href^="mailto:"] {
```

```
                padding-left: 23px;
                background: transparent url(icon-email.png) no-repeat center left;
            }
        </style>
    </head>
    <body>

    <h1>Recipes for Cheese</h1>

    <p class="intro">Cheese is a remarkably versatile food, available in literally
    hundreds of varieties with different flavors and textures.</p>

    <div class="content">

        <h2>Submit a recipe</h2>

        <p class="intro">We would love to hear from you about your delicious recipes
        for cheese. Please complete our form (all fields required) or email us at
        <a href="mailto:recipes@example.com">recipes@example.com</a>.</p>

        <form method="post" action="">
            <div>
                <label for="submit-name">Name</label>
                <input type="text" name="name" id="submit-name">
            </div>
            <div>
                <label for="submit-email">Email</label>
                <input type="text" name="email" id="submit-email">
            </div>
            <div>
                <label for="submit-recipe-name">Recipe Name</label>
                <input type="text" name="recipe-name" id="submit-recipe-name">
            </div>
            <div>
                <label for="submit-ingredients">Ingredients</label>
                <textarea name="ingredients" id="submit-ingredients" rows="5" cols="50">
                </textarea>
            </div>
            <div>
                <label for="submit-recipe">Recipe</label>
                <textarea name="recipe" id="submit-recipe" rows="5" cols="50">
                </textarea>
            </div>
            <div>
                <input type="submit" value="Send recipe">
            </div>
        </form>

    </div>

    </body>
    </html>
```

2. Save the preceding CSS and markup as `example_14-5.html`. This example results in the output in Figure 14-5.

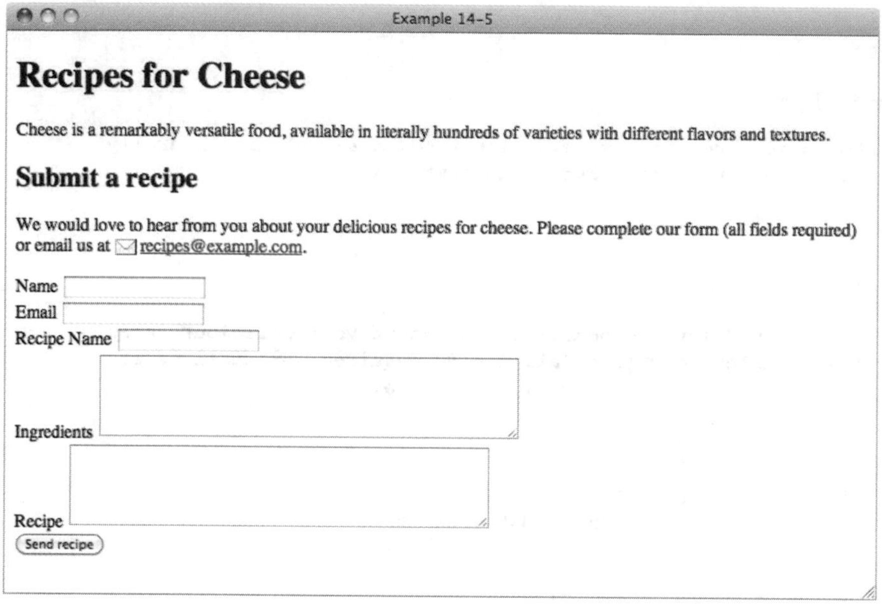

FIGURE 14-5

How It Works

In Example 14-5, you used a combined type, attribute, and a value selector with the ^ character indicating that you want to match the start of the value with your string, `a[href^="mailto:"]`; you added an envelope icon as a background image.

Selection Based on Attribute Values That End with a String

The next substring attribute selector chooses elements with attributes whose value ends with a string. The syntax is:

```
input[id$="name"] {
    border: 2px dashed #000;
}
```

The selector of the preceding rule uses the dollar sign to signify that the selector matches the end of the attribute value. This changes all `input` elements with an `id` attribute value that ends in the string `name`.

The following Try It Out shows how to use attributes that end with a string as a selector.

TRY IT OUT Attribute Selector: Attribute Ends with a String

Example 14-6

To use a selector based on the presence of an attribute with a value that ends with a given string, follow these steps.

1. Enter the following markup:

```
<!DOCTYPE html PUBLIC "-//W3C//DTD HTML 4.01//EN"
    "http://www.w3.org/TR/html4/strict.dtd">
<html lang="en">
<head>
    <meta http-equiv="Content-Type" content="text/html; charset=utf-8">
    <title>Example 14-6</title>
    <style type="text/css">
        input[id$="name"] {
            border: 2px dashed #000;
        }
    </style>
</head>
<body>

<h1>Recipes for Cheese</h1>

<p class="intro">Cheese is a remarkably versatile food, available in literally
hundreds of varieties with different flavors and textures.</p>

<div class="content">

    <h2>Submit a recipe</h2>

    <p class="intro">We would love to hear from you about your delicious recipes
    for cheese. Please complete our form (all fields required) or email us at
    <a href="mailto:recipes@example.com">recipes@example.com</a>.</p>

    <form method="post" action="">
        <div>
            <label for="submit-name">Name</label>
            <input type="text" name="name" id="submit-name">
        </div>
        <div>
            <label for="submit-email">Email</label>
            <input type="text" name="email" id="submit-email">
        </div>
        <div>
            <label for="submit-recipe-name">Recipe Name</label>
            <input type="text" name="recipe-name" id="submit-recipe-name">
        </div>
        <div>
            <label for="submit-ingredients">Ingredients</label>
            <textarea name="ingredients" id="submit-ingredients" rows="5" cols="50">
            </textarea>
        </div>
        <div>
```

```
                   <label for="submit-recipe">Recipe</label>
                   <textarea name="recipe" id="submit-recipe" rows="5" cols="50">
                   </textarea>
             </div>
             <div>
                   <input type="submit" value="Send recipe">
             </div>
       </form>

   </div>

   </body>
   </html>
```

2. Save the preceding CSS and markup as `example_14-6.html`. This example results in the output in Figure 14-6.

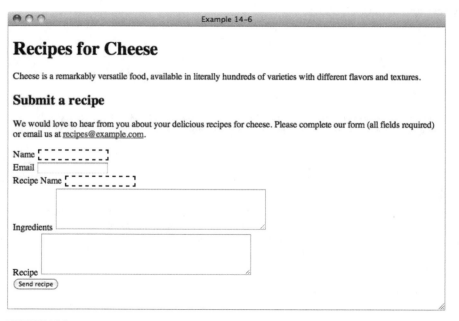

FIGURE 14-6

How It Works

In Example 14-6, you used a combined type, attribute, and a value selector with the $ character, indicating that you want to match the end of the value with your string, `input[id$="name"]`; you added a border to all `input` elements with `id` attribute values ending in `name`.

Selection Based on Attribute Values That Contain a String

The final type of attribute substring selector is a wildcard attribute substring selector. It selects an element that contains an attribute whose value contains a string anywhere in the value: at the beginning, the end, or anywhere in the middle. This attribute substring selector uses an asterisk in the syntax to indicate that the selector is looking anywhere inside the value:

```
[name*="recipe"] {
    border: 2px dashed #000;
}
```

The following Try It Out shows how to use attributes that contain a string as a selector.

TRY IT OUT **Attribute Selector: Attribute Contains a String**

Example 14-7

To use a selector based on the presence of an attribute with a value that contains a given string, follow these steps.

1. Enter the following markup:

```
<!DOCTYPE html PUBLIC "-//W3C//DTD HTML 4.01//EN"
    "http://www.w3.org/TR/html4/strict.dtd">
<html lang="en">
<head>
    <meta http-equiv="Content-Type" content="text/html; charset=utf-8">
    <title>Example 14-7</title>
    <style type="text/css">
        [name*="recipe"] {
            border: 2px dashed #000;
        }
    </style>
</head>
<body>

<h1>Recipes for Cheese</h1>

<p class="intro">Cheese is a remarkably versatile food, available in literally
hundreds of varieties with different flavors and textures.</p>

<div class="content">

    <h2>Submit a recipe</h2>

    <p class="intro">We would love to hear from you about your delicious recipes
    for cheese. Please complete our form (all fields required) or email us at
    <a href="mailto:recipes@example.com">recipes@example.com</a>.</p>

    <form method="post" action="">
        <div>
            <label for="submit-name">Name</label>
            <input type="text" name="name" id="submit-name">
        </div>
        <div>
```

```
                    <label for="submit-email">Email</label>
                    <input type="text" name="email" id="submit-email">
            </div>
            <div>
                    <label for="submit-recipe-name">Recipe Name</label>
                    <input type="text" name="recipe-name" id="submit-recipe-name">
            </div>
            <div>
                    <label for="submit-ingredients">Ingredients</label>
                    <textarea name="ingredients" id="submit-ingredients" rows="5" cols="50">
                    </textarea>
            </div>
            <div>
                    <label for="submit-recipe">Recipe</label>
                    <textarea name="recipe" id="submit-recipe" rows="5" cols="50">
                    </textarea>
            </div>
            <div>
                    <input type="submit" value="Send recipe">
            </div>
        </form>

    </div>

    </body>
    </html>
```

2.   Save the preceding CSS and markup as `example_14-7.html`. This example results in the output
in Figure 14-7.

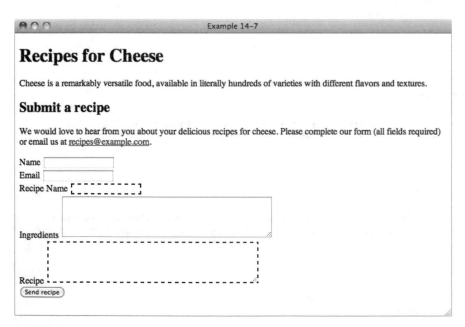

FIGURE 14-7

How It Works

In Example 14-7, you used a combined attribute and value selector with the * character indicating that you want to match values that contain the given string, [name*="recipe"]; you added a border to all elements with name attribute values containing the string recipe.

PSEUDO-ELEMENTS :FIRST-LETTER AND :FIRST-LINE

Pseudo-elements represent certain aspects of a document not easily modifiable with plain markup. Pseudo-elements may be used to modify the formatting of the first letter of a paragraph, or the first line of a paragraph, for example.

The pseudo-elements :first-letter and :first-line refer to the first letter and first line of an element containing text. When you design a website, it is helpful to have control over how you present content. With the :first-letter and :first-line pseudo-elements, you can control the formatting of the first letter and first line of a paragraph completely from CSS. You may add an increased font size or other font effects, apply a background color or image, or use just about any text effect supported by CSS and the browser.

 WARNING *CSS 3 changes pseudo-element syntax to use a double colon (: :) preceding each pseudo-element. For example,* p::first-letter *refers to the first letter of a paragraph instead of* p:first-letter. *This syntax distinguishes pseudo-elements from pseudo-classes, which use a single colon syntax, as in* a:hover, *which is a reference to a pseudo-class.*

However, this form is not supported in any version of IE, but the single colon version is, and also continues to be supported by all other major browsers so it is my recommendation that you use :first-letter and :first-line instead of ::first-letter and ::first-line.

The following Try It Out shows how to use :first-letter and :first-line pseudo-elements to style content.

TRY IT OUT   :first-letter and :first-line Pseudo-elements

Example 14-8

To style the first letter or first line of text, follow these steps.

1.   Enter the following markup:

```
<!DOCTYPE html PUBLIC "-//W3C//DTD HTML 4.01//EN"
    "http://www.w3.org/TR/html4/strict.dtd">
<html lang="en">
```

```html
<head>
    <meta http-equiv="Content-Type" content="text/html; charset=utf-8">
    <title>Example 14-8</title>
    <style type="text/css">
        .intro:first-letter {
            font-size: 1.7em;
        }

        .intro:first-line {
            font-style: italic;
        }
    </style>
</head>
<body>

<h1>Recipes for Cheese</h1>

<p class="intro">Cheese is a remarkably versatile food, available in literally
hundreds of varieties with different flavors and textures.</p>

<div class="content">

    <h2>Submit a recipe</h2>

    <p class="intro">We would love to hear from you about your delicious recipes
    for cheese. Please complete our form (all fields required) or email us at
    <a href="mailto:recipes@example.com">recipes@example.com</a>.</p>

    <form method="post" action="">
        <div>
            <label for="submit-name">Name</label>
            <input type="text" name="name" id="submit-name">
        </div>
        <div>
            <label for="submit-email">Email</label>
            <input type="text" name="email" id="submit-email">
        </div>
        <div>
            <label for="submit-recipe-name">Recipe Name</label>
            <input type="text" name="recipe-name" id="submit-recipe-name">
        </div>
        <div>
            <label for="submit-ingredients">Ingredients</label>
            <textarea name="ingredients" id="submit-ingredients" rows="5" cols="50">
            </textarea>
        </div>
        <div>
            <label for="submit-recipe">Recipe</label>
            <textarea name="recipe" id="submit-recipe" rows="5" cols="50">
            </textarea>
        </div>
        <div>
            <input type="submit" value="Send recipe">
```

```
        </div>
      </form>

  </div>

  </body>
  </html>
```

2. Save the preceding CSS and markup as `example_14-8.html`. This example results in the output in Figure 14-8.

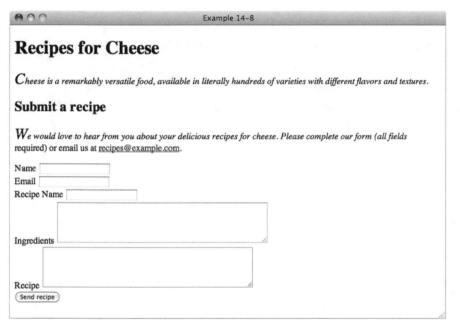

FIGURE 14-8

How It Works

In Example 14-8, you used `:first-letter` to increase the text size of the first letter and `:first-line` to italicize the first line of each intro paragraph.

STRUCTURAL PSEUDO-CLASSES

Much like the direct child and next sibling selectors earlier in this chapter, structural pseudo-classes are used to refer to an element's position in a document.

:first-child

The :first-child structural pseudo-class applies only when an element is the first child of another element.

 NOTE *All major browsers except for IE 6 support the* :first-child *structural pseudo-class.*

:last-child

The :last-child structural pseudo-class applies only when an element is the last child of another element.

 NOTE *IE 6, 7, and 8 do not support the* :last-child *structural pseudo-class. All other major browsers, including IE9, do.*

:nth-child(n)

The :nth-child(n) structural pseudo-class applies only when an element is the nth child of another element; in other words, if the value in the brackets is 3, the third child element will be selected.

 NOTE *IE 6, 7, and 8 do not support the* :nth-child(n) *structural pseudo-class. All other major browsers, including IE9, do.*

The following Try It Out shows how to use :first-child, :last-child and :nth-child(n) pseudo-classes to style content.

TRY IT OUT **Using Child Structural Pseudo-Classes**

Example 14-9

To use a selector based on the presence of an attribute with a value that starts with a given string, follow these steps.

1. Enter the following markup:

```
<!DOCTYPE html PUBLIC "-//W3C//DTD HTML 4.01//EN"
    "http://www.w3.org/TR/html4/strict.dtd">
<html lang="en">
```

```
<head>
    <meta http-equiv="Content-Type" content="text/html; charset=utf-8">
    <title>Example 14-9</title>
    <style type="text/css">
        form div:first-child {
            background: #CC5;
        }

        form div:last-child {
            background: #000;
        }

        form div:nth-child(4) {
            background: #CCF;
        }
    </style>
</head>
<body>

<h1>Recipes for Cheese</h1>

<p class="intro">Cheese is a remarkably versatile food, available in literally
hundreds of varieties with different flavors and textures.</p>

<div class="content">

    <h2>Submit a recipe</h2>

    <p class="intro">We would love to hear from you about your delicious recipes
    for cheese. Please complete our form (all fields required) or email us at
    <a href="mailto:recipes@example.com">recipes@example.com</a>.</p>

    <form method="post" action="">
        <div>
            <label for="submit-name">Name</label>
            <input type="text" name="name" id="submit-name">
        </div>
        <div>
            <label for="submit-email">Email</label>
            <input type="text" name="email" id="submit-email">
        </div>
        <div>
            <label for="submit-recipe-name">Recipe Name</label>
            <input type="text" name="recipe-name" id="submit-recipe-name">
        </div>
        <div>
            <label for="submit-ingredients">Ingredients</label>
            <textarea name="ingredients" id="submit-ingredients" rows="5" cols="50">
            </textarea>
        </div>
        <div>
            <label for="submit-recipe">Recipe</label>
            <textarea name="recipe" id="submit-recipe" rows="5" cols="50">
            </textarea>
```

```
            </div>
            <div>
                <input type="submit" value="Send recipe">
            </div>
        </form>

    </div>

    </body>
    </html>
```

2. Save the preceding CSS and markup as `example_14-9.html`. This example results in the output in Figure 14-9.

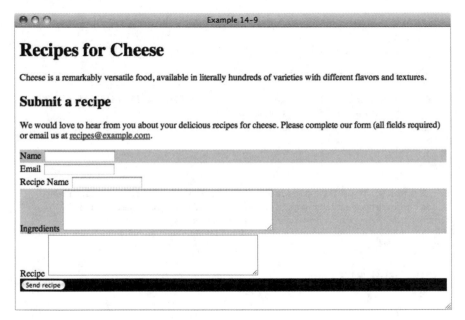

FIGURE 14-9

How It Works

In Example 14-9, you used `:first-child`, `:last-child` and `:nth-child(n)` structural pseudo-classes to apply background colors to the first, last, and fourth child `div` elements of the form.

It is important to understand which way these pseudo-classes work:

```
    div:first-child
```

This selector targets a `div` element that is the first child of another element, *not* an element that is the first child of a `div`.

EXERCISES

1. What is the syntax for using direct child selectors?

2. What is the syntax for using next sibling selectors?

3. How would you select an element based on an attribute value?

4. How would you select an element based only on the start of an attribute value string?

5. How would you style the first letter and first line of a paragraph of text?

6. How would you style only the first link in a list of links?

► WHAT YOU LEARNED IN THIS CHAPTER

In this chapter, I showed you what is possible with advanced CSS selectors. You learned the following:

TOPIC	KEY CONCEPTS
Direct child selectors	Direct child selectors make descendant selectors more specific, applying styles only to direct child elements instead of all descendant elements.
Next sibling selectors	Direct adjacent sibling combinators, or as I have termed them, next sibling selectors, apply style if two elements, appearing back-to-back in a document as siblings, have the same parent.
Attribute selectors	Attribute selectors delegate style depending on the presence of attributes or attribute values.
Pseudo-elements	Pseudo-elements are used for situations where it would be difficult to use real markup, such as in the styling of the first letter or first line of a paragraph.
Structural pseudo-classes	Structural pseudo-classes are used to style elements based on their position in the document.

15

Styling for Print

WHAT YOU WILL LEARN IN THIS CHAPTER:

➤ The benefits of print style sheets

➤ Applying styles based on media types

➤ Controlling page breaks

➤ The `content` property in print

You can use a specific style sheet to style content for print. In Chapter 2, you saw the differences between length units used for a computer screen and length units used for print. This is one of the key reasons that separate style sheets for print exist. Specifying measurements designated for computer screens, such as pixel units, can potentially be inconsistent in printed documents, whereas real-world, absolute length units, such as inches, centimeters, points, and so on are ideally suited for print.

BENEFITS OF PRINT STYLE SHEETS

A style sheet written explicitly for print enables developers to exclude irrelevant portions of a web document from the printed version. For example, no document navigation is required in a printed version. Additionally, because color documents have some expense associated with them, depending on the type of printer and what type of ink or toner the printer uses, it is also often better to exclude background images or other aspects of the design that result in greater consumption of expensive ink or toner. For these reasons, print versions of web documents are often simplified to simple black and white productions of the original document. Only foreground images relevant to the document are retained. In fact browsers, by default, strip out all background images and background color; to print these, the user must specifically enable them before printing.

CSS provides several properties for controlling the presentation of paged media, such things as where page breaks occur, the size of the page margins, and the size of the page itself. At the time of this writing, a sparse selection of those properties is actually implemented in current browsers, and there is no sign that browsers are going to improve any time soon.

APPLYING STYLES BASED ON MEDIA

In order to print in CSS, you need a way of differentiating styles intended for print from styles intended for the computer screen. CSS can apply to a variety of documents, not just HTML, and CSS can be used on a variety of different devices and media.

To target different media, you use the media attribute, which is applied to the `<link />` element, or the `<style>` element. Or, from within a style sheet, you can target different media using @media rules. You see examples of these later in this section. First, let's examine the different types of media that CSS can theoretically be applied to. The different types of media are outlined in the following table.

MEDIA	PURPOSE
all	Suitable for all devices
braille	Intended for Braille tactical feedback devices
embossed	Intended for paged Braille printers
handheld	Intended for handheld devices
print	Intended for presentation to a printer (In a browser, use print preview to view the print style sheet.)
projection	Intended for projected presentations
screen	Intended for presentation on a color computer screen
speech | aural	Intended for presentation to a speech synthesizer (called aural in CSS 2, changed to speech in CSS 2.1)
tty	Intended for media using a fixed-pitch character grid (such as teletypes, terminals, or portable devices with limited display capabilities)
tv	Intended for television (low resolution, low color, limited scrollability)

The default value is all.

 NOTE Only screen, print, and all values are widely supported in desktop browsers.

As you can see in the preceding table, CSS can target a wide variety of media types. For this chapter, you need only be concerned with the screen, print, and all media. Each medium can be supplied as a value to the media attribute. For example, if you wanted a style sheet to apply only to styles presented in a PC or Mac browser, or smartphone browsers such as those on iPhone or Android devices, you would add the attribute media= "screen" to either the <link /> or <style> elements:

```
<style type="text/css" media="screen"></style>

<link rel="stylesheet" type="text/css" href="print.css" media="print">
```

The following Try It Out shows the media attribute in action.

TRY IT OUT   Applying Styles for Print

Example 15-1

To use a direct child selector, follow these steps.

1.   Enter the following markup:

```
<!DOCTYPE html PUBLIC "-//W3C//DTD HTML 4.01//EN"
    "http://www.w3.org/TR/html4/strict.dtd">
<html lang="en">
<head>
    <meta http-equiv="Content-Type" content="text/html; charset=utf-8">
    <title>Example 15-2</title>
    <style type="text/css" media="print">
        label {
            float: left;
            display: block;
            width: 3cm;
        }

        input {
            width: 7cm;
            border: none;
            border-bottom: 1px solid #000;
        }

        textarea {
            display: block;
            width: 10cm;
            height: 6cm;
            margin-top: 1cm;
            border-bottom: 1px solid #000;
        }

        form div {
            overflow: hidden;
            margin: 0.5cm 0;
        }

        .submit {
```

```
                display: none;
            }
    </style>
</head>
<body>

<h1>Recipes for Cheese</h1>

<p class="intro">Cheese is a remarkably versatile food, available in literally
hundreds of varieties with different flavors and textures.</p>

<div class="content">

    <h2>Submit a recipe</h2>

    <p class="intro">We would love to hear from you about your delicious recipes
    for cheese. Please complete our form (all fields required) or email us at
    <a href="mailto:recipes@example.com">recipes@example.com</a>.</p>

    <form method="post" action="">
        <div>
            <label for="submit-name">Name</label>
            <input type="text" name="name" id="submit-name">
        </div>
        <div>
            <label for="submit-email">Email</label>
            <input type="text" name="email" id="submit-email">
        </div>
        <div>
            <label for="submit-recipe-name">Recipe Name</label>
            <input type="text" name="recipe-name" id="submit-recipe-name">
        </div>
        <div>
            <label for="submit-ingredients">Ingredients</label>
            <textarea name="ingredients" id="submit-ingredients" rows="5"
            cols="50"></textarea>
        </div>
        <div>
            <label for="submit-recipe">Recipe</label>
            <textarea name="recipe" id="submit-recipe" rows="5"
            cols="50"></textarea>
        </div>
        <div class="submit">
            <input type="submit" value="Send recipe">
        </div>
    </form>

</div>

</body>
</html>
```

2. Save the preceding CSS and markup as example_15-1.html. This example results in the output
in Figure 15-1.

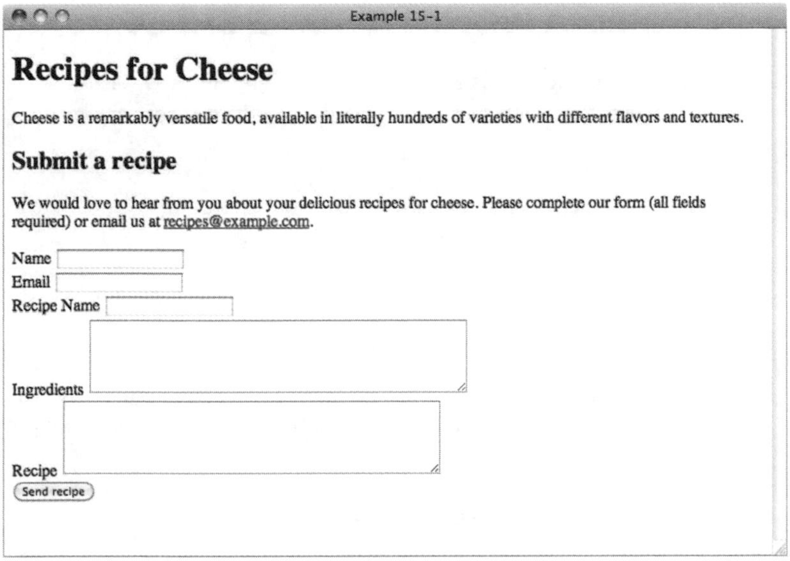

FIGURE 15-1

3. In your browser menu, select the print command, and, when given the option, select preview. This will show you what the page will look like when it is printed, and is a much cheaper way to test than to print each page out every time you make a change. You will see output similar to that in Figure 15-2.

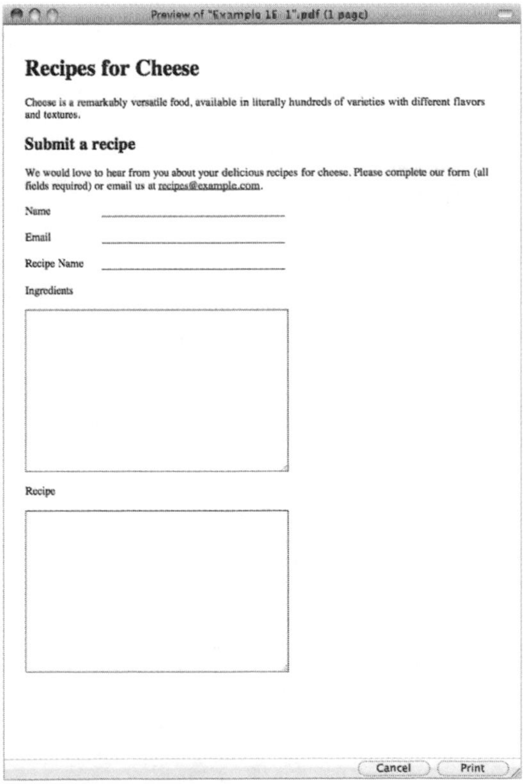

How It Works

In Example 15-1, you applied your styles to print only by adding a media attribute with a value of print to your style element.

In Figure 15-1 you can see that the page in our browser just has the browser default styling; but for print, shown in Figure 15-2, you have used a variety of familiar properties to position the form labels and give your input and textarea elements styles that you would expect in a printed document.

You have also hidden the div that contains the submit input because this is content that does not make sense outside of a web browser.

FIGURE 15-2

CONTROLLING STYLES FOR MEDIA WITHIN A STYLE SHEET

Another way to target styles for a particular media type is the @media rule. This is used within a style sheet to enclose rules where you can make style sheet adjustments based on medium, for example:

```
@media print {
    h1 {
        font-size: 50pt;
        text-align: center;
    }
}
```

You can see that a new syntax is enclosing the two rules that refer to the body element; these are the @media rules. The top @media rule applies to onscreen display, and the bottom @media rule applies to print display.

 NOTE *It is widely thought that most people find sans-serif fonts more readable on screen but serif fonts more readable in print. This is why most websites use a sans-serif font for body copy whereas most books and newspapers are printed with a serif font.*

In the following Try It Out, you review @media rules.

TRY IT OUT Applying Styles for Print

Example 15-2

To use a direct child selector, follow these steps.

1. Enter the following markup:

```
<!DOCTYPE html PUBLIC "-//W3C//DTD HTML 4.01//EN"
    "http://www.w3.org/TR/html4/strict.dtd">
<html lang="en">
<head>
    <meta http-equiv="Content-Type" content="text/html; charset=utf-8">
    <title>Example 15-2</title>
    <style type="text/css">
        @media screen {
            h1 {
                font-size: 3em;
                color: #A00;
            }
        }
        @media print {
            h1 {
                font-size: 50pt;
                text-align: center;
```

```
            }
        }
    </style>
</head>
<body>

<h1>Recipes for Cheese</h1>

<p class="intro">Cheese is a remarkably versatile food, available in literally
hundreds of varieties with different flavors and textures.</p>

<div class="content">

    <h2>Submit a recipe</h2>

    <p class="intro">We would love to hear from you about your delicious recipes
    for cheese. Please complete our form (all fields required) or email us at
    <a href="mailto:recipes@example.com">recipes@example.com</a>.</p>

    <form method="post" action="">
        <div>
            <label for="submit-name">Name</label>
            <input type="text" name="name" id="submit-name">
        </div>
        <div>
            <label for="submit-email">Email</label>
            <input type="text" name="email" id="submit-email">
        </div>
        <div>
            <label for="submit-recipe-name">Recipe Name</label>
            <input type="text" name="recipe-name" id="submit-recipe-name">
        </div>
        <div>
            <label for="submit-ingredients">Ingredients</label>
            <textarea name="ingredients" id="submit-ingredients" rows="5"
            cols="50"></textarea>
        </div>
        <div>
            <label for="submit-recipe">Recipe</label>
            <textarea name="recipe" id="submit-recipe" rows="5"
            cols="50"></textarea>
        </div>
        <div class="submit">
            <input type="submit" value="Send recipe">
        </div>
    </form>

</div>

</body>
</html>
```

2. Save the preceding CSS and markup as example_15-2.html. This example results in the output in Figure 15-3.

Recipes for Cheese

Cheese is a remarkably versatile food, available in literally hundreds of varieties with different flavors and textures.

Submit a recipe

We would love to hear from you about your delicious recipes for cheese. Please complete our form (all fields required) or email us at recipes@example.com.

Name

Email

Recipe Name

Ingredients

Recipe

Send recipe

FIGURE 15-3

3. In your browser menu, select the print command, and, when given the option, select preview. You will see output similar to that in Figure 15-4.

How It Works

In Example 15-2, you applied separate styles to screen and print using @media rules.

In Figure 15-3 you can see that the page in our browser shows that the font-size: 3em; and color: #A00; declarations have been picked up, making the h1 larger and dark red in color. This is because this rule is itself wrapped in an @media screen rule.

In Figure 15-4, you will see that the same h1 element has not been made red by the previous rule, but that the font-size: 50pt; and text-align: center; declarations have been picked up, making the h1 even larger and the text centered. This rule is wrapped in an @media screen rule, meaning that the styles will only apply in print.

FIGURE 15-4

In the next section, I describe how to control page breaks in printed content.

CONTROLLING PAGE BREAKS

Two print properties, or paged media properties, as they are referred to by the W3C, that all popular browsers have in common are `page-break-before` and `page-break-after`. These properties are outlined in the following table.

PROPERTY	VALUE
page-break-before	auto | always | avoid | left | right Initial value: auto
page-break-after	auto | always | avoid | left | right Initial value: auto

The `page-break-before` and `page-break-after` properties dictate where a page break should be made depending on where an element appears in a document.

 NOTE *The only keywords reliably supported across all browsers are* always *and* auto.

A value of `always` for `page-break-before` and `page-break-after` means that a page break must occur before or after the selected block level elements generated box (for example, the following declaration will force a page break after the element, as you will see in Figure 15-5 when you apply the following rule):

Available for download on Wrox.com

```
<!DOCTYPE html PUBLIC "-//W3C//DTD HTML 4.01//EN"
    "http://www.w3.org/TR/html4/strict.dtd">
<html lang="en">
<head>
    <meta http-equiv="Content-Type" content="text/html; charset=utf-8">
    <title>Figure 15-5</title>
    <style type="text/css" media="print">
        h1 {
            page-break-after: always;
        }
    </style>
</head>
<body>

<h1>Recipes for Cheese</h1>

<p class="intro">Cheese is a remarkably versatile food, available in literally
```

```
hundreds of varieties with different flavors and textures.</p>

<div class="content">

    <h2>Submit a recipe</h2>

    <p class="intro">We would love to hear from you about your delicious recipes
    for cheese. Please complete our form (all fields required) or email us at
    <a href="mailto:recipes@example.com">recipes@example.com</a>.</p>

    <form method="post" action="">
        <div>
            <label for="submit-name">Name</label>
            <input type="text" name="name" id="submit-name">
        </div>
        <div>
            <label for="submit-email">Email</label>
            <input type="text" name="email" id="submit-email">
        </div>
        <div>
            <label for="submit-recipe-name">Recipe Name</label>
            <input type="text" name="recipe-name" id="submit-recipe-name">
        </div>
        <div>
            <label for="submit-ingredients">Ingredients</label>
            <textarea name="ingredients" id="submit-ingredients" rows="5"
            cols="50"></textarea>
        </div>
        <div>
            <label for="submit-recipe">Recipe</label>
            <textarea name="recipe" id="submit-recipe" rows="5"
            cols="50"></textarea>
        </div>
        <div class="submit">
            <input type="submit" value="Send recipe">
        </div>
    </form>

</div>

</body>
</html>
```

code snippet /chapter15/figure_15-5.html

In the style sheet that you see in Figure 15-5, you apply the declaration
page-break-after: always; to the h1 element, forcing a page break after the h1 so that
subsequent content appears on a new page.

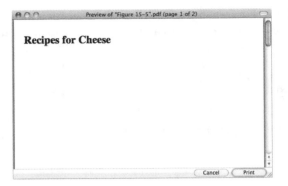

FIGURE 15-5

The `page-break-before` property works the same way as `page-break-after`, but it forces a page break before an element.

THE CONTENT PROPERTY

The `content` property is a way for us to insert content into a page using CSS. This content is not strictly part of the page, so it is not accessible to most assistive technology such as screen readers, which read out the content of pages. While it has applications beyond print that are outside of the scope of this book, it has one particular use which warrants its inclusion here.

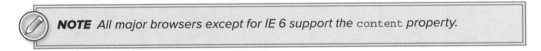

NOTE *All major browsers except for IE 6 support the* `content` *property.*

There is one interesting trick you can use when printing web pages that makes use of the `content` property that I will cover in brief.

One of the main drawbacks of printing web pages is that, by default, the URLs of any links are lost to us; for example:

```
<h1><a href="/">Recipes for Cheese</a></h1>
```

This results in Figure 15-6

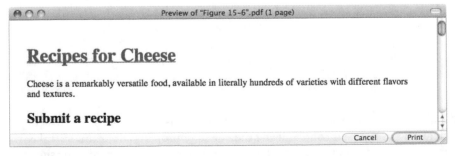

FIGURE 15-6

You can guess from the style of the heading that this is a link, but there is no way other than going back to the site in your browser of knowing where the link goes. With a little bit of CSS magic, you can fix this problem:

Available for download on Wrox.com

```
<!DOCTYPE html PUBLIC "-//W3C//DTD HTML 4.01//EN"
    "http://www.w3.org/TR/html4/strict.dtd">
<html lang="en">
<head>
    <meta http-equiv="Content-Type" content="text/html; charset=utf-8">
    <title>Figure 15-7</title>
    <style type="text/css" media="print">
        a:link:after,
        a:link:after {
          content: " (http://example.com" attr(href) ") ";
        }
    </style>
</head>
<body>

<h1><a href="/">Recipes for Cheese</a></h1>

<p class="intro">Cheese is a remarkably versatile food, available in literally
hundreds of varieties with different flavors and textures.</p>

<div class="content">

    <h2>Submit a recipe</h2>

</div>

</body>
</html>
```

code snippet /chapter15/figure_15-7.html

This results in Figure 15-7.

FIGURE 15-7

As you can see, the text is now followed by the URL of the link. This makes use of the `:after` pseudo-class, which allows us to insert content using the `content` property. `attr(href)` takes the `href` property from our link and uses it in the content. We prefix it with the domain our site is hosted on (here I've used `http://example.com`), and added some brackets to separate the link from the main text.

Don't worry if this is hard to understand; this is code that you can copy and paste to your own print style sheets. I hope it will encourage you to delve deeper into CSS to find further useful tricks.

EXERCISES

1. Which media values apply to desktop browsers?

2. Write the opening tag for the `<style>` element, targeting the styles to print.

3. What does the `page-break-before` property do?

4. Write a sample style sheet that includes three rules; the first rule applies to all media types, the second rule applies to onscreen layout, and the third applies to print.

▶ **WHAT YOU LEARNED IN THIS CHAPTER**

In this chapter, I showed you what is possible with advanced CSS selectors. You learned the following:

TOPIC	KEY CONCEPTS
Applying styles for a specific media type	Use the media property on `style` and `link` elements, or the `@media` rule within style sheets.
Controlling page breaks when printing	You can use `page-break-before` and `page-break-after` to specify where page breaks should be made.
Inserting content with CSS	Use the `content` property to add content such as the URLs for links when printing.

16

Customizing the Mouse Cursor

WHAT YOU WILL LEARN IN THIS CHAPTER:

➤ How to customize the cursor

➤ The different cursors that can be used

CSS provides the `cursor` property to control the type of cursor displayed for a particular element. When you build advanced web applications, it can be useful to change the cursor to indicate to users when they can perform certain actions, such as re-sizing or dragging elements. This should always be done with care because to use an inappropriate cursor would be confusing to your users. Done correctly it can potentially make custom interactions more usable.

THE CURSOR PROPERTY

The following table outlines the `cursor` property and its possible values.

PROPERTY	VALUE
cursor	`[<uri> ,]* [auto	crosshair	default	pointer	move	e-resize	ne-resize	nw-resize	n-resize	se-resize	sw-resize	s-resize	w-resize	text	wait	help	progress]`
Initial value: auto	
Non-standard extensions to cursor	`hand｜all-scroll｜col-resize｜row-resize｜no-drop｜ not-allowed｜vertical-text`

NOTE *Safari and Chrome do not support non-standard cursor keywords. Opera for the Mac does not support* *-resize *keywords, or non-standard cursor keywords. Opera for Windows supports* *-resize *keywords, but not non-standard keywords. Firefox for the Mac does not support the* all-scroll *keyword, but Firefox for Windows does. IE supports all possible options.*

The notation in the preceding table shows that you can provide a keyword to change the cursor displayed while the user's mouse pointer is hovering over an element.

CUSTOM POINTERS

It is possible with the use of the uri value to specify a custom cursor based on an image. In practice this is almost never done, and it is not recommended as the user is better served by using familiar mouse cursors. Custom cursors are not covered in this book.

To demonstrate how the cursor can be changed using a keyword, consider the example in the following Try It Out.

TRY IT OUT   **Changing the Mouse Cursor**

Example 16-1.

To see the different mouse cursors that can be displayed, follow these steps.

1.   Enter the following markup into your text editor:

```
<!DOCTYPE html PUBLIC "-//W3C//DTD HTML 4.01//EN"
    "http://www.w3.org/TR/html4/strict.dtd">
<html lang="en">
<head>
    <meta http-equiv="Content-Type" content="text/html; charset=utf-8">
    <title>Example 16-2</title>
    <style type="text/css">
        .crosshair {
            cursor: crosshair;
        }
        .pointer {
            cursor: pointer;
        }
        .move {
            cursor: move;
        }
        .e-resize {
            cursor: e-resize;
        }
        .w-resize {
```

```css
        cursor: w-resize;
    }
    .ne-resize {
        cursor: ne-resize;
    }
    .sw-resize {
        cursor: sw-resize;
    }
    .n-resize {
        cursor: n-resize;
    }
    .s-resize {
        cursor: s-resize;
    }
    .nw-resize {
        cursor: nw-resize;
    }
    .se-resize {
        cursor: se-resize;
    }
    .text {
        cursor: text;
    }
    .wait {
        cursor: wait;
    }
    .help {
        cursor: help;
    }
    .progress {
        cursor: progress;
    }
    .hand {
        cursor: hand;
    }
    .all-scroll {
        cursor: all-scroll;
    }
    .col-resize {
        cursor: col-resize;
    }
    .row-resize {
        cursor: row-resize;
    }
    .no-drop {
        cursor: no-drop;
    }
    .not-allowed {
        cursor: not-allowed;
    }
    .vertical-text {
        cursor: vertical-text
    }
    </style>
</head>
```

```
<body>

    <h1>Cursor Types</h1>

    <ul>
        <li class="crosshair">Crosshair</li>
        <li class="pointer">Pointer</li>
        <li class="move">Move</li>
        <li class="e-resize">E-Resize</li>
        <li class="w-resize">W-Resize</li>
        <li class="ne-resize">NE-Resize</li>
        <li class="sw-resize">SW-Resize</li>
        <li class="n-resize">N-Resize</li>
        <li class="s-resize">S-Resize</li>
        <li class="nw-resize">NW-Resize</li>
        <li class="se-resize">SE-Resize</li>
        <li class="text">Text</li>
        <li class="wait">Wait</li>
        <li class="help">Help</li>
        <li class="progress">Progress</li>
        <li class="hand">Hand</li>
        <li class="all-scroll">All-Scroll</li>
        <li class="col-resize">Col-Resize</li>
        <li class="row-resize">Row-Resize</li>
        <li class="no-drop">No-Drop</li>
        <li class="not-allowed">Not-Allowed</li>
        <li class="vertical-text">Vertical-Text</li>
    </ul>

</body>

</html>
```

2. Save the preceding markup as `example_16-1.html`, and then load it into a browser.

How It Works

Hovering over each of the list items triggers a different cursor as specified for the associated class.

CURSOR COMPATIBILITY

To assist you in anticipating the differences in cursors between browsers and operating systems, I've prepared the following table. The cursors in the following table indicate what cursor is used for that browser when the keyword is supported. This is just a sample. The cursors displayed often have as much to do with the operating system as the browser, and it is possible for users to change themes within operating systems to use different cursors. Chrome support is the same as for Safari.

CURSOR	IE 6 WIN XP	IE 7 VISTA	FIREFOX MAC	FIREFOX WIN	SAFARI MAC	OPERA MAC	OPERA WIN
default							
crosshair							
pointer							
move							
e-resize							
w-resize							
ne-resize							
sw-resize							
n-resize							
s-resize							
nw-resize							
se-resize							
text							
wait							
help							
progress							
hand							

continues

(continued)

CURSOR	IE 6 WIN XP	IE 7 VISTA	FIREFOX MAC	FIREFOX WIN	SAFARI MAC	OPERA MAC	OPERA WIN
all-scroll	✦	✦		✥			
col-resize	⊣⊢	⊣⊢	⊣⊢	←‖→			
row-resize	≑	≑	≑	↕			
no-drop	🖑⊘	🖑⊘	⊘	⊘			
not-allowed	⊘	⊘	⊘	⊘			
vertical-text	⊢⊣	⊢⊣	⊢⊣	⊢⊣			

> **NOTE** *In the preceding table, where a cell is empty, the* cursor *keyword is unsupported by that browser on that platform.*

By far the most commonly used cursor is pointer, which is particularly useful for indicating that an element is interactive when functionality is added with JavaScript. It is also quite common to see the pointer cursor used on button and input submit elements as they behave in a similar way to links but don't have this style by default.

EXERCISES

1. What is the syntax for specifying a cursor?

2. What browser(s) supports all cursor keywords?

▶ **WHAT YOU LEARNED IN THIS CHAPTER**

In this chapter you learned how to customize the mouse cursor. To recap, in this chapter you learned the following:

TOPIC	KEY CONCEPTS
Applying cursors	How to apply cursor styles to an element
Support for cursors	Which browsers support which cursors

17

Controlling Opacity and Visibility

WHAT YOU WILL LEARN IN THIS CHAPTER:

➤ How to modify the opacity of an element

➤ How to set the visibility of an element

The last CSS I will teach you is how to change the opacity of an element, that is how transparent an element is, and also how to set the visibility of an element, allowing you to hide it from view.

THE OPACITY PROPERTY

First, you'll look at the opacity property; it has a very simple syntax, as you can see from the following table.

PROPERTY	VALUE
opacity	<number> Initial value: 1

An opacity value of 1 indicates that an element is fully opaque. An opacity value of 0 on the other hand makes the element completely invisible. You can specify opacity to two decimal places.

 NOTE *All major browsers, except IE 6, 7, and 8, support the opacity property. There are proprietary methods of setting opacity in IE versions less than 9 that I won't cover here, but see Appendix B for links to more information.*

You should make sure that transparency is an optional part of the visual design, so that users of modern browsers are rewarded with a prettier visual experience, but the site remains attractive and usable in older browsers.

Let's Try It Out!

TRY IT OUT Using the opacity Property

Example 17-1

To demonstrate the use of the opacity property, follow these steps.

1. Enter the following markup:

```
<!DOCTYPE html PUBLIC "-//W3C//DTD HTML 4.01//EN"
    "http://www.w3.org/TR/html4/strict.dtd">
<html lang="en">
<head>
    <meta http-equiv="Content-Type" content="text/html; charset=utf-8">
    <title>Example 17-1</title>
    <style type="text/css">
        body {
            width: 600px;
            margin: 1em auto;
        }

        h1 {
            float: left;
            margin-top: 0;
        }

        .header {
            background: #000;
            color: #FFF;
            padding: 1em;
        }

        .header .intro {
            clear: both;
        }

        .navigation {
            float: right;
            margin: 0;
            list-style: none;
        }

        .navigation li {
            float: left;
        }

        .navigation a {
            display: block;
            margin-left: 0.5em;
            padding: 0.5em;
            border: 1px solid #CCC;
            background: #FFF;
```

```
            color: #233;
            text-decoration: none;
        }

        li {
            opacity: 1;
        }

        li.current {
            opacity: 0.5;
        }

        li.last {
            opacity: 0;
        }
    </style>

</head>
<body>

<div class="header">

    <h1>Recipes for Cheese</h1>

    <ul class="navigation">
        <li><a href="#">Home</a></li>
        <li class="current"><a href="#">Recipes</a></li>
        <li class="last"><a href="#">Suggestions</a></li>
    </ul>

    <p class="intro">Cheese is a remarkably versatile food, available in literally
    hundreds of varieties with different flavors and textures.</p>

</div>

<div class="recipe">

    <h2>Welsh Rarebit</h2>

    <p class="intro">Welsh Rarebit is a savory dish made from melted cheese, often
    Cheddar, on toasted bread, and a variety of other ingredients such as mustard,
    egg, or bacon. Here is one take on this classic.</p>

    <ol>
        <li>Lightly toast the bread</li>
        <li>Place on a baking tray, and spread with butter.</li>
        <li>Add the grated Cheddar cheese and 2 tablespoons of beer to a saucepan.
        Place the saucepan over a medium heat, and stir the cheese continuously
        until it has melted. Add a teaspoon of wholegrain mustard and grind in a
        little pepper. Keep stirring.</li>
        <li>When thick and smooth, pour over each piece of toast spreading it to
        the edges to stop the toast from burning.</li>
        <li>Place under the grill for a couple of minutes or until golden
        brown.</li>
```

```
            </ol>

        </div>

    </body>
</html>
```

2. Save the preceding CSS and markup as `example_17-1.html`. This example results in the output in Figure 17-1 in Safari and other desktop browsers.

FIGURE 17-1

How It Works

In Example 17-1, I have added a black background to elements with the class of `header` and a white background to each of the `opacity` elements in the navigation. I have also added classes of `current` and `last` to the navigation `li` elements.

All `li` elements are styled as follows:

```
li {
    opacity: 1;
}
```

An `opacity` value of `1` is the default, and so in normal cicumstances you would specify this unless you needed to override an inherited opacity value. As you can see in Figure 17-1, the background to the first navigation link remains a solid white.

The second `li` element with a class of `current` is styled as follows:

```
li.current {
    opacity: 0.5;
}
```

An `opacity` value of `0.5` makes the `li` element 50% transparent. Figure 17-1 shows that the background to the link is now gray, as you would expect with a black background behind a semi-transparent white background.

The third `li` element with a class of `last` is styled as follows:

```
li.last {
    opacity: 0;
}
```

An `opacity` value of `0` makes the `li` element completely transparent; in Figure 17-1, the link has been made invisible.

Play around with the `opacity` values to see `opacity` levels between these three levels of transparency.

Example 17-1 shows that an `opacity` value of `0` makes elements invisible, but there is a property that gives you much more control over the visibility of elements: the imaginatively named `visibility` property.

THE VISIBILITY PROPERTY

The `visibility` property has a very simple syntax, as you can see from the following table.

PROPERTY	VALUE
visibility	visible | hidden Initial value: visible

There isn't much that should surprise you here; the following code will make an element invisible:

`visibility: hidden;`

While this code will make an element visible:

`visibility: visible`

An element with a `visibility` value of `hidden` still remains in the normal document flow and takes up space; it is just not visible on screen and is ignored by most assistive technologies such as screen readers. Interactive elements such as links and buttons are no longer clickable or accessible by screen reader. Other than the space it takes up on the page, a hidden element is effectively not there.

To see this in action, and for the last time in this book, let's Try It Out.

Using the visibility Property

Example 17-2

To demonstrate the use of the visibility property, follow these steps.

1. Enter the following markup:

```
<!DOCTYPE html PUBLIC "-//W3C//DTD HTML 4.01//EN"
    "http://www.w3.org/TR/html4/strict.dtd">
<html lang="en">
<head>
    <meta http-equiv="Content-Type" content="text/html; charset=utf-8">
    <title>Example 17-2</title>
    <style type="text/css">
        body {
            width: 600px;
            margin: 1em auto;
        }

        h1 {
            float: left;
            margin-top: 0;
        }

        .header .intro {
            clear: both;
        }

        .navigation {
            float: right;
            margin: 0;
            list-style: none;
        }

        .navigation li {
            float: left;
        }

        .navigation a {
            display: block;
            margin-left: 0.5em;
            padding: 0.5em;
            border: 1px solid #CCC;
            background: #FFF;
            color: #233;
            text-decoration: none;
        }

        .recipe {
            visibility: hidden;
            border: 1px solid #000;
```

```
            }

            .recipe ol {
                visibility: visible;
            }
    </style>

</head>
<body>

<div class="header">

    <h1>Recipes for Cheese</h1>

    <ul class="navigation">
        <li><a href="#">Home</a></li>
        <li><a href="#">Recipes</a></li>
        <li><a href="#">Suggestions</a></li>
    </ul>

    <p class="intro">Cheese is a remarkably versatile food, available in literally
    hundreds of varietios with different flavors and textures.</p>

</div>

<div class="recipe">

    <h2>Welsh Rarebit</h2>

    <p class="intro">Welsh Rarebit is a savory dish made from melted cheese, often
    Cheddar, on toasted bread, and a variety of other ingredients such as mustard,
    egg, or bacon. Here is one take on this classic.</p>

    <ol>
        <li>Lightly toast the bread</li>
        <li>Place on a baking tray, and spread with butter.</li>
        <li>Add the grated Cheddar cheese and 2 tablespoons of beer to a saucepan.
        Place the saucepan over a medium heat, and stir the cheese continuously
        until it has melted. Add a teaspoon of wholegrain mustard and grind in a
        little pepper. Keep stirring.</li>
        <li>When thick and smooth, pour over each piece of toast spreading it to
        the edges to stop the toast from burning.</li>
        <li>Place under the grill for a couple of minutes or until golden
        brown.</li>
    </ol>

</div>

</body>
</html>
```

2. Save the preceding CSS and markup as `example_17-2.html`. This example results in the output in Figure 17-2 in Safari and other desktop browsers.

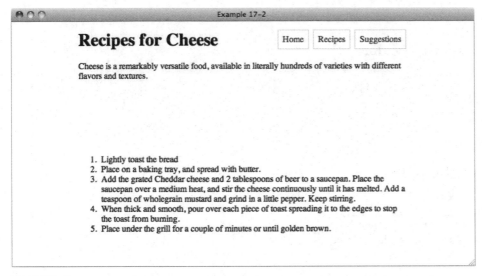

FIGURE 17-2

How It Works

In Example 17-2, I have applied a style of `visibility: hidden;` to elements with the class of `recipe`. This makes this element and its descendants invisible. As you (can't!) see in Figure 17-2, the `h2` and `p` elements that are children of the `div` with the class of `recipe` are no longer displayed but still take up space in the layout.

The `ol` element that is also a child of the `div` with the class of `recipe` is visible, and that is because I have also applied the following rule:

```
.recipe ol {
    visibility: visible;
}
```

That's right; you can make elements inside invisible elements visible again!

In the next chapter, you look at styling content for mobile devices.

EXERCISES

1. What range of values is valid for the `opacity` property?

2. What value would you give the `opacity` property to make an element fully transparent, effectively making it invisible?

3. What other property can you use to make an element invisible, and what value would you use?

▶ **WHAT YOU LEARNED IN THIS CHAPTER**

In this chapter, I showed you some of the challenges of writing CSS for mobile devices. You learned the following:

TOPIC	KEY CONCEPTS
Opacity	The `opacity` property can be used with a range of values, from `0`, which makes an element completely transparent; to `1`, which makes an element fully opaque.
Visibility	The visibility of an element can be controlled with the `font` property. Invisible elements reserve space in a page.

18

Styling Content for Mobile Devices

WHAT YOU WILL LEARN IN THIS CHAPTER:

➤ The differences between desktop and mobile development

➤ How to apply styles based on screen size

In Chapter 15 you saw how you could apply styles that applied only when printed with the media attribute and @media rule. Mobile browsers offer a similar challenge to developers as their capabilities and limitations can be very different to those of desktop browsers.

WHY MOBILE IS IMPORTANT

A February 2011 report for YouGov revealed that in the US one in five mobile phone users access the Internet on their phone every day, while in the UK the proportion was even higher with one in three accessing the Web with their mobile phone every day. Similar usage patterns can be found the world over, with the trend towards mobile use increasing every year as devices become more sophisticated. The future of the Web may well be on a small screen device such as a mobile phone.

The same report also found that over a quarter of mobile phone users in both the US and the UK were discouraged from accessing the Web on their mobile phones, not because their devices were hard to use, but because the websites that they wanted to access did not display or function correctly on their phones.

With such large numbers of potential users, but so many being put off by poor user experience, there is a great and increasing need to write CSS in such a way as to be mobile friendly.

DEVELOPING FOR MOBILE

Interacting with a mobile device is very different from using a browser on a desktop computer. On a desktop, you mostly rely on two input devices: the mouse and the keyboard. On a mobile device, the keyboard is not applicable to general browsing (for example, you can't scroll down a page by hitting the space bar in a mobile browser), and the mouse is replaced with either a keypad or joystick-like device for moving around a page or with a touch interface.

With the keypad method of input, you control a cursor in the same way as with a mouse on the desktop, so interactions such as hover states on links will function. With a touch-screen device, hovering doesn't have an equivalent; under most circumstances, tapping on a link will activate it immediately.

The small screen of a mobile device also changes the way users interact with a site. Most modern mobile browsers support zooming in one form or another, either by tapping on the screen to enlarge a certain area or using gestures to change the zoom level on devices that support multi-touch events (that is, actions where more than one finger is used).

Until the user zooms in to the area of the page they are interested in, content may be too small to read or easily identify, and navigating the page can be particularly cumbersome for keypad users.

All of these issues mean that you have to give some specific attention to the design and layouts of sites on mobile devices, in particular:

➤ Do not set an absolute size on the width of your site.

➤ Display the main content in a single column.

➤ Clearly indicate links, buttons, and other interactive controls.

➤ Do not assume a hover state.

In the next section, I briefly cover testing for mobile devices.

TESTING MOBILE DEVICES

As you read in Chapter 1, there are 4 main families of desktop browser rendering engines:

➤ Webkit used by Safari and Chrome

➤ Trident used by Internet Explorer

➤ Gecko used by Firefox

➤ Presto used by Opera

Of these, Webkit and Presto are the most strongly represented in the mobile browser space, with the mobile Safari browser from Apple and the Android browser from Google using the Webkit rendering engine, and Opera Mobile and Opera Mini using Presto. The Windows Phone 7 had the Mobile IE 7 browser using the Trident rendering engine. Mozilla has a Firefox mobile browser that uses the Gecko rendering engine, as you might expect.

So far mobile and desktop browsers look very similar, but these common browsers are just the tip of the iceberg. Peter-Paul Koch, an expert on mobile browsers, maintains a table of the most common mobile browsers, a table that at the time of writing includes 20 browsers, 14 Operating Systems, and 14 different device vendors! Take a look for yourself at `www.quirksmode.org/mobile/mobilemarket.html`.

Testing for all of the different browsers is not practical for most people, and the reality is that, as with desktop browsers, you need to be able to identify which browsers and devices will give you good coverage of the market.

This is a much too complicated subject for this book, and anything I might write would soon be out-of-date, so instead I will give you a link to an article Mr. Koch wrote for the A List Apart website, which, as well as giving an excellent overview of the mobile market as of November 2010, includes advice on testing.

The article lives at `www.alistapart.com/articles/smartphone-browser-landscape/`.

Of particular interest to you as you read this chapter may be the guide to mobile phone emulators at `http://mobiforge.com/emulators/page/mobile-emulators`, which will give you links to both online and installable emulators.

The screen shots in this chapter use the iPhone Simulator supplied by Apple for application development.

In the next section, I will show you how to apply styles specifically to mobile devices.

MEDIA QUERIES

As you saw in Chapter 15, you can in theory target different media using the `media` attribute, which is applied to the `link` or `style` element, or from within a style sheet, using `@media` rules. The different types of media are repeated in the following table.

MEDIA	PURPOSE
all	Suitable for all devices.
braille	Intended for Braille tactical feedback devices.
embossed	Intended for paged Braille printers.
handheld	Intended for handheld devices.
print	Intended for presentation when printed. Use print preview to view the result of using a print style sheet.
projection	Intended for projected presentations.
screen	Intended for presentation on a color computer screen.
speech I aural	Intended for presentation to a speech synthesizer (called aural in CSS 2, changed to speech in CSS 2.1).
tty	Intended for media using a fixed-pitch character grid (such as teletypes, terminals, or portable devices with limited display capabilities).
tv	Intended for television (low resolution, low color, limited scrollability).

The default value is `all`.

As you found in Chapter 15, only the `screen`, `print`, and `all` values are widely supported on desktop browsers, but you may have noticed a `handheld` value is available, intended for use for handheld devices.

Unfortunately, support for media types is no better in the mobile world, and virtually all mobile browsers ignore the `handheld` media type.

All is not lost, however. In modern mobile browsers, the `media` attribute and `@media` rule support more than just basic media types; enter media queries!

```
<style type="text/css" media="screen and (max-device-width: 480px)">
</style>

<link rel="stylesheet" type="text/css" href="mobile.css"
   media="screen and (max-device-width: 480px)">

<style type="text/css">
    @media screen and (max-device-width: 480px) {

    }
</style>
```

As you can see from the preceding code, we can use media queries anywhere that we can use the `media` attribute or `@media` rule. Here I am targeting `screen` devices, a media type that modern mobile phones support, in order to avoid conflicting CSS on any other type of device that also uses a small screen, and additionally specifying a `max-device-width` with a value of `480px`.

`device-width` is a media feature, which describes the width of the screen of a device; using the `max` prefix I am targeting my CSS at devices that have a screen width up to a maximum of `480px`. This targets most mobile phones with modern browsers and provides good support coverage. Let's Try It Out.

TRY IT OUT   Applying Styles for Mobile Devices

Example 18-1

To use styles only for mobile devices, follow these steps.

1. Enter the following markup:

```
<!DOCTYPE html PUBLIC "-//W3C//DTD HTML 4.01//EN"
    "http://www.w3.org/TR/html4/strict.dtd">
<html lang="en">
<head>
    <meta http-equiv="Content-Type" content="text/html; charset=utf-8">
    <title>Example 18-1</title>
    <style type="text/css">
        body {
```

```
            width: 600px;
            margin: 1em auto;
        }

        h1 {
            float: left;
            margin-top: 0.2em;
        }

        .navigation {
            float: right;
        }

        .navigation li {
            display: inline;
        }

        .navigation a {
            margin-left: 0.5em;
            padding: 0.5em;
            border: 1px solid #CCC;
        }

        .intro {
            clear: both;
        }

        @media screen and (max-device-width: 480px) {
            body {
                width: auto;
                margin: 1em;
            }

            h1,
            .navigation {
                float: none;
            }
        }
    </style>

</head>
<body>

<h1>Recipes for Cheese</h1>

<ul class="navigation">
    <li><a href="#">Home</a></li>
    <li><a href="#">Recipes</a></li>
    <li><a href="#">Suggestions</a></li>
</ul>

<p class="intro">Cheese is a remarkably versatile food, available in
```

```
literally hundreds of varieties with different flavors and textures.</p>

<div class="recipe">

    <h2>Welsh Rarebit</h2>

    <p class="intro">Welsh Rarebit is a savory dish made from melted
    cheese, often Cheddar, on toasted bread, and a variety of other
    ingredients such as mustard, egg, or bacon. Here is one take on
    this classic.</p>

    <ol>
        <li>Lightly toast the bread</li>
        <li>Place on a baking tray, and spread with butter.</li>
        <li>Add the grated Cheddar cheese and 2 tablespoons of beer to
        a saucepan. Place the saucepan over a medium heat, and stir the
        cheese continuously until it has melted. Add a teaspoon of
        wholegrain mustard and grind in a little pepper. Keep
        stirring.</li>
        <li>When thick and smooth, pour over each piece of toast
        spreading it to the edges to stop the toast from burning.</li>
        <li>Place under the grill for a couple of minutes or until
        golden brown.</li>
    </ol>

</div>

</body>
</html>
```

2. Save the preceding CSS and markup as `example_18-1.html`. This example results in the rendered output in Figure 18-1 in Safari and other desktop browsers.

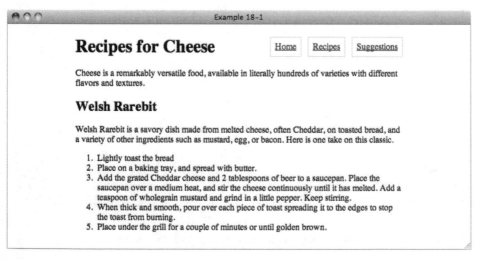

FIGURE 18-1

3. Now open the same page in a browser on a mobile device or a mobile browser simulator (see earlier in this chapter or in Appendix B for links to available simulators). You will see output similar to that in Figure 18-2.

How It Works

In Example 18-1, you applied separate styles to desktop browsers and mobile browsers using @media rules.

In Figure 18-1, you can see that the page in your browser looks much the same as it has in examples in previous chapters, with the page title on the left and the navigation on the right.

Figure 18-2 shows the same page in the iPhone simulator. Here the page title and navigation have been put on separate lines, and unlike the desktop version the content fills the full width of the page.

You can see this more clearly when you compare Figure 18-2 to Figure 18-3, which is the page without the addition of mobile device media queries.

FIGURE 18-2

In Figure 18-3 you will see that without the addition of mobile-targeted CSS there is a lot of wasted space, as the content does not fit the full width of the screen, making the navigation links in particular virtually unreadable unless the user zooms in.

FIGURE 18-3

Another interesting media feature is `orientation`, which accepts values of `portrait` and `landscape`. `portrait` is defined as the screen width less than or equal to the height; `landscape` is when the screen width is more than the height.

Adding `orientation` queries means that we can display different content depending on which way a device is being held, so in the following code I only position the navigation on a separate line if the orientation is `portrait`.

```
<!DOCTYPE html PUBLIC "-//W3C//DTD HTML 4.01//EN"
    "http://www.w3.org/TR/html4/strict.dtd">
<html lang="en">
<head>
    <meta http-equiv="Content-Type" content="text/html; charset=utf-8">
    <title>Figure 18-4</title>
    <style type="text/css">
        body {
            width: 600px;
            margin: 1em auto;
        }

        h1 {
            float: left;
            margin-top: 0.2em;
        }

        .navigation {
            float: right;
        }

        .navigation li {
            display: inline;
        }

        .navigation a {
            margin-left: 0.5em;
            padding: 0.5em;
            border: 1px solid #CCC;
        }

        .intro {
            clear: both;
        }

        @media screen and (max-device-width: 480px) {
            body {
                width: auto;
                margin: 1em;
            }
        }

        @media screen and (max-device-width: 480px) and
            (orientation: portrait) {
            h1,
            .navigation {
```

```
                    float: none;
                }
            }
        </style>

</head>
<body>

<h1>Recipes for Cheese</h1>

<ul class="navigation">
    <li><a href="#">Home</a></li>
    <li><a href="#">Recipes</a></li>
    <li><a href="#">Suggestions</a></li>
</ul>

<p class="intro">Cheese is a remarkably versatile food, available in
literally hundreds of varieties with different flavors and textures.</p>

<div class="recipe">

    <h2>Welsh Rarebit</h2>

    <p class="intro">Welsh Rarebit is a savory dish made from melted
    cheese, often Cheddar, on toasted bread, and a variety of other
    ingredients such as mustard, egg, or bacon. Here is one take on
    this classic.</p>

    <ol>
        <li>Lightly toast the bread</li>
        <li>Place on a baking tray, and spread with butter.</li>
        <li>Add the grated Cheddar cheese and 2 tablespoons of beer to
        a saucepan. Place the saucepan over a medium heat, and stir the
        cheese continuously until it has melted. Add a teaspoon of
        wholegrain mustard and grind in a little pepper. Keep
        stirring.</li>
        <li>When thick and smooth, pour over each piece of toast
        spreading it to the edges to stop the toast from burning.</li>
        <li>Place under the grill for a couple of minutes or until
        golden brown.</li>
    </ol>

</div>

</body>
</html>
```

Figure 18-4 shows my iPhone simulator in portrait orientation, and it looks as before. The content fills the full width of the screen and the navigation is below the page title. Now see what happens when I flip the orientation to landscape.

In Figure 18-5 the content still fits the fill width of the screen, but the navigation and page title are on the same line as in the desktop browser version.

FIGURE 18-4   **FIGURE 18-5**

There are many other media features available to developers; see Appendix B for a link to a full list. Media queries aren't just about supporting mobile devices. They're a key aspect in what's being called Responsive Design, where the CSS is mixed with media queries to create several layouts depending on the media properties. As you progress in your knowledge of CSS you will see them used in different ways, but I hope this chapter gives you a good basic knowledge.

That's the end of this chapter and almost the end of the book. In the final chapter, I close with a summary of what I've covered and some of my thoughts on the future of CSS.

EXERCISES

1. Which media value was intended to apply to mobile devices but which has poor real world support?

2. Write a sample style sheet that includes two rules; the first rule applies to all media types, and the second rule applies to mobile.

▶ WHAT YOU LEARNED IN THIS CHAPTER

In this chapter, I showed you some of the challenges of writing CSS for mobile devices. You learned the following:

TOPIC	KEY CONCEPTS
The benefits of writing mobile specific CSS	The Web is widely accessed on mobile devices, with more people using the mobile Web every year. Sites designed for desktop browsers can be difficult to use on a mobile, but some simple changes can help enormously.
The state of the mobile landscape	There are a wide variety of mobile browsers, operating systems and devices in wide use, and it is impossible for most developers to test on them all.
Using media queries	`media` attributes on `link` and `style` tags, and `@media` rules in CSS files and `style` elements can be used to write CSS for mobile devices.

19

Closing Comments

In this final chapter of the book, I will give a brief summary of what I hope you have learned, as well as my thoughts on the future of CSS.

CSS SUMMARY

CSS is a key technology for developing websites, the language by which you apply styles to pages to make them more attractive and usable. Without CSS, the Web would be a less beautiful place!

We've covered a lot of CSS in this book, and I hope you now have a firm grounding in the basics, as well as a few advanced tricks in your toolbox.

You should now know:

> What Cascading Style Sheets are, and the benefits to using them (Chapter 1)

> The parts that make up CSS, and how to add style sheets to web pages (Chapter 2)

> How to target elements for styling in HTML with CSS (Chapter 3)

> What the C in CSS stands for, and how to determine which of conflicting rules will apply (Chapter 4)

> How to style text, determining the font and size, and modifying text in many other ways (Chapters 5 and 6)

> How to apply background colors and images to web pages (Chapter 7 and Appendix D)

> The principles of the box model, and how to use margins, padding and borders to create the basics of a layout (Chapter 8)

> How to create more complex layouts by floating content (Chapter 9)

> The ways that HTML lists can be styled, and used to create navigation for a website (Chapter 10)

> Further ways to create layouts by positioning content relative to HTML elements or the browser viewport, and how to layer content (Chapter 11)

➤ How to style HTML tables, controlling borders and the presentation of individual table cells (Chapter 12)

➤ How to create a complete layout with HTML and CSS, and how to use custom fonts and add gradient backgrounds (Chapter 13)

➤ The advanced selectors available to you in the most modern browsers to allow even more fine control over the styling of content (Chapter 14)

➤ How to style printed content, including outputting text that only appears in the printed version (Chapter 15)

➤ The different mouse cursors that can be applied using CSS (Chapter 16)

➤ Making content transparent or invisible with CSS (Chapter 17)

➤ How to apply styles that only take effect in Mobile phone browsers (Chapter 18)

FUTURE OF CSS

Browser support in the current age of rapid browser releases is ever improving, with browser vendors competing to be the most up-to-date, and experimenting with new features that might go on to become part of future CSS recommendations.

As the older versions of Internet Explorer fall out of use, you will be able to write leaner and meaner CSS; until then, you will go through a painful period of supporting out-of-date technologies, but be heartened by the fact that even before you are able to put IE 6 to rest, the expectation that websites must look the same in all browsers is fading. As I promote in this book, CSS will be written in a progressive manner, with users of older browsers seeing a basic design, allowing them to focus more on cutting-edge browsers, giving users the best possible experience.

The Web is going mobile, and CSS authors will increasingly be creating and implementing layouts tailored for mobile devices and designing mobile applications.

Exciting innovations, such as animation in CSS, will encourage talented designers to push the boundaries of what web browsers are capable of, and, as CSS authors, you and I will be the ones that get to build beautiful and engaging sites with a potential audience greater than that of any other form of art.

The future is bright for CSS.

CLOSING STATEMENT

My aim in this book is to teach you the fundamentals of CSS in the way professional web designers and developers use it. From the start, my intention is that not only will you complete this book able to implement the design for a website but that you will be able to do so in a robust, professional, and standards-aware way.

With this foundation, I hope you enjoy writing CSS as much as I do and are able to experience the same great feeling of satisfaction I get when seeing a website come to life in a browser.

Answers to Exercises

CHAPTER 1

1. What are the key benefits of CSS?

    A. Benefits include:

     ➤ Separation of styling from HTML with CSS enables the appearance of an entire site to be updated from a single file or set of files.

     ➤ Using external CSS files, the styles for a site need only be downloaded once, instead of once for every page.

     ➤ Users of a website can compose style sheets of their own, potentially making websites more accessible.

     ➤ Support for multiple style sheets can enable a developer to provide more than one look for a website to users.

     ➤ Style sheets allow content to be targeted towards specific devices, for example, printers or mobile phones.

2. Name the five main web browsers used today.

    A. Internet Explorer, Firefox, Chrome, Safari and Opera.

3. Which is the latest version of Internet Explorer?

    A. Internet Explorer 9.

CHAPTER 2

1. Name the different components that make up a CSS rule?

    A. Rules are made up of selectors and declarations, and declarations are further made up of properties and values.

2. What's the difference between when `width: auto;` is applied to a `<table>` as opposed to a `<div>` element?

   A. A `<table>` shrinks to fit its contents, a `<div>` expands to fill its container.

3. Complete the sequence: Declaration, Property,

   A. Value.

4. Convert the color RGB(234, 123, 45) to hexadecimal.

   A. `#EA7B2D`.

5. What is the shortened hexadecimal notation of `#FFFFFF`?

   A. `#FFF`.

6. If I have a style sheet located at `www.example.com/stylesheet.css`, and a web page located at `www.example.com/index.html`, what markup would I include in index.html to include `stylesheet.css` via a relative path?

   A. You would include a `link` element with a `div` attribute which points to the file, using a relative path:

```
<link rel="stylesheet" type="text/css" href="stylesheet.css">
```

   or an absolute path:

```
<link rel="stylesheet" type="text/css" href="/stylesheet.css">
```

CHAPTER 3

1. How would you apply a style to an element based on its class?

   A. By preceding the class name in a selector with a dot:

```
.example-class {
}
```

2. How many class names can one element have?

   A. As many as you like.

3. How would you apply a style to an element based on its ID?

   A. By preceding the class name in a selector with a hash mark or pound sign:

```
#example-id {
}
```

4. How would you apply a style to an element based on its class and type?

   A. Add the class name, with the preceding dot to the end of the element name, with no space in between:

```
div.example-class {
}
```

5. If you wanted to style a link a different color when the user's mouse hovers over it, what might the selector look like?

    A. The selector would at minimum look like `a:hover`, though `a.classname:hover`, `a#idname:hover`, and so on, are acceptable answers as well.

CHAPTER 4

1. In the following style sheet, determine the specificity of each selector.

    A.

```
ul#hmenu ul.menu  /* 1,1,2 */
ul#hmenu li li:hover /* 1,1,3 */
ul#hmenu ul.menu ul.menu /* 1,2,3 */
ul#hmenu li#menu-204 ul.menu ul.menu /* 2,2,4 */
ul#hmenu li#menu-848 ul.menu ul.menu ul.menu ul.menu /* 2,4,6 */
ul#hmenu li#menu-990 ul.menu ul.menu /* 2,2,4 */
ul#hmenu > li.menu.eas + li.menu.eas ul.menu ul.menu ul.menu /* 1,7,6 */
li.menu /* 11 */
li.menu-highlight /* 11 */
ul.menu li a /* 13 */
ul.menu li a span /* 14 */
ul.menu span.arrow   /* 22 */
```

2. According to the following style sheet, what color is the link?

```
a.context:link {
    color: blue;
}
a.context:visited {
    color: purple;
}
a.context:hover {
    color: green;
}
a.context:active {
    color: red;
}
```

    A. It depends on what state the link is in. If the link is unvisited, the link is blue. If the link is visited, it's purple. If the user is hovering their mouse over the link, it's green, and if the user is clicking on the link, it's red regardless of whether it has been visited or not.

3. According to the following style sheet, what color is the link?

```
a.context:visited {
    color: purple;
}
a.context:hover {
    color: green;
}
```

```
a.context:active {
    color: red;
}
a.context:link {
    color: blue;
}
```

A. The link is blue, regardless of its state, since the :link selector appears last and it has the same specificity as the other selectors.

4. According to the following style sheet, what color is the link?

```
a.context:link {
    color: blue;
}
a.context:visited {
    color: purple !important;
}
a.context:hover {
    color: green;
}
a.context:active {
    color: red;
}
```

A. It depends on the state; if the link is unvisited, it's blue. If the link is unvisited and the user is hovering their mouse over the link, it's green. If the link is unvisited and the user is clicking on the link, it's red. If the link is visited, it's purple, regardless of whether the user is hovering over the link or clicking it.

CHAPTER 5

1. Why aren't the values of the font-weight property 100 through 900, bolder, and lighter used in real-world web design?

A. Because commonly available fonts are either bold or they aren't, and since there is only one variation, bold and normal, the other values aren't used.

2. How could the following rules be better written?

```
p {
    font-family: Arial, sans-serif;
    font-weight: bold;
    font-size: 24px;
    color: crimson;
}
p.copy {
    font-style: italic;
    font-weight: bold;
    line-height: 2em;
}
p#footer {
    font-size: 12px;
    line-height: 2em;
    font-family: Helvetica, Arial, sans-serif;
}
```

A.

```
p {
    font: bold 24px Arial, sans-serif;
    color: crimson;
}
p.copy {
    font-style: italic;
    font-weight: bold;
    line-height: 2em;
}
p#footer {
    font: 12px/2em Helvetica, Arial, sans-serif;
}
```

The second rule, which begins with the selector p.copy, had no change, because there is no font-size and no font-family specified in the rule, which are both required for the font shorthand property. Another acceptable approach would be to repeat the font-size and font-family as defined in the first rule, since it applies to all <p> elements. If you repeated the font-size and font-family from the first rule, another acceptable answer would be:

```
p.copy {
    font: italic bold 24px/2em Arial, sans-serif;
}
```

3. What's wrong with the following rule?

```
p {
    font-size: 24;
}
```

A. It is missing a length unit. Measurements that don't include a length unit are illegal, unless the specification specifically says it is allowed.

4. Would the declaration font-size: 75%; make the font size larger or smaller?

A. Smaller. Values under 100% result in a smaller font size, and values larger than 100% result in a larger font size.

CHAPTER 6

1. If you wanted to reduce the spacing between letters, how will you do so? Provide an example declaration.

A. Provide a negative length value to the letter-spacing property, such as letter-spacing: -1px;

2. How do you remove the underlines from links, but restore the underlines when the links are focused on or hovered over?

A. With the following rules:

```
a {
    text-decoration: none;
```

```
        }
        a:focus,
        a:hover {
            text-decoration: underline;
        }
```

3.   When indenting text in a paragraph, how is a percentage value calculated?

A.   Providing a percentage value to the `text-indent` property causes the indentation to be calculated based on the width of the parent element of the target element.

4.   What are the keywords that CSS offers for changing the case of text within an element?

A.   `lowercase`, `uppercase`, and `capitalize`.

5.   If you wanted to preserve line breaks and spacing as formatted in the source code, what CSS declaration would you use?

A.   `white-space: pre;`

CHAPTER 7

1.   What are two properties that you can use to specify a background color in a web page?

A.   The `background-color` and `background` properties.

2.   What declaration causes a background image to be tiled only along the x-axis?

A.   `background-repeat: repeat-x;`.

3.   What keyword value can you use to turn off tiling of a background image?

A.   `no-repeat`.

4.   If you wanted to offset an image ten pixels from the left and ten pixels from the top, what declaration would you use?

A.   `background-position: 10px 10px;`

5.   If you wanted a background image to scroll with the document, what declaration would you use?

A.   `background-attachment: scroll;`

6.   When a background image is said to be "fixed," what HTML element is the background image position relative to?

A.   The viewport.

7.   Write a declaration that contains all five background properties in one.

A.   The declaration should look something like:

```
background: white url(image.png) repeat scroll center center;
```

The individual components of the value are background-color, background-image, background-repeat, background-attachment, and background-position (vertical and horizontal).

CHAPTER 8

1. From left to right, what are the seven box model properties that make up the left, center, and right sides of a box?

A. `margin-left, border-left, padding-left, width, padding-right, border-right, margin-right.`

2. How do you left-, center-, and right-align a block-level box (using the standard method)?

A. To left-align: `margin-right: auto;` or `margin: 0 auto 0 0;`

To center-align: `margin: 0 auto;` or `margin: 0 auto 0 auto;` or `margin-left: auto; margin-right: auto;`

To right-align: `margin-left: auto;` or `margin: 0 0 0 auto;`

3. When the `margin` shorthand property has four values, what side of the target element does each value apply margin to, in order?

A. Top, right, bottom, left.

4. What are the three keyword values of the `border-width` property?

A. `thin, medium,` and `thick.`

5. If the `border-color` shorthand property has three values, what side of the target element does each value apply to, in order?

A. Top, right and left, bottom.

6. Name the shorthand properties that encompass the `border-width, border-style,` and `border-color` properties.

A. `border-top, border-right, border-bottom, border-left,` and `border.`

7. Describe briefly the two situations in which `margin` collapsing occurs?

A. Between adjacent sibling elements where the bottom margin of the top element comes into contact with the top margin of the bottom element, or between nested elements where the top margin of any nested element comes into contact with the top margin of its container element, and likewise when the bottom margin of a nested element comes into contact with the bottom margin of its container element.

8. What are the four keywords of the `overflow` property?

A. `visible, auto, scroll,` and `hidden.`

CHAPTER 9

1. When an element is floated, what rule governs its dimensions?

A. The shrink-to-fit rules; the element only expands enough to accommodate the content inside.

2. What happens when an inline element, such as a `<span>` element, is floated?

A. It becomes a block element with shrink-to-fit sizing.

3. What are the three keywords of the `float` property?

A. `left`, `right`, and `none`.

4. If an element is floated to the right, and you don't want the following element to wrap around it, what declaration would you apply to that element?

A. `clear: right;` or `clear: both;`

5. What declarations would you use to create subscript and superscript text?

A. `vertical-align: sub;` and `vertical-align: super;`

6. When vertically aligning an inline element to the `middle`, how is the element positioned on the line?

A. It is centered at the center point of the lowercase letter x.

7. What is the difference between the `text-top` and `top` keywords of the `vertical-align` property?

A. In some browsers, nothing. The `text-top` keyword aligns to the top of the tallest lowercase letter, and the `top` keyword aligns to the top of the line box.

8. If you are aligning table cells to the baseline, what determines the baseline?

A. The tallest content in the first row of the table.

CHAPTER 10

1. Name the keywords of the `list-style-type` property supported by all major browsers?

A. `disc`, `circle`, `square`, `decimal`, `lower-roman`, `upper-roman`, `none`.

2. What properties does the `list-style` property allow you to specify in a single declaration?

A. `list-style-type`, `list-style-image`, `list-style-position`.

3 Can size and position be controlled with the `list-style-image` property? If so, how?

A. No, size and position cannot be controlled with the `list-style-image` property.

CHAPTER 11

1. What is the default value of the `top`, `right`, `bottom`, and `left` properties?

A. The `auto` keyword.

2. What are offset properties used for?

A. To control the position of elements with a position value of absolute, relative, or fixed.

3. If the `<body>` element has a sole child that is positioned absolutely, what point of reference is used for its positioning?

A. The browser's viewport.

4. If the `<body>` element has a sole child that is positioned relatively, with an id name of *relative-element*, and that relatively positioned element has a child that is absolutely positioned, what point of reference is used for the absolutely positioned element?

A. The element with the id name relative-element.

5. If the element from Exercise 4, *relative-element*, has a fixed position child, what point of reference is used for its positioning?

A. The browser's viewport.

6. You have five elements that are all absolutely positioned siblings, but no `z-index` is specified for any of them. In what order will they be stacked? Provide the `z-index` declaration for each element, in order.

A. `z-index: 1;, z-index: 2;, z-index: 3;, z-index: 4;, z-index: 5;`.

CHAPTER 12

1. Describe what the `table-layout: fixed;` declaration does.

A. It forces an HTML table to honor explicitly defined widths, instead of auto sizing to accommodate content.

2. When sizing using the `table-layout: fixed;` declaration, how does the browser determine the width of table columns?

A. First the browser takes into account the `width` property as applied to the `<table>` element, then the browser takes into account the width property as applied to `<col />` elements. If none is found, it goes to the `width` property as applied to the `<td>` or `<th>` elements that appear in the first row of the table. If no width is defined, each column is given equal width.

3. What purpose does the optional `<thead>` element serve?

A. It contains table headers, when you print a table that spans multiple pages. Its contents are repeated at the top of each printed page.

4. In what containing element does the main table data appear?

A. The `<tbody>` element.

CHAPTER 13

1. What is the first step in implementing a web page from a design?

A. Start with good, semantic, and valid HTML. Use a validator to make sure you have not made any mistakes in your markup, and view the page with only the default browser styles to check if all of the content makes sense and is in a logical order.

2. Which rule is used to add support for custom fonts?

A. The @font-face rule.

3. What are the drawbacks to using custom fonts?

A. They need to be downloaded with the page, which will make the overall page download longer. Until the font has been downloaded, text that uses the custom font may not be displayed.

4. What are vendor prefixes?

A. Vendor prefixes are strings that preface not yet finalized or experimental CSS properties or values, so that browser vendors can implement new features that may be subject to change. The main prefixes are –ms- for Internet Explorer, -moz- for Firefox, -webkit- for Chrome and Safari, and –o- for Opera.

5. How would you apply a gradient background, and what must you do to support browsers that don't implement gradient backgrounds?

A. You would add a gradient using the two vendor prefixed background-image property values, -moz-linear-gradient and –webkit-gradient, the proprietary Internet Explorer -ms-filter property, and the non-prefixed linear-gradient value for the background-image property that is likely to become the standard, as follows:

```
html {
    height: 100%;
    background-color: #233;
    background-image: -moz-linear-gradient(top, #233, #FFF);
    background-image: -webkit-gradient(linear, left top, left bottom,
        from(#233), to(#FFF));
    -ms-filter: "progid:DXImageTransform.Microsoft.Gradient
        (StartColorStr=#223333, EndColorStr=#FFFFFF)";
    background-image: linear-gradient(top, #233, #FFF);
}
```

You should always specify a background-color for browsers that do not support background gradients.

CHAPTER 14

1. What is the syntax for using direct child selectors?

A. A direct child selector looks like:

```
body > .intro {
}
```

This selector targets elements with the class of intro that are direct children of the body element.

2. What is the syntax for using next sibling selectors?

A. A next sibling selector looks like:

```
h1 + .intro {
}
```

This selector targets elements with class of intro that directly follow an h1 element.

3. How would you select an element based on an attribute value?

A. An attribute value selector looks like:

```
element[attribute="value"]
```

4. How would you select an element based only on the start of an attribute value string?

A. With a caret character following the attribute string, and before the equals character as follows:

```
element[attribute^="value"]
```

5. How would you style the first letter and first line of a paragraph of text?

A. With the :first-letter and :first-line pseudo-element selectors as follows:

```
.intro:first-letter,
.intro:first-line {
}
```

6. How would you style only the first link in a list of links?

A. With the :first-child structural pseudo-class:

```
ul:first-child a {
}
```

CHAPTER 15

1. Which media values apply to desktop browsers?

A. Screen, print, and all.

2. Write the opening tag for the <style> element, targeting the styles to print.

A. `<style type='text/css' media='print'>`

3. What does the page-break-before property do?

A. It forces a page break to happen before the beginning of an element.

4. Write a sample style sheet that includes three rules; the first rule applies to all media types, the second rule applies to onscreen layout, and the third applies to print.

A. Your style sheet may differ, but it should look something like the following.

```
@media all {
    p {
        /* Your declarations appear here */
    }
}
@media screen {
```

```
    p {
        /* Your declarations appear here */
    }
}
@media print {
    p {
        /* Your declarations appear here */
    }
}
```

The following is also a valid answer:

```
p {
    /* Your declarations appear here */
}
@media screen {
    p {
        /* Your declarations appear here */
    }
}
@media print {
    p {
        /* Your declarations appear here */
    }
}
```

CHAPTER 16

1. What is the syntax for specifying a cursor?

A. The syntax is as follows:

`cursor: pointer;`

2. What browser(s) supports all cursor keywords?

A. Internet Explorer.

CHAPTER 17

1. What range of values is valid for the opacity property?

A. opacity values can range from 0 to 1.

2. What value would you give the opacity property to make an element fully transparent, effectively making it invisible?

A. You would give it a value of 0. To make the element completely opaque you would use a value of 1.

3. What other property can you use to make an element invisible, and what value would you use?

A. You would use the visibility property with a value of hidden as follows:

`visibility: hidden;`

CHAPTER 18

1. Which media value was intended to apply to mobile devices but which has poor real-world support?

   A. The `handheld` value.

2. Write a sample style sheet that includes two rules; the first rule applies to all media types, and the second rule applies to mobile.

   A. A style sheet that looks something like the following would apply styles to all media types, and separate rules for mobile browsers or other small screen devices.

   ```
   body {
   }

   @media screen and (max-device-width: 480px) {
       body {
       }
   }
   ```

Additional CSS Resources

TEXT EDITORS

Windows

Notepad++: http://sourceforge.net/projects/notepad-plus/

Crimson Editor: www.crimsoneditor.com

HTML-kit: www.chami.com/html-kit

Mac

TextWrangler: www.barebones.com

TextMate: http://macromates.com/

Other

List of editors: http://en.wikipedia.org/wiki/List_of_HTML_editors

Adobe Dreamweaver: www.adobe.com/products/dreamweaver

BROWSERS

Internet Explorer: www.microsoft.com/uk/windows/internet-explorer/

Internet Explorer test browser images: www.microsoft.com/downloads/en/details.aspx?FamilyID=21eabb90-958f-4b64-b5f1-73d0a413c8ef&displaylang=en

Firefox: www.firefox.com/

Chrome: www.google.com/chrome

Safari: www.apple.com/safari

Opera: www.opera.com/

Yahoo! Graded Browser Support: http://developer.yahoo.com/yui/articles/gbs/

HTML

W3C HTML Validator: http://validator.w3.org/

Valid Doctype list: www.w3.org/QA/2002/04/valid-dtd-list.html

CSS

W3C CSS2.1 recommendation: www.w3.org/TR/CSS2/

W3C CSS3 recommendation: www.w3.org/Style/CSS/current-work

W3C CSS Validator: jigsaw.w3.org/css-validator/

CSS3 support information: www.css3.info/

Specificity: http://meyerweb.com/eric/css/link-specificity.html

Commonly installed Font Families: www.codestyle.org/css/font-family/index.shtml

Font Family stacks: www.codestyle.org/css/font-family/BuildBetterCSSFontStacks.shtml

Box model switching: www.quirksmode.org/css/box.html

Conditional Comments: www.quirksmode.org/css/condcom.html

IE hacks: http://webstandardstips.com/2008/11/18/css-hacks-for-ie-only-style-rules/

position: fixed; in IE6: www.gunlaug.no/contents/wd_additions_15.html

http://ryanfait.com/resources/fixed-positioning-in-internet-explorer/

Sprites: www.alistapart.com/articles/sprites

Gradient Backgrounds for all browsers: http://robertnyman.com/2010/02/15/css-gradients-for-all-web-browsers-without-using-images/

Gradient Background generator: http://gradients.glrzad.com/

Free embeddable fonts: www.theleagueofmoveabletype.com/

Print style sheets: www.alistapart.com/articles/goingtoprint/

Cross browser opacity: www.impressivewebs.com/css-opacity-reference/

http://blogs.msdn.com/b/ie/archive/2010/08/17/ie9-opacity-and-alpha.aspx

The mobile landscape: www.alistapart.com/articles/smartphone-browser-landscape/

Mobile Emulators: http://mobiforge.com/emulators/page/mobile-emulators

CSS Media Queries: www.w3.org/TR/css3-mediaqueries/

CSS Reference

REFERENCE CONVENTIONS

The following conventions are used to outline browser compatibility for each CSS feature:

➤ **Y = Yes.** The feature is implemented completely per the W3C specification of what that feature is.

➤ **N = No.** The feature is not implemented.

➤ **B = Buggy.** The feature is implemented but has unexpected side effects.

➤ **P = Partial.** The feature is partially implemented.

➤ **A = Alternative.** The feature is not implemented but an alternative proprietary feature is available that provides the same functionality.

➤ **I = Incorrect.** The feature is implemented but does not conform to the W3C definition of what that feature provides.

The CSS level that reference material refers to is provided in the CSS column. At the time of this writing, there are four CSS specifications:

➤ **CSS Level 1:** The reference material provided is outlined in the CSS Level 1 Recommendation made 17 December 1996.

➤ **CSS Level 2:** The reference material provided is outlined in the W3C CSS Level 2 Recommendation made 12 May 1998.

➤ **CSS Level 2.1:** The reference material provided is outlined in the W3C CSS Level 2.1 Working Draft made 11 April 2006.

➤ **CSS Level 3:** The reference material provided refers to a W3C CSS Level 3 Candidate Recommendation (at the time of this writing portions of CSS 3 are still in development; references refer to those parts of CSS 3 in Candidate Recommendation status).

SELECTORS

SELECTOR	CSS	IE 6.0	IE 7.0	IE 8.0	IE 9.0	FF 3.6	O 11.1	S 5.0
Universal `* { color: blue; }`	3	Y	Y	Y	Y	Y	Y	Y
Type `div { color: blue; }`	3	Y	Y	Y	Y	Y	Y	Y
Descendant `div p { color: blue; }`	3	Y	Y	Y	Y	Y	Y	Y
Direct Child `div > p { color: blue; }`	3	N	Y	Y	Y	Y	Y	Y
Direct Adjacent Sibling `p + p { color: blue; }`	3	N	Y	Y	Y	Y	Y	Y
Indirect Adjacent Sibling `p ~ p { color: blue; }`	3	N	B	B	Y	Y	Y	Y
Attribute Existence `input[type] { color: blue; }`	3	N	Y	Y	Y	Y	Y	Y

Attribute's value matches value exactly
`input[type=text]`
`{ color: blue; }`
	3	N	Y	Y	Y	Y	Y	Y

Attribute's value is a space-separated list of words, e.g.,
`rel="copyright copyleft copyeditor`
`"a[rel~="copyright"]`
`{ color: blue; }`
	3	N	Y	Y	Y	Y	Y	Y

Attribute's value begins with a value or is the value exactly; value provided may be a hyphen-separated list of words, e.g.,
`hreflang="en-us"`
`link[hreflang|="en"]`
`{ color: blue; }`
	3	N	Y	Y	Y	Y	Y	Y

Attribute's value begins with …
`a[href^=http://www.somesite`
`.com] { color: blue; }`
	3	N	Y	Y	Y	Y	Y	Y

SELECTOR	CSS	IE 6.0	IE 7.0	IE 8.0	IE 9.0	FF 3.6	O 11.1	S 5.0

Attribute's value contains . . .
`a[href*=somesite]`
`{ color: blue; }`
	3	N	Y	Y	Y	Y	Y	Y

Attribute's value ends with . . .
`a[href$=html]`
`{ color: blue; }`
	3	N	Y	Y	Y	Y	Y	Y

Class `div.class { color: blue; }`	3	Y	Y	Y	Y	Y	Y	Y

Multiple classes, e.g.,
`class="class1 class2"`
`.class1.class2 { color: blue; }`
	3	N	Y	Y	Y	Y	Y	Y

IE 6 supports multiple class syntax on the element, but not chaining class selectors in the style sheet.

SELECTOR	CSS	IE 6.0	IE 7.0	IE 8.0	IE 9.0	FF 3.6	O 11.1	S 5.0
ID `div#id { color: blue; }`	3	Y	Y	Y	Y	Y	Y	Y

PSEUDO-CLASSES

PSEUDO-CLASS	CSS	IE 6.0	IE 7.0	IE 8.0	IE 9.0	FF 3.6	O 11.1	S 5.0
`:link`	3	Y	Y	Y	Y	Y	Y	Y
`:visited`	3	Y	Y	Y	Y	Y	Y	Y
`:hover`	3	P	Y	Y	Y	Y	Y	Y
`:active`	3	P	P	P	Y	Y	Y	Y
`:focus`	3	P	Y	Y	Y	Y	Y	Y
`:target`	3	N	N	N	Y	Y	Y	Y
`:lang`	3	N	N	N	Y	Y	Y	N
`:root`	3	N	N	N	Y	Y	Y	Y
`:first-child`	3	N	Y	Y	Y	Y	Y	Y
`:last-child`	3	N	N	N	Y	Y	Y	Y
`:empty`	3	N	N	N	Y	Y	Y	Y
`:not`	3	N	N	N	Y	Y	Y	Y

PSEUDO-ELEMENTS

PSEUDO-ELEMENT	CSS	IE 6.0	IE 7.0	IE 8.0	IE 9.0	FF 3.6	O 11.1	S 5.0
CSS 3 :: (double-colon) syntax	3	Y	N	N	Y	Y	Y	Y
:first-line	3	Y	Y	Y	Y	Y	Y	Y
:first-letter	3	Y	Y	Y	Y	Y	Y	Y
:before	3	N	N	Y	Y	Y	Y	Y
:after	3	N	N	Y	Y	Y	Y	Y
:selection	3	N	N	N	Y	A	N	Y

COLOR PROPERTIES

PROPERTY	CSS	IE 6.0	IE 7.0	IE 8.0	IE 9.0	FF 3.6	O 11.1	S 5.0
color	2.1	Y	Y	Y	Y	Y	Y	Y

Value:	<color>
Initial value:	Depends on browser
Applies to:	All elements
Inherited:	Yes

<color> refers to one of the following:

➤ A color keyword: body { color: black; }

➤ A hexadecimal value: body { color: #000000; }

➤ Short hexadecimal value: body { color: #000; }

➤ RGB value: body { color: rgb(0, 0, 0); }

➤ RGB percentage: body { color: rgb(0% ,0%, 0%); }

PROPERTY	CSS	IE 6.0	IE 7.0	IE 8.0	IE 9.0	FF 3.6	O 11.1	S 5.0
opacity	3	A	A	A	Y	Y	Y	Y

Value:	<alphavalue>
Initial value:	1
Applies to:	All elements
Inherited:	No

PROPERTY	CSS	IE 6.0	IE 7.0	IE 8.0	IE 9.0	FF 3.6	O 11.1	S 5.0

Introduced in CSS 3, the `opacity` property accepts a floating-point value between 0.0 (fully transparent) and 1.0 (fully opaque).

IE 6 and IE 7 provide an alternative, proprietary `filter` property to achieve a similar effect.

FONT PROPERTIES

PROPERTY	CSS	IE 6.0	IE 7.0	IE 8.0	IE 9.0	FF 3.6	O 11.1	S 5.0
`font-family`	2.1	Y	Y	Y	Y	Y	Y	Y
Value:	`[[<family-name>	<generic-family>] [, <family-name>| <generic-family>]*]`							
Initial value:	Varies from browser to browser							
Applies to:	All elements							
Inherited:	Yes							

`<family-name>` Refers to the name of a font installed on the user's operating system and supported by the browser, for instance: Arial and Times New Roman. A comma-separated list of fonts may be provided; font names containing spaces must be enclosed with quotations.

`<generic-family>` Refers to fonts not native to a particular operating system and provided by the browser. The following are all of the generic font families:

➤ serif (Times New Roman, or Times)

➤ sans-serif (Arial or Helvetica)

➤ cursive (Zapf-Chancery)

➤ fantasy (Western)

➤ monospace (Courier)

`font-style`	2.1	Y	Y	Y	Y	Y	Y	Y
Value:	`normal	italic	oblique`							
Initial value:	`normal`							
Applies to:	All elements							
Inherited:	Yes							

continues

(continued)

PROPERTY	CSS	IE 6.0	IE 7.0	IE 8.0	IE 9.0	FF 3.6	O 11.1	S 5.0
font-variant	2.1	Y	Y	Y	Y	Y	Y	Y
Value:	normal | small-caps							
Initial value:	normal							
Applies to:	All elements							
Inherited:	Yes							
font-weight	2.1	Y	Y	Y	Y	Y	Y	Y
Value:	normal | bold | bolder | lighter | 100 | 200 | 300 | 400 | 500 | 600 | 700 | 800 | 900							
Initial value:	normal							
Applies to:	All elements							
Inherited:	Yes							
font-size	2.1	Y	Y	Y	Y	Y	Y	Y
Value:	<absolute-size> | <relative-size> | <length> | <percentage>							
Initial value:	medium							
Applies to:	All elements							
Inherited:	Yes							
Percentage value:	Refers to parent element's font size							

<absolute-size> refers to one of the keywords: xx-small \| x-small \| small \| medium \| large \| xx-large

<relative-size> refers to one of the keywords: larger \| smaller

PROPERTY	CSS	IE 6.0	IE 7.0	IE 8.0	IE 9.0	FF 3.6	O 11.1	S 5.0
font	2.1	Y	Y	Y	Y	Y	Y	Y
Value:	[[<font-style> || <font-variant> || <font-weight>]? <font-size> [/ <line-height>]? <font-family>] | caption | icon | menu | message-box | small-caption | status-bar							
Initial value:	Not defined for shorthand properties							
Applies to:	All elements							
Inherited:	Yes							

BACKGROUND PROPERTIES

PROPERTY	CSS	IE 6.0	IE 7.0	IE 8.0	IE 9.0	FF 3.6	O 11.1	S 5.0
background-color	2.1	Y	Y	Y	Y	Y	Y	Y
Value:	<color> | transparent							
Initial value:	transparent							
Applies to:	All elements							
Inherited:	No							
background-image	2.1	Y	Y	Y	Y	Y	Y	Y
Value:	<uri> | none							
Initial value:	none							
Applies to:	All elements							
Inherited:	No							
background-repeat	2.1	Y	Y	Y	Y	Y	Y	Y
Value:	repeat | repeat-x | repeat-y | no-repeat							
Initial value:	repeat							
Applies to:	All elements							
Inherited:	No							
background-attachment	2.1	P	Y	Y	Y	Y	Y	Y
Value:	scroll | fixed							
Initial value:	repeat							
Applies to:	All elements							
Inherited:	No							

IE 6 only supports the fixed keyword when applied to the <body> element. The fixed keyword may be applied to any element in IE 7 and above.

background-position	3	Y	Y	Y	Y	Y	Y	Y
Value:	[<percentage> | <length>]{1,2} | [[top | center | bottom] || [left | center | right]]							
Initial value:	0% 0%							
Applies to:	All elements							

continues

(continued)

PROPERTY	CSS	IE 6.0	IE 7.0	IE 8.0	IE 9.0	FF 3.6	O 11.1	S 5.0
Inherited:	No							
Percentage values:	Are determined based on the size of the element itself							
background	2.1	Y	Y	Y	Y	Y	Y	Y
Value:	`<background-color> || <background-image> || <background-repeat> || <background-attachment> || <background-position>`							
Initial value:	Not defined for shorthand properties							
Applies to:	All elements							
Inherited:	No							
Percentage values:	Are determined based on the size of the element itself							

TEXT PROPERTIES

PROPERTY	CSS	IE 6.0	IE 7.0	IE 8.0	IE 9.0	FF 3.6	O 11.1	S 5.0
word-spacing	2.1	Y	Y	Y	Y	Y	Y	Y
Value:	`normal	<length>`							
Initial value:	`normal`							
Applies to:	All elements							
Inherited:	Yes							
letter-spacing	2.1	Y	Y	Y	Y	Y	Y	Y
Value:	`normal	<length>`							
Initial value:	`normal`							
Applies to:	All elements							
Inherited:	Yes							
text-decoration	2.1	Y	Y	Y	Y	Y	Y	Y
Value:	`none	[underline || overline || line-through || blink]`							
Initial value:	`none`							

PROPERTY	CSS	IE 6.0	IE 7.0	IE 8.0	IE 9.0	FF 3.6	O 11.1	S 5.0
	Applies to:	All elements						
	Inherited:	No						
text-transform	2.1	Y	Y	Y	Y	Y	Y	Y
	Value:	capitalize | uppercase | lowercase | none						
	Initial value:	none						
	Applies to:	All elements						
	Inherited:	Yes						
text-align	2.1	Y	Y	Y	Y	Y	Y	Y
	Value:	left | right | center | justify						
	Initial value:	left						
	Applies to:	Block-level elements, table cells, and inline blocks						
	Inherited:	Yes						
text-indent	2.1	Y	Y	Y	Y	Y	Y	Y
	Value:	<length> | <percentage>						
	Initial value:	0						
	Applies to:	Block-level elements, table cells, and inline blocks						
	Inherited:	Yes						
	Percentage value:	Refers to the width of the containing block						
line-height	2.1	Y	Y	Y	Y	Y	Y	Y
	Value:	normal | <number> | <length> | <percentage>						
	Initial value:	normal						
	Applies to:	All elements						
	Inherited:	Yes						
	Percentage value:	Refers to the font size of the element the line-height is applied to						
vertical-align	2.1	Y	Y	Y	Y	Y	Y	Y
	Value:	baseline | sub | super | top | text-top | middle | bottom | text-bottom | <percentage> | <length>						

continues

(continued)

PROPERTY	CSS	IE 6.0	IE 7.0	IE 8.0	IE 9.0	FF 3.6	O 11.1	S 5.0
Initial value:	baseline							
Applies to:	Inline-level and 'table-cell' elements							
Inherited:	No							
Percentage value:	Is determined by the line-height of the element							
white-space	2	Y	Y	Y	Y	Y	Y	Y
Value:	normal | pre | nowrap							
Initial value:	normal							
Applies to:	All elements							
Inherited:	Yes							

BOX MODEL PROPERTIES

PROPERTY	CSS	IE 6.0	IE 7.0	IE 8.0	IE 9.0	FF 3.6	O 11.1	S 5.0
margin-top margin-right margin-bottom margin-left	2.1	Y	Y	Y	Y	Y	Y	Y
Value:	<length> | <percentage> | auto							
Initial value:	0							
Applies to:	All elements							
Inherited:	No							
Percentage value:	Refers to the width of the containing block							
margin	2.1	Y	Y	Y	Y	Y	Y	Y
Value:	[<length> | <percentage> | auto] {1, 4}							
Initial value:	Not defined for shorthand properties							
Applies to:	All elements							
Inherited:	No							
Percentage value:	Refers to the width of the containing block							

PROPERTY	CSS	IE 6.0	IE 7.0	IE 8.0	IE 9.0	FF 3.6	O 11.1	S 5.0
padding-top padding-right padding-bottom padding-left	2.1	Y	Y	Y	Y	Y	Y	Y
Value:	`<length>	<percentage>`						
Initial value:	0							
Applies to:	All elements							
Inherited:	No							
Percentage value:	Refers to the width of the containing block							
padding	2.1	Y	Y	Y	Y	Y	Y	Y
Value:	`[<length>	<percentage>] {1,4}`						
Initial value:	Not defined for shorthand properties							
Applies to:	All elements							
Inherited:	No							
Percentage value:	Refers to the width of the containing block							
border-top-width border-right-width border-bottom-width border-left-width	2.1	Y	Y	Y	Y	Y	Y	Y
Value:	`thin	medium	thick	<length>`						
Initial value:	medium							
Applies to:	All elements							
Inherited:	No							
border-width	2.1	Y	Y	Y	Y	Y	Y	Y
Value:	`[thin	medium	thick	<length>] {1,4}`						
Initial value:	Not defined for shorthand properties							
Applies to:	All elements							
Inherited:	No							

continues

(continued)

PROPERTY	CSS	IE 6.0	IE 7.0	IE 8.0	IE 9.0	FF 3.6	O 11.1	S 5.0

`border-top-color`
`border-right-color`
`border-bottom-color`
`border-left-color`
	2.1	P	Y	Y	Y	Y	Y	Y

Value:	`<color>` | `transparent`
Initial value:	The value of the `color` property
Applies to:	All elements
Inherited:	No

IE 6 does not support the `transparent` keyword.

PROPERTY	CSS	IE 6.0	IE 7.0	IE 8.0	IE 9.0	FF 3.6	O 11.1	S 5.0
`border-color`	2.1	P	Y	Y	Y	Y	Y	Y

Value:	`[ <color>` | `transparent ] {1,4}`
Initial value:	See individual properties
Applies to:	All elements
Inherited:	No

IE 6 does not support the `transparent` keyword.

PROPERTY	CSS	IE 6.0	IE 7.0	IE 8.0	IE 9.0	FF 3.6	O 11.1	S 5.0

`border-top-style`
`border-right-style`
`border-bottom-style`
`border-left-style`
	2.1	P	P	Y	Y	Y	Y	Y

Value:	`none` | `dotted` | `dashed` | `solid` | `double` | `groove` | `ridge` | `inset` | `outset`
Initial value:	`none`
Applies to:	All elements
Inherited:	No

IE 6 renders the `dotted` keyword as `dashed`.

PROPERTY	CSS	IE 6.0	IE 7.0	IE 8.0	IE 9.0	FF 3.6	O 11.1	S 5.0
`border-style`	2.1	P	P	Y	Y	Y	Y	Y

Value:	`[none` | `dotted` | `dashed` | `solid` | `double` | `groove` | `ridge` | `inset` | `outset ] {1,4}`
Initial value:	Not defined for shorthand properties

PROPERTY	CSS	IE 6.0	IE 7.0	IE 8.0	IE 9.0	FF 3.6	O 11.1	S 5.0
Applies to:	All elements							
Inherited:	No							

IE 6 renders the `dotted` keyword as `dashed`.

PROPERTY	CSS	IE 6.0	IE 7.0	IE 8.0	IE 9.0	FF 3.6	O 11.1	S 5.0

`border-top`
`border-right`
`border-bottom`
`border-left`
	2.1	Y	Y	Y	Y	Y	Y	Y

Value:	`<border-width> || <border-style> || <border-color>`							
Initial value:	Not defined for shorthand properties							
Applies to:	All elements							
Inherited:	No							
`border`	2.1	Y	Y	Y	Y	Y	Y	Y
Value:	`<border-width> || <border-style> || <border-color>`							
Initial value:	Not defined for shorthand properties							
Applies to:	All elements							
Inherited:	No							
`width`	2.1	I	Y	Y	Y	Y	Y	Y
Value:	`<length>	<percentage>	auto`							
Initial value:	`auto`							
Applies to:	All elements, but non-replaced inline elements, table rows, and row groups							
Inherited:	No							

IE 6 incorrectly resizes elements if the content inside of the element is larger than its width; this is fixed in IE 7 and above.

PROPERTY	CSS	IE 6.0	IE 7.0	IE 8.0	IE 9.0	FF 3.6	O 11.1	S 5.0
`min-width`	2.1	N	Y	Y	Y	Y	Y	Y
Value:	`<length>	<percentage>`							
Initial value:	0							

continues

(continued)

PROPERTY		CSS	IE 6.0	IE 7.0	IE 8.0	IE 9.0	FF 3.6	O 11.1	S 5.0
	Applies to:	All elements, but non-replaced inline elements and table elements							
	Inherited:	No							
max-width		2.1	N	Y	Y	Y	Y	Y	Y
	Value:	`<length>` | `<percentage>` | none							
	Initial value:	none							
	Applies to:	All elements, but non-replaced inline elements and table elements							
	Inherited:	No							
height		2.1	I	Y	Y	Y	Y	Y	Y
	Value:	`<length>` | `<percentage>` | auto							
	Initial value:	auto							
	Applies to:	All elements, but non-replaced inline elements, table rows, and row groups							
	Inherited:	No							

IE 6 incorrectly resizes elements if the content inside of the element is larger than its height.

min-height		2.1	P	Y	Y	Y	Y	Y	Y
	Value:	`<length>` | `<percentage>`							
	Initial value:	0							
	Applies to:	All elements, but non-replaced inline elements, table rows, and row groups							
	Inherited:	No							

IE 6 only supports the min-height property when applied to `<td>`, `<th>`, or `<tr>` elements.

max-height		2.1	N	Y	Y	Y	Y	Y	Y
	Value:	`<length>` | `<percentage>` | none							
	Initial value:	none							
	Applies to:	All elements, but non-replaced inline elements, table rows, and row groups							
	Inherited:	No							

VISUAL EFFECTS

PROPERTY	CSS	IE 6.0	IE 7.0	IE 8.0	IE 9.0	FF 3.6	O 11.1	S 5.0
overflow	2.1	I	Y	Y	Y	Y	Y	Y
Value:	visible | hidden | scroll | auto							
Initial value:	visible							
Applies to:	Block-level and replaced elements							
Inherited:	No							

IE 6 incorrectly resizes element width / height when `overflow: visible;` is applied in addition to explicit width or height, and the contents overflow. This is fixed in IE 7 and above.

overflow-x	3	Y	Y	Y	Y	Y	N	N
Value:	visible | hidden | scroll | auto							
Initial value:	visible							
Applies to:	Block-level and replaced elements							
Inherited:	No							

overflow-y	3	Y	Y	Y	Y	Y	N	N
Value:	visible | hidden | scroll | auto							
Initial value:	visible							
Applies to:	Block-level and replaced elements							
Inherited:	No							

clip	2.1	Y	Y	Y	Y	Y	Y	Y
Value:	<shape> | auto							
Initial value:	auto							
Applies to:	Absolutely positioned elements							
Inherited:	No							

Under CSS 2 the only valid `<shape>` value is `rect(<top>, <right>, <bottom>, <left>)`, where `rect()` provides the dimensions of a rectangle and `<top>`, `<right>`, `<bottom>`, `<left>` are `<length>` values.

visibility	2.1	P	P	P	P	P	P	P
Value:	visible | hidden | collapse							
Initial value:	visible							

continues

(continued)

PROPERTY		CSS	IE 6.0	IE 7.0	IE 8.0	IE 9.0	FF 3.6	O 11.1	S 5.0
	Applies to:	All elements							
	Inherited:	Yes							

No browser supports the `collapse` keyword, presumably because it essentially provides the same effect as `display: none;`

POSITIONING

PROPERTY		CSS	IE 6.0	IE 7.0	IE 8.0	IE 9.0	FF 3.6	O 11.1	S 5.0
display		2.1	P	P	Y	Y	Y	Y	Y
	Values:	`inline` | `block` | `list-item` | `run-in` | `inline-block` | `table` | `inline-table` | `table-row-group` | `table-header-group` | `table-footer-group` | `table-row` | `table-column-group` | `table-column` | `table-cell` | `table-caption` | `none`							
	Initial value:	`inline`							
	Applies to:	All elements							
	Inherited:	No							

IE 5.5 and 6 only support the keywords `block`, `none`, `inline`, `inline-block`, `table-header-group` and `table-footer-group`. IE 6 additionally supports the `list-item` keyword. Firefox does not support the keywords `inline-block`, `run-in`, or `compact`.

PROPERTY		CSS	IE 6.0	IE 7.0	IE 8.0	IE 9.0	FF 3.6	O 11.1	S 5.0
position		2.1	P	Y	Y	Y	Y	Y	Y
	Value:	`static` | `relative` | `absolute` | `fixed`							
	Initial value:	`static`							
	Applies to:	All elements							
	Inherited:	No							

IE 6 does not support the `fixed` keyword.

PROPERTY		CSS	IE 6.0	IE 7.0	IE 8.0	IE 9.0	FF 3.6	O 11.1	S 5.0
top		2.1	Y	Y	Y	Y	Y	Y	Y
	Value:	`<length>` | `<percentage>` | `auto`							
	Initial value:	`auto`							

PROPERTY		CSS	IE 6.0	IE 7.0	IE 8.0	IE 9.0	FF 3.6	O 11.1	S 5.0
	Applies to:	Positioned elements							
	Inherited:	No							
	Percentage value:	Refers to height of containing block							
`right`		2.1	Y	Y	Y	Y	Y	Y	Y
	Value:	`<length>` | `<percentage>` | `auto`							
	Initial value:	`auto`							
	Applies to:	Positioned elements							
	Inherited:	No							
	Percentage value:	Refers to width of containing block							
`bottom`		2.1	Y	Y	Y	Y	Y	Y	Y
	Value:	`<length>` | `<percentage>` | `auto`							
	Initial value:	`auto`							
	Applies to:	Positioned elements							
	Inherited:	No							
	Percentage value:	Refers to height of containing block							
`left`		2.1	Y	Y	Y	Y	Y	Y	Y
	Value:	`<length>` | `<percentage>` | `auto`							
	Initial value:	`auto`							
	Applies to:	Positioned elements							
	Inherited:	No							
	Percentage value:	Refers to width of containing block							
`top + bottom = height`		2.1	N	Y	Y	Y	Y	Y	Y

When both the `top` and `bottom` offset properties are applied to an element positioned absolutely or fixed, height is implied.

`left + right = width`		2.1	N	Y	Y	Y	Y	Y	Y

When both the `left` and `right` offset properties are applied to an element positioned absolutely or fixed, width is implied.

continues

(continued)

PROPERTY	CSS	IE 6.0	IE 7.0	IE 8.0	IE 9.0	FF 3.6	O 11.1	S 5.0
float	2.1	Y	Y	Y	Y	Y	Y	Y
Value:	left | right | none							
Initial value:	none							
Applies to:	All elements							
Inherited:	No							
clear	2.1	Y	Y	Y	Y	Y	Y	Y
Value:	none | left | right | both							
Initial value:	none							
Applies to:	Block-level elements							
Inherited:	No							
z-index	2.1	Y	Y	Y	Y	Y	Y	Y
Value:	auto | <integer>							
Initial value:	auto							
Applies to:	Positioned elements							
Inherited:	No							

TABLE PROPERTIES

PROPERTY	CSS	IE 6.0	IE 7.0	IE 8.0	IE 9.0	FF 3.6	O 11.1	S 5.0
caption-side	2.1	N	N	Y	Y	Y	Y	Y
Value:	top | bottom							
Initial value:	top							
Applies to:	'table-caption' elements							
Inherited:	Yes							
table-layout	2.1	Y	Y	Y	Y	Y	Y	Y
Value:	auto | fixed							
Initial value:	auto							

PROPERTY		CSS	IE 6.0	IE 7.0	IE 8.0	IE 9.0	FF 3.6	O 11.1	S 5.0
	Applies to:	'table' and 'inline-table' elements							
	Inherited:	No							
border-collapse		2.1	Y	Y	Y	Y	Y	Y	Y
	Value:	collapse | separate							
	Initial value:	separate							
	Applies to:	'table' and 'inline-table' elements							
	Inherited:	Yes							
border-spacing		2.1	N	N	Y	Y	Y	Y	Y
	Value:	<length> <length> ?							
	Initial value:	0							
	Applies to:	'table' and 'inline-table' elements							
	Inherited:	Yes							
empty-cells		2.1	N	N	Y	Y	Y	Y	Y
	Value:	show | hide							
	Initial value:	show							
	Applies to:	'table-cell' elements							
	Inherited:	Yes							

USER INTERFACE

PROPERTY		CSS	IE 6.0	IE 7.0	IE 8.0	IE 9.0	FF 3.6	O 11.1	S 5.0
cursor		2.1	Y	Y	Y	Y	Y	P	Y
	Value:	[<uri> ,]* [auto | crosshair | default | pointer | move | e-resize | ne-resize | nw-resize | n-resize | se-resize | sw-resize | s-resize | w-resize | text | wait | help | progress]							
	Initial value:	auto							
	Applies to:	All elements							
	Inherited:	Yes							

continues

(continued)

PROPERTY	CSS	IE 6.0	IE 7.0	IE 8.0	IE 9.0	FF 3.6	O 11.1	S 5.0
`outline-width`	2.1	N	N	Y	Y	Y	Y	Y
Value:	`<border-width>`							
Initial value:	`medium`							
Applies to:	All elements							
Inherited:	No							
`outline-style`	2.1	N	N	Y	Y	Y	Y	Y
Value:	`<border-style>`							
Initial value:	`none`							
Applies to:	All elements							
Inherited:	No							
`outline-color`	2.1	N	N	Y	Y	Y	Y	Y
Value:	`<color>	invert`							
Initial value:	`invert`							
Applies to:	All elements							
Inherited:	No							
`outline`	2.1	N	N	Y	Y	Y	Y	Y
Value:	`<'outline-color'> || <'outline-style'> || <'outline-width'>`							
Initial value:	Not defined for shorthand properties							
Applies to:	All elements							
Inherited:	No							

GENERATED CONTENT, AUTOMATIC NUMBERING, AND LISTS

PROPERTY	CSS	IE 6.0	IE 7.0	IE 8.0	IE 9.0	FF 3.6	O 11.1	S 5.0
`content`	2.1	N	N	Y	Y	Y	Y	Y
Value:	`normal	none	[<string>	<uri>	<counter>	attr(<identifier>)	open-quote	close-quote	no-open-quote	no-close-quote]+`							

PROPERTY	CSS	IE 6.0	IE 7.0	IE 8.0	IE 9.0	FF 3.6	O 11.1	S 5.0
Initial value:	normal							
Applies to:	::before and ::after pseudo-elements							
Inherited:	No							
quotes	2.1	N	N	Y	Y	Y	Y	Y
Value:	[<string> <string>]+ | none							
Initial value:	Varies from browser to browser							
Applies to:	All elements							
Inherited:	Yes							
counter-reset	2.1	N	N	Y	Y	N	Y	Y
Value:	[<identifier> <integer>?]+ | none							
Initial value:	none							
Applies to:	All elements							
Inherited:	No							
counter-increment	2.1	N	N	Y	Y	N	Y	Y
Value:	[<identifier> <integer>?]+ | none							
Initial value:	none							
Applies to:	All elements							
Inherited:	No							
list-style-type	2.1	P	P	P	P	P	P	Y
Value:	disc | circle | square | decimal | decimal-leading-zero | lower-roman | upper-roman | lower-greek | lower-latin | upper-latin | armenian | georgian | none							
Initial value:	disc							
Applies to:	Elements with 'display: list-item'							
Inherited:	Yes							
list-style-image	2.1	Y	Y	Y	Y	Y	Y	Y
Value:	<uri> | none							
Initial value:	none							

continues

(continued)

PROPERTY		CSS	IE 6.0	IE 7.0	IE 8.0	IE 9.0	FF 3.6	O 11.1	S 5.0
	Applies to:	Elements with `'display: list-item'`							
	Inherited:	Yes							
`list-style-position`		2.1	Y	Y	Y	Y	Y	Y	Y
	Value:	`inside` | `outside`							
	Initial value:	`outside`							
	Applies to:	Elements with `'display: list-item'`							
	Inherited:	Yes							
`list-style`		2.1	P	P	Y	Y	P	P	Y
	Value:	`<'list-style-type'> || <'list-style-position'> || <'list-style-image'>`							
	Initial value:	Not defined for shorthand properties.							
	Applies to:	Elements with `'display: list-item'`							
	Inherited:	Yes							

D

CSS Colors

This appendix references the available CSS color keywords as documented in the W3C CSS 3 candidate recommendation. With the exception of IE 6 not supporting the spelling of *lightgray* with an *a*, as in its American spelling, and IE 6 not supporting other gray color keywords spelled with an "e", as in the British spelling, all of the following keywords are supported in all of the major browsers.

The following sections show colors as sorted from light hue to dark hue.

Reds

COLOR KEYWORD	HEXADECIMAL	RGB
lavenderblush	#FFF0F5	255, 240, 245
mistyrose	#FFE4E1	255, 228, 225
pink	#FFC0CB	255, 192, 203
lightpink	#FFB6C1	255, 182, 193
orange	#FFA500	255, 165, 0
lightsalmon	#FFA07A	255, 160, 122
darkorange	#FF8C00	255, 140, 0
coral	#FF7F50	255, 127, 80
hotpink	#FF69B4	255, 105, 180

continues

(continued)

COLOR KEYWORD	HEXADECIMAL	RGB
tomato	#FF6347	255, 99, 71
orangered	#FF4500	255, 69, 0
deeppink	#FF1493	255, 20, 147
fuchsia	#FF00FF	255, 0, 255
magenta	#FF00FF	255, 0, 255
red	#FF0000	255, 0, 0
salmon	#FA8072	250, 128, 114
lightcoral	#F08080	240, 128, 128
violet	#EE82EE	238, 130, 238
darksalmon	#E9967A	233, 150, 122
plum	#DDA0DD	221, 160, 221
crimson	#DC143C	220, 20, 60
palevioletred	#DB7093	219, 112, 147
orchid	#DA70D6	218, 112, 214
thistle	#D8BFD8	216, 191, 216
indianred	#CD5C5C	205, 92, 92
mediumvioletred	#C71585	199, 21, 133
mediumorchid	#BA55D3	186, 85, 211
firebrick	#B22222	178, 34, 34
darkorchid	#9932CC	153, 50, 204
darkviolet	#9400D3	148, 0, 211
mediumpurple	#9370DB	147, 112, 219
darkmagenta	#8B008B	139, 0, 139
darkred	#8B0000	139, 0, 0
purple	#800080	128, 0, 128
maroon	#800000	128, 0, 0

Blues

COLOR KEYWORD	HEXADECIMAL	RGB
azure	#F0FFFF	240, 255, 255
aliceblue	#F0F8FF	240, 248, 255
lavender	#E6E6FA	230, 230, 250
lightcyan	#E0FFFF	224, 255, 255
powderblue	#B0E0E6	176, 224, 230
lightsteelblue	#B0C4DE	176, 196, 222
paleturquoise	#AFEEEE	175, 238, 238
lightblue	#ADD8E6	173, 216, 230
blueviolet	#8A2BE2	138, 43, 226
lightskyblue	#87CEFA	135, 206, 250
skyblue	#87CEEB	135, 206, 235
mediumslateblue	#7B68EE	123, 104, 238
slateblue	#6A5ACD	106, 90, 205
cornflowerblue	#6495ED	100, 149, 237
cadetblue	#5F9EA0	95, 158, 160
indigo	#4B0082	75, 0, 130
mediumturquoise	#48D1CC	72, 209, 204
darkslateblue	#483D8B	72, 61, 139
steelblue	#4682B4	70, 130, 180
royalblue	#4169E1	65, 105, 225
turquoise	#40E0D0	64, 224, 208
dodgerblue	#1E90FF	30, 144, 255
midnightblue	#191970	25, 25, 112
aqua	#00FFFF	0, 255, 255
cyan	#00FFFF	0, 255, 255

continues

(continued)

COLOR KEYWORD	HEXADECIMAL	RGB
darkturquoise	#00CED1	0, 206, 209
deepskyblue	#00BFFF	0, 191, 255
darkcyan	#008B8B	0, 139, 139
blue	#0000FF	0, 0, 255
mediumblue	#0000CD	0, 0, 205
darkblue	#00008B	0, 0, 139
navy	#000080	0, 0, 128

Greens

COLOR KEYWORD	HEXADECIMAL	RGB
mintcream	#F5FFFA	245, 255, 250
honeydew	#F0FFF0	240, 255, 240
greenyellow	#ADFF2F	173, 255, 47
yellowgreen	#9ACD32	154, 205, 50
palegreen	#98FB98	152, 251, 152
lightgreen	#90EE90	144, 238, 144
darkseagreen	#8FBC8F	143, 188, 143
olive	#808000	128, 128, 0
aquamarine	#7FFFD4	127, 255, 212
chartreuse	#7FFF00	127, 255, 0
lawngreen	#7CFC00	124, 252, 0
olivedrab	#6B8E23	107, 142, 35
mediumaquamarine	#66CDAA	102, 205, 170
darkolivegreen	#556B2F	85, 107, 47
mediumseagreen	#3CB371	60, 179, 113

COLOR KEYWORD	HEXADECIMAL	RGB
limegreen	#32CD32	50, 205, 50
seagreen	#2E8B57	46, 139, 87
forestgreen	#228B22	34, 139, 34
lightseagreen	#20B2AA	32, 178, 170
springgreen	#00FF7F	0, 255, 127
lime	#00FF00	0, 255, 0
mediumspringgreen	#00FA9A	0, 250, 154
teal	#008080	0, 128, 128
green	#008000	0, 128, 0
darkgreen	#006400	0, 100, 0

Yellows

COLOR KEYWORD	HEXADECIMAL	RGB
lightgoldenrodyellow	#FAFAD2	250, 250, 210
ivory	#FFFFF0	255, 255, 240
lightyellow	#FFFFE0	255, 255, 224
floralwhite	#FFFAF0	255, 250, 240
lemonchiffon	#FFFACD	255, 250, 205
cornsilk	#FFF8DC	255, 248, 220
khaki	#F0E68C	240, 230, 140
yellow	#FFFF00	255, 255, 0
gold	#FFD700	255, 215, 0
darkkhaki	#BDB76B	189, 183, 107

Browns

COLOR KEYWORD	HEXADECIMAL	RGB
snow	#FFFAFA	255, 250, 250
seashell	#FFF5EE	255, 245, 238
oldlace	#FDF5E6	253, 245, 230
linen	#FAF0E6	250, 240, 230
antiquewhite	#FAEBD7	250, 235, 215
beige	#F5F5DC	245, 245, 220
papayawhip	#FFEFD5	255, 239, 213
blanchedalmond	#FFEBCD	255, 235, 205
bisque	#FFE4C4	255, 228, 196
moccasin	#FFE4B5	255, 228, 181
navajowhite	#FFDEAD	255, 222, 173
peachpuff	#FFDAB9	255, 218, 185
wheat	#F5DEB3	245, 222, 179
sandybrown	#F4A460	244, 164, 96
palegoldenrod	#EEE8AA	238, 232, 170
burlywood	#DEB887	222, 184, 135
goldenrod	#DAA520	218, 165, 32
tan	#D2B48C	210, 180, 140
chocolate	#D2691E	210, 105, 30
peru	#CD853F	205, 133, 63
rosybrown	#BC8F8F	188, 143, 143
darkgoldenrod	#B8860B	184, 134, 11
brown	#A52A2A	165, 42, 42
sienna	#A0522D	160, 82, 45
saddlebrown	#8B4513	139, 69, 19

Grays

COLOR KEYWORD	HEXADECIMAL	RGB
white	#FFFFFF	255, 255, 255
ghostwhite	#F8F8FF	248, 248, 255
whitesmoke	#F5F5F5	245, 245, 245
gainsboro	#DCDCDC	220, 220, 220
lightgray	#D3D3D3	211, 211, 211
lightgrey	#D3D3D3	211, 211, 211
silver	#C0C0C0	192, 192, 192
darkgray	#A9A9A9	169, 169, 169
darkgrey	#A9A9A9	169, 169, 169
gray	#808080	128, 128, 128
grey	#808080	128, 128, 128
lightslategray	#778899	119, 136, 153
lightslategrey	#778899	119, 136, 153
slategray	#708090	112, 128, 144
slategrey	#708090	112, 128, 144
dimgray	#696969	105, 105, 105
dimgrey	#696969	105, 105, 105
darkslategray	#2F4F4F	47, 79, 79
darkslategrey	#2F4F4F	47, 79, 79
black	#000000	0, 0, 0

INDEX